COMMON SENSE CATHOLICISM

For my grandson, Grant William

BILL DONOHUE

Common Sense Catholicism

How to Resolve Our Cultural Crisis

IGNATIUS PRESS   SAN FRANCISCO

Cover image from allvision/us.fotolia.com

Cover design by Carl Olson

© 2019 by Ignatius Press, San Francisco
All rights reserved
ISBN 978-1-62164-209-1
Library of Congress Control Number 2018948283
Printed in the United States of America ∞

CONTENTS

INTRODUCTION

Stupidity and the Collapse of Common Sense

Survey after survey shows that most Americans believe we are going in the wrong direction. They are asking lots of questions. Why does everything seem to be out of whack? What's happening to our society? Why have right and wrong switched places? Why is incivility so commonplace? Why are standards dropping in school and in the workplace? Whatever happened to decency? Why do so many people see religion as the enemy? Why is respect for authority and tradition vanishing? We seem to be coming apart at the seams.

It wasn't always this way, and it doesn't have to be this way. Getting back on track, however, requires that we figure out what happened and why, and then apply the right remedies.

To understand what ails us, we need to put aside the notion that our problems are fundamentally political and economic in nature. They are not. American society is in trouble largely because our social and cultural house is broken. The social fabric is coming apart, and our culture is in a state of decline.

There are many reasons why we are on the wrong track, but there is one factor that is of overriding importance: we have adopted policies, norms, and values that are at odds with some very fundamental truths governing human nature. It's as though everything we have learned about the human condition throughout history has been totally discarded, if not trampled on, so bizarre is our predicament. To say this lacks common sense is an understatement. In fact, the collapse of common sense is driving our derailment.

Fortunately, we are not without answers to what ails us. They are found in the wisdom of Catholic social thought, teachings that respect the limits of the human condition and that are grounded in common sense.

The first thing we need to realize is that bad things are not always the result of bad people—stupid people, yes, but not necessarily bad people. By "stupid", I do not mean "badly educated". Indeed, most of our problems are the direct consequence of highly educated persons, many of whom are intellectuals. But how can they be educated yet stupid?

Going to school and reading a lot of books are to be commended, but they are no guard against stupidity. Indeed, from my years spent as a college professor, I can testify that some of the stupidest people I have ever met teach college. It is not as though they are incompetent in their field of study—most are well trained—it's just that many of them can barely function. To put it differently, they have a hard time navigating in the real world. That's why they like the classroom: it's safe.

Stupidity is not a lack of knowledge. For example, if someone doesn't know how to hard-boil an egg, he is not stupid: he simply hasn't learned how to do it. Stupidity is many things, but, most of all, it is a lack of common sense, as in sound judgment. Unfortunately, there are many ideological strains of thought that are not grounded in common sense. Fortunately, the teachings of the Catholic

Church are a rich source of accumulated wisdom, which can help us acquire prudence.

Thomas Jefferson knew the difference between a practical man and a bookworm. "State a moral case to a ploughman and a professor. The former will decide it as well [as] and often better than the latter, because he has not been led astray by artificial rules."[1] George Orwell has this to say about people who deny basic facts when they contradict their cherished ideas: "One has to belong to the intelligentsia to believe things like that: no ordinary man could be such a fool."[2] William F. Buckley Jr. famously said, "I would rather be governed by the first 2000 people in the Boston telephone directory than by the 2000 people on the faculty of Harvard University."[3] G.K. Chesterton had no patience for "some of the lunacies of those who call themselves cultured", noting that they lack "common sense, as it would have been understood by the common people".[4]

Jefferson, Orwell, Buckley, and Chesterton were getting at the same subject: the stupidity of many intellectuals. Of course, we can all act foolishly, so why did Jefferson pan the professors? Why did Orwell single out intellectuals? Why did Buckley want to be governed by ordinary men, and not the Harvard faculty? Why did Chesterton speak

[1] Thomas Jefferson to Peter Carr, Paris, August 10, 1787, quoted in Robert Curry, *Common Sense Nation: Unlocking the Forgotten Power of the American Idea* (New York: Encounter Books, 2015), p. 29.

[2] George Orwell, "Notes on Nationalism", *England Your England and Other Essays* (London: Secker and Warburg, 1953), posted at George Orwell, http://orwell.ru/library/essays/nationalism/english/e_nat.

[3] "William F. Buckley Jr Harvard Faculty Quote", YouTube video, posted by Legal Insurrection, December 16, 2015, 0:35, https://www.youtube.com/watch?v=2nf_bu-kBr4.

[4] G.K. Chesterton, *The Common Man* (New York: Sheed and Ward, 1950), p. 1.

about their "lunacies"? These four learned men were anything but anti-intellectual, so what did they see in these
people that made them wince? The absence of common
sense explains it all.

Merriam-Webster defines "common sense" as "sound
and prudent judgment based on a simple perception of the
situation or facts". Notice that the definition says nothing
about education. That's one reason why it is entirely possible to be well educated yet not possess common sense.
This is especially true of intellectuals—*they are more likely
to lack common sense.* To put it another way, they are more
likely to lack practical experience, and, as a result, their
judgment about mundane conditions is often flawed. "We
are all born ignorant," said Benjamin Franklin, "but one
must work hard to remain stupid."[5] Many intellectuals
work very hard at it.

It cannot be emphasized too strongly that the criticisms
about intellectuals made in this book do not apply to all
of them; they are meant to apply to blue-sky thinkers and
hard-core ideologues. Such intellectuals are likely to work
in a college or a university, and they are clearly overrepre-
sented in the humanities and the social sciences, although
they can also be found in the theoretical and applied sciences. Driven more by emotion than by reason, they are
not interested in the pursuit of truth. Intellectuals who
are worthy of our respect do not share those characteristics; they have their feet on the ground and are persuaded
by logic, reason, and empirical evidence. It is unfortunate
that we do not have more of them.

Bruce G. Charlton is a professor with common sense.
The British scholar teaches at the University of Buckingham

---

[5] Ann Witmer, "Ben Franklin Still Electrifies Philadelphia", *Patriot News*,
October 27, 2013, p. D9.

and wrote a splendid piece for *Medical Hypotheses*, "Clever Sillies—Why the High IQ Lack Common Sense". In it, he notes that "it has often been observed that high IQ types are lacking in 'common sense'—and especially when it comes to dealing with other human beings." His research led him to conclude that "the most intelligent people have personalities which over-use abstract analysis in the social domain", and this implies that "the most intelligent people are predisposed to have silly ideas and to behave maladaptively when it comes to solving social problems."[6]

Charlton is being too kind: the brainy ones he describes are not only unable to solve social problems—they are responsible for creating them. Indeed, he seems to recognize this himself when he writes that "the fatal flaw of modern ruling elites lies in their lack of common sense—especially the misinterpretations of human psychology and socio-political affairs." He ventures to say that "this lack of common sense is intrinsic and incorrigible."[7]

Charlton is on to something. The highly educated tend to overanalyze events, employing abstract ideas to think about human behavior. It can be said that they are capable of solving the world's most daunting problems, so long as they never leave the classroom. Too many do, however, and that is where the danger lies. Worse, those in the business of disseminating ideas, which is what intellectuals do, ineluctably shape the thinking of decision makers in all segments of society. The trickle-down effect is not only real; it demonstrates the power of these savants.

The "modern ruling elites", as Charlton calls them, do indeed misinterpret human psychology and sociopolitical

---

[6] Bruce G. Charlton, "Clever Sillies—Why the High IQ Lack Common Sense", *Medical Hypotheses*, (2009): 867–870, http://medicalhypotheses.blogspot.com/2009/11/clever-sillies-why-high-iq-lack-common.html.

[7] Ibid.

affairs. But why? They do so largely because they misunderstand, if not ignore, mandates inscribed in human
nature. To be precise, by not giving due deference to the
biological, social, and cultural attributes found in every
society, the ruling elites have crafted policies, norms, and
values that simply do not work. We should be taking our
cues from human nature—Catholicism certainly does—
not turning our back on it.

Noted anthropologist Donald E. Brown spent many
years detailing hundreds of human traits that are universally recognized; no society is without them.[8] Common
sense suggests that our social institutions, norms, and values be respectful of those attributes, and not run rough-
shod over them. But that is exactly what we have done.
Thus, the ensuing mess.

For example, we know from Brown's contributions
that humans of all ages need to express their emotions
and attach themselves to others, typically family members.
Similarly, sociologist Amitai Etzioni says that we all need
recognition and affection, and when these needs are not
met, trouble follows.[9]

Leave it to the intellectuals to get this wrong. The great
nineteenth-century philosopher John Stuart Mill was raised
by his father, a first-class scholar, to be a genius. The young
Mill was taught Greek when he was three years old, and by
eight he had read such classics as Aesop's fables. Between
ages eight and twelve, he learned Latin and read the works of
Virgil, Horace, Ovid, and Cicero. He also learned geome-
try, algebra, and calculus. Poetry, economics, history, physics, astronomy—there was nothing he didn't learn. But he
had no friends. His father was crafting an intellectual giant,

---

[8] Donald E. Brown, *Human Universals* (New York: McGraw-Hill, 1991).

[9] Amitai Etzioni, "Man and Society: The Inauthentic Condition", *Human Relations* 22, no. 4 (August 1969): 327.

not a normal boy, and he kept him away from children his own age. Totally unhappy, and emotionally starved, he contemplated suicide when he turned twenty.[10]

It could have been worse. Mill could have finished the job. Some may say that his father made a mistake, but that is too kind. This was child abuse. Children, like adults, need to express their emotions and attach themselves to others. Mill may have gotten recognition from his father, but there was no affection. There was also no common sense—Mill's father had none of it.

Getting Human Nature Right

If there is one subject that has delighted intellectuals throughout the ages, it is the makings of the good society. We can all agree that the rallying cry of the French Revolution—liberty, equality, fraternity—is about ends that most people want. But we don't have to look any further than to the intellectual architects of the French Revolution, Rousseau being first among them, to realize that they misapprehended how to achieve those ends.

Just as Charlton noted, when it comes to human psychology and sociopolitical affairs, the highly educated are typically in over their heads. In this case, the abstract ideas entertained by the French intellectuals, coupled with their lack of common sense, allowed them to hold a seriously flawed conception of human nature.

There is nothing more serious in intellectual affairs than getting human nature wrong: it's a slippery slope that, once stepped on, destines all policies to ruin. The geniuses who gave us Robespierre not only failed to deliver liberty,

[10] John Stuart Mill, *Autobiography*, ed. John M. Robson (London: Penguin Books, 1989), pp. 27–32, 116–17.

equality, and fraternity; they also succeeded in providing oppression, inequality, division, and mass murder.

The French Revolution failed because the philosophes—what the French called their intellectuals—mistakenly thought that man is basically good but was corrupted by society. All that was needed, they thought, was to put the "right persons" in charge, allowing them to make the necessary adjustments. Once we remake our social institutions, norms, and values, they thought, we will remake man, ridding him of his corrupted ways. He will then return to his benign state of nature.

By contrast, Catholicism understands original sin: we are a fallen people. With God's grace, we are capable of great good; with Satan's influence, we are also capable of great evil. Social progress can be made, but there is no such thing as perfectibility on earth; it is a pipe dream. Worse, attempts by ruling elites to orchestrate the perfect society—such as the attempts of Hitler, Stalin, Mao, and Pol Pot—yield nothing but genocide. With good reason, the *Catechism of the Catholic Church* says, "Ignorance of the fact that man has a wounded nature inclined to evil gives rise to serious errors in the areas of education, politics, social action,[11] and morals" (407).

Those who founded America were not all practicing Christians, but they all respected Christianity. They also had a very common sense understanding of human nature. They knew that man was self-interested, capable of great good and great evil. By getting human nature right, they were able to craft institutions that directed man's self-interest to serve the best interests of society.

James Madison was a first-class intellectual who possessed common sense. He exhibited this when he questioned, "But what is government itself but the greatest of

[11] Cf. John Paul II, encyclical letter *Centesimus annus* (May 1, 1991), no. 25.

all reflections on human nature? If men were angels, no government would be necessary."[12] He and the writers who influenced the Founders were men who had their feet planted squarely on the ground; they were anything but blue-sky thinkers.

Americans enjoy freedom today largely because the Founders instituted a system of government based on man's self-interest. They allowed for three vertical levels of governance—federal, state, and local—and for three competing horizontal branches at the national level—executive, legislative, and judicial. By dividing power, they denied its monopolization, thus ensuring freedom. As Madison put it, "Ambition must be made to counteract ambition."[13]

We also enjoy prosperity. This, too, is a direct result of the Founders' accurate conception of human nature. Their preference for a market economy was based on the premise that man's self-interest, economically speaking, is best achieved by appealing to the greatest number of persons. To enrich ourselves, we must please others.

The assumptions about human nature that guided the Founders were quintessentially Christian. That is why they succeeded. But we have been abandoning common sense policies that yielded progress, replacing them with unworkable programs based on unrealistic assumptions about the human condition.

What Makes Intellectuals Tick?

The average person makes decisions based on real-life experiences. By a process of elimination, we learn to negotiate

---

[12] Alexander Hamilton, James Madison, and John Jay, *The Federalist Papers*, ed. Clinton Rossiter (New York: American Library, 1961), no. 51, p. 322.
[13] Ibid.

the everyday world, deciding through a process of trial and error what works best. Most of us are not dreamers—we are realists. Not so for the big-time thinkers.

In his book *Intellectuals*, English historian Paul Johnson noted how incredibly egotistical the great modern minds of Western civilization were.[14] They saw themselves as superior to the common man and indeed looked down their noses at the bourgeoisie, never mind the unwashed masses. True children of the Enlightenment, they believed they possessed the answers to current social conditions, solutions that escaped the grasp of ordinary folks.

Does God exist? Intellectuals are too smart to believe in something they cannot prove (although they have no problem believing in their own unprovable utopian schemes), and, as such, they are happy to agree with Karl Marx that religion is the opiate of the masses. They are guilty of what Catholicism calls pride, the sin that allows us to think that we are wholly self-sufficient, needing no guidance from the Almighty.

Because intellectuals do not believe that there is a Creator, they cannot admit to the existence of a created and fixed human nature: there is no such thing as nature, or nature's God. This allows them to believe—it is central to their dogmatic beliefs—that they possess the power to reconstruct human nature. Indeed, they typically downplay, or deny, the existence of human universals, traits that are common to individuals and societies throughout history.

The ego of the great modern thinkers also accounts for their tendency to rely on education, science, and technology to resolve what ails us. They believe that they can remold anything. The answers to our troubles, they contend, can be rationally conceived and imposed at will.

[14] Paul Johnson, *Intellectuals* (New York: Harper and Row, 1988).

Yet they seriously misunderstand the human condition, promote policies that are bound to fail, and then try to fix the problems caused by these policies. And because their reach is large—the effect they have on cultural elites, in particular, is huge—the damage done by their surrogates is incalculable.

This isn't normal. This is cultural schizophrenia. Intellectuals complain about the poor outcomes that are a direct consequence of their ideas, and then they try to rectify matters by imposing policies unrelated to the cause. Worse, when they are told that their ideas defy common sense, they respond just the way George Orwell said Big Brother acts when challenged. He wrote, "The very existence of external reality was tacitly denied by their philosophy. The heresy of heresies was common sense."[15]

Imagine a doctor who makes the wrong diagnosis, offers the wrong treatment, and then expresses horror at the results. Imagine him then blaming the patient, forcing him to undergo treatment that only exacerbates the problem. This is what our policy experts are doing. They misdiagnose social problems, recommend the wrong programs, and are baffled by the results. Then they blame everyone but themselves, imposing a new set of unworkable policies. But unlike the incompetent doctor, they get either tenure or a raise.

We are dealing with stupidity. Common sense has all but collapsed. Moreover, given the anti-Catholic animus that many intellectuals harbor, they are not in a position to access the wisdom that the Church has to offer.

If we are going to get our nation back on track, we have to come to our senses and start rendering decisions based on real-life experiences and accumulated wisdom,

---

[15] George Orwell, *1984* (New York: Penguin Books, 1950), p. 80.

not on untested ideas drawn on the blackboard. Economist Thomas Sowell captures this point well: "The ignorance, prejudices, and groupthink of an educated elite are still ignorance, prejudice, and groupthink—and for those with one percent of the knowledge in a society to be guiding or controlling those with the other 99 percent is as perilous as it is absurd."[16]

Liberty, Equality, Fraternity

The ends that the architects of the French Revolution sought were noble, but their vision of liberty, equality, and fraternity was seriously flawed. Similarly, the deep thinkers who influence our laws and public policies hold to misinterpretations of these three goals.

Does "liberty" mean the right to do wrong, or do rights have a value independent of their exercise? Does the exercise of rights assume a degree of virtue, or does it not matter? Should the differences between men and women affect social and cultural decisions, or should we develop policies that discount those differences? Should policies that seek greater economic equality center more on the family or on anti-discrimination legislation? Is tradition a resource worth safeguarding, or does it stand in the way of a meaningful sense of community? Is religion a social asset or a liability?

Intellectuals have an uncanny ability to choose the wrong alternative. Their idea of liberty knows few bounds and pays lip service to individual responsibilities. They view the differences between the sexes as a social construction

[16] Thomas Sowell, *Intellectuals and Society* (New York: Basic Books, 2012), p. 20.

having little to do with biology. Their way of achieving economic equality gives short shrift to the role of the family, focusing more on combating racism. Their vision of fraternity is expansive, viewing the whole society—if not the world—as one big family; tradition and religion are deterrents to this conceptualization and must be censored.

These interpretations of liberty, equality, and fraternity represent radical libertarianism, radical egalitarianism, and radical collectivism, all seen through the lens of rationalism. To be sure, the mind is certainly capable of entertaining all sorts of social outcomes, but when fanciful ideas that don't square with the limits of the human condition are put into practice, they wreak havoc. The correctives that follow only magnify the problems, and that is because the decision makers typically double down by refusing to change course.

We are not destined to fail. The right outcomes can be had, but for this to happen, intellectuals and our ruling elites need to drop their aversion to common sense and one of its chief custodians—Catholicism. If this proves too elusive, thoughtful Catholics will have to make their case with greater vigor. The good news is that objective social science data support a Catholic interpretation of what ails us and what needs to be done about it.

For instance, a mature understanding of liberty, as found in Catholicism, gives primacy to individual responsibilities, not to rights. It stresses duty and rejects license. It also realizes that moral harms, that is, pernicious behaviors that debase society, exist.

Equality in the Catholic tradition is centered on the human dignity that inheres in every man and woman, independent of station in life or demographic characteristics. But Catholicism also understands that there are natural differences between men and women, grounded in our

nature; they should be seen as complementary, not conflicting, characteristics. For Catholicism, the greatest engine
of economic equality rests not in schools or government
programs but in the family, especially the intact family.

Fraternity in Catholic social teachings is best expressed
at the micro level—in the social networks that constitute
family and neighborhood. Tradition is to be valued, not
subject to the multicultural knife. Similarly, the public role
of religion must be promoted, not just protected; even
nonbelievers benefit from the social capital that religion
affords. Most important, tradition and religion bind us in a
way that has no rival.

It can be said with certainty that there is no tension
between the Catholic interpretation of liberty, equality,
and fraternity, and the ability realistically to achieve these
ends. In other words, human universal traits are in harmony with Catholic social teachings; they are in utter disharmony with the perspective afforded by the dominant
culture and the intellectuals who shape it.

Americans are an impatient people. Our economic,
scientific, and technological achievements are stunning,
inviting us to think that all we need to do is develop new
ideas to resolve social problems. We have yet to learn that
it is infinitely easier to put a man on the moon than it is
to make the irresponsible responsible. Even more to the
point, we have yet to learn that, for the most part, the ones
least capable of playing the role of Mr. Fix-It are members
of the professorial class.

It takes more than common sense to turn things around,
but without it, we have no compass. Fortunately, centuries
of Catholic social thought provide us with a rich body of
ideas to draw on; it would behoove us to do so with alac-
rity. We can begin by recognizing that those who have
their heads in the clouds are not well situated to offer any

cogent advice on how to resolve what ails us. They created our cultural crisis and are thus incapable of rectifying it.

Americans are resilient—we can be kicked around, but we always bounce back. Just as important, we are practical—we tend to opt for what works, putting theory aside. We need to rely more on wisdom than on knowledge, and more on experience than on ideology. Not to do so is to ensure the triumph of stupidity, yielding outcomes that even intellectuals abhor.

PART I: LIBERTY

Freedom, Properly Understood

Throughout most of American history, it was illegal to burn the American flag on a courthouse lawn, but it was legal to erect a Nativity scene on the same spot. Now the reverse is true. Without debating the constitutional questions involved, it must be asked: Are we freer now than we were before? To put it differently, shouldn't advances in freedom make us feel freer?

Freedom is one of the most defining American characteristics, but in most of the world, the kind of personal freedom enjoyed by Americans is relatively unknown. Tyranny is much more common and always has been. The Chinese and the Japanese were so accustomed to living in tyranny that they had no word for "freedom" until the nineteenth century. American-style freedom, as in personal autonomy, is certainly not a need: throughout history, most people neither sought nor experienced this kind of radical liberty.

Donald E. Brown lists more than three hundred human universals, but freedom is not among them. The closest we get is the universal sense of rights and obligations that stem from various social roles and statuses. For example, fathers and mothers have rights and responsibilities in every society, but that is a far cry from the inalienable rights that inhere in every individual, regardless of status.[1] Notice, too, that rights do not exist by themselves: they are always attached to responsibilities. That association, however, is no longer the rule in the Western world. Indeed, the very suggestion that individuals have responsibilities to others is seen as increasingly controversial. That is one reason we are experiencing a cultural crisis.

Linking rights to responsibilities is certainly not controversial to Catholicism. In fact, no other institution in history has conjoined the two attributes as tightly as the Catholic Church has—seeing them as virtually inseparable. This carries even greater weight when we consider that the Catholic Church pioneered individual rights: the Church's opposition to arbitrary authority was the first institutional foray against the overreach of government. Over the centuries, the Church Fathers took the lead, crafting a seminal understanding of freedom.

Building on this tradition, in the late nineteenth century, Pope Leo XIII offered one of the most cogent expositions of freedom that the modern world has ever seen. No one has a right to do wrong, he insisted, arguing that "liberty is to be regarded as legitimate in so far only as it affords greater facility for doing good, but no farther."[2] In other words, liberty must always be tied to doing good for others. This view is expressly countercultural: the reigning understanding of liberty is the right of the individual to do as he pleases, save for directly trespassing on the rights of others.

The *Catechism of the Catholic Church* holds that all persons possess "inalienable" rights, liberties that the government must respect (1738). But to be legitimate, as Pope

---

[1] Donald E. Brown, *Human Universals* (New York: McGraw-Hill, 1991), p. 138.

[2] Leo XIII, encyclical letter *Libertas* (June 20, 1888), no. 42.

Leo XIII indicated, individual rights must always be in service to the good. The *Catechism* is very clear about this: "There is no true freedom except in the service of what is good and just. The choice to disobey and do evil is an abuse of freedom and leads to 'the slavery of sin' (cf. Rom 6:17)" (1733). Freedom, as the Church teaches, is the right to do what we ought to do.

This is not a popular way of thinking about freedom. But it meets the definition of freedom, properly understood. Any right that is abused is no friend to freedom: rights are not exercised in a vacuum, so when they are abused, someone else loses. Common sense suggests that a society that truly values freedom will not celebrate conditions where one individual's liberties come at the expense of someone else's rights. The choice to do evil, as the Church teaches, is the negation of freedom.

Now contrast this perspective with the view favored by many intellectuals, the one that is woven into their thinking. Take, for instance, Sigmund Freud's idea of liberty. He conceded that because man must live in society, civilization demands that he harness his instincts. This would seem to be a fairly pedestrian concession, but for Freud, it was reluctantly granted. "Primitive man", he said, "was better off in knowing no restrictions of instinct."[3] But primitive man was a predator—that is what happens when our primordial interests go unchecked. Why Freud would prefer such conditions to a more civilized outcome tells us how fanciful his idea of freedom is. It is a colossal example of the collapse of common sense.

The Freudian appeal is evidenced in our preoccupation with autonomy. Pop culture has been promoting radical autonomy since the 1960s. Its message to young people—in

---

[3] Sigmund Freud, *Civilization and Its Discontents* (New York: W.W. Norton, 1961), pp. 62, 87.

music, on television, and in the movies—is that the freer
we are from rules and regulations, especially religious ones,
the better off we will be. Sanctions are oppressive, inhibiting our innermost desires and wants. Sexual freedom, in
particular, depends on a full-blown sense of autonomy: the
shackles of tradition must be severed once and for all. We
may then approximate the state that primitive man knew.

The resulting condition, however, is anything but rosy.
Neighborhoods where self-discipline has broken down
have the highest rates of out-of-wedlock births and violent crime.

Rights Are a Means, Not an End

Freedom is inconceivable without a panoply of individual rights. Less settled is whether rights are an end or a
means to an end. The dominant culture promotes the former interpretation: the mere exercise of individual rights is
something good, requiring no justification. The Founders
and the Church Fathers disagree. In their eyes, rights are a
means to an end, the end being the good society.

The Founders, and especially the Framers of the First
Amendment, were heavily influenced by Sir William
Blackstone. He wrote authoritatively about the common
law, or what sociologists call the mores, that is, the unwritten laws reflected by religion and tradition. For Blackstone, common sense provided much of the content of the
common law: it was simply a matter of common sense, he
said, to distinguish between liberty and license; the former
commands our respect; the latter does not.

The Founders prized freedom of speech not as an end
in itself, but as a means toward the creation of a free society. Reasonable men and women can disagree on what it

takes to make society better, making it all the more important to protect free speech. Without the guarantee that
political discourse will be protected, many will be afraid to
voice their concerns, thus ill serving the prospect of reaching a desired end. Libel and sedition, however, do not
serve the desired ends, and should therefore be outlawed.[4]

The late Jesuit scholar Francis Canavan understood this
instrumentalist conception of freedom as well as anyone.
Why is freedom of speech valuable? It is guaranteed by
the Constitution "to protect and facilitate the achievement
of rational ends by communication among free and ordi-
narily intelligent people. Chief among these ends is the
successful functioning of the democratic political process."
For Canavan, "end or purpose is also a limiting principle,
regulating and restricting the uses of means to those which
in some way contribute to the end."[5]

His view was widely shared by the Founders. Political scientist David Lowenthal notes that they "understood
freedom to require limits that would prevent harm to others and to the republic. They did not include the abuse
of freedom, or license, in the notion of freedom itself."[6]
To buttress this point, Lowenthal quotes from one of the
most influential legal writers of the nineteenth century,
Supreme Court judge Joseph Story.

Story strongly defended the First Amendment right to
free speech, but he had no tolerance for any interpretation not grounded in common sense. The idea that the
First Amendment was intended "to secure to every citizen
an absolute right to speak, or write, or print whatever he

[4] David Lowenthal, *No Liberty for License: The Forgotten Logic of the First Amendment* (Dallas: Spence Publishing, 1997), pp. 10–11.

[5] Francis Canavan, *Freedom of Expression: Purpose as Limit* (Durham, N.C.: Carolina Academic Press, 1984), p. 6.

[6] Lowenthal, *No Liberty for License*, p. xiii.

might please, without any responsibility ... is a supposition too wild to be indulged by any rational man. This would be to allow every citizen a right to destroy at his pleasure the reputation, the peace, the property, and even the personal safety of every other citizen."[7]

It follows that if rights are to serve a good end, we cannot counsel the exercise of rights that serve evil. John Winthrop, founder of the Massachusetts Bay Colony, had good common sense. The only liberty he accepted was "a liberty to [do] that which is good, just, and honest."[8] He found objectionable the liberty to do good or evil. Similarly, Saint John Paul II repeatedly stressed that freedom must always be ordered to what we are morally obliged to do. That way, every exercise of freedom winds up serving others, thus underscoring our social being.

This is not an exclusively Christian interpretation of freedom. The utilitarian philosopher Jeremy Bentham did not have his head in the clouds when he took up this issue. "Is not the liberty to do evil, evil? If not, what is it? Do we not say that it is necessary to take away liberty from idiots and bad men, because they abuse it?"[9]

If the right of the individual to abridge the rights of others makes no sense, it also makes no sense to allow the government to facilitate the process. For example, a free society should not tolerate a government that does evil. Abraham Lincoln, according to political philosopher Harry Jaffa, "insisted that the case for popular government depended upon a standard of right and wrong independent of mere opinion and one which was not justified merely

[7] Ibid., p. 29.

[8] John Winthrop, "On Liberty", Constitution Society, http://www .constitution.org/bcp/winthlib.htm.

[9] Sidney Hook, *Paradoxes of Freedom* (Buffalo, N.Y.: Prometheus Books, 1987), p. 10.

by the counting of heads."[10] That is why it did not matter to Lincoln whether a majority preferred slavery for African Americans. That majority was morally wrong.

The same could be said about invoking public opinion to make the case for abortion rights. Moral theologian Monsignor William Smith, who taught young men for decades at Saint Joseph's Seminary in the New York Archdiocese, took apart the abortion stance with precision: "Human rights do not rest on consensus. Respect for the human rights of blacks, Jewish people—any minority—does not rest on consensus. That is why we call them inalienable rights."[11] Polls may be a good barometer of prevailing social currents, but they should have no bearing on defining right and wrong.

There is not a single society in history that has failed to distinguish right from wrong. Brown found that although not every society defines right and wrong the same way, there are some behaviors, such as murder, that are universally proscribed. Every society employs sanctions, punishments for crimes against the people; removal from the social unit is commonplace.[12]

Given the need to distinguish right from wrong, it makes no sense to promote moral relativism. Yet that is exactly what the learned ones do. It is true that individuals may hold to their own conception of right and wrong, but no society can function without a moral consensus—that is, a general agreement as to what constitutes morally acceptable and unacceptable behavior. Those who

[10] Robert D. McFadden, "Harry V. Jaffa, Conservative Scholar and Muse for Goldwater, Dies at 96", *New York Times*, January 13, 2015, p. A19.

[11] Joan Desmond, "Mario Cuomo, 1932–2015: His Controversial Legacy", *National Catholic Register*, January 5, 2015, http://www.ncregister.com /daily-news/mario-cuomo-1932-2015-his-controversial-legacy.

[12] Brown, *Human Universals*, p. 139.

advocate otherwise are responsible for our cultural crisis: they are fostering nihilism, a radical individualism that is at odds with basic social needs.

Pope Benedict XVI warned us about a "dictatorship of relativism"—a condition in which moral absolutes are seen as impediments to liberty. He counseled against the "widespread relativism which acknowledges nothing as definitive and, even more, tends to make its ultimate measure the individual and his personal caprice".[13] This conception of morality and freedom sees the individual as a self-directing agent, one who goes about society making up his own ideas of right and wrong. There is no role for the common good, just the good of the individual. Not only is this conception sociologically preposterous, but it invites everyone to indulge his base appetites in the name of liberty.

Thanks to Supreme Court justice Oliver Wendell Holmes, the cultural disdain for morality found a respectable place in law. According to Amherst College professor Hadley Arkes, it was Holmes' desire that "every word of moral significance could be banished from the law altogether, and other words adopted which could convey legal ideas uncolored by anything outside the law."[14] Holmes got what he wanted: an endless array of judicial decisions that completely ignore the moral basis of law. This lacks common sense. All of us look to the law for at least some guidance on matters of right and wrong, so when rulings are made without reference to traditional understandings of morality, the outcome must necessarily reflect the clinically pure reasoning of unelected judges. How can it be

---

[13] Benedict XVI, address to the bishops of Angola and São Tomé (March 20, 2009).

[14] Hadley Arkes, "The Moral Turn", *First Things*, May 2017, p. 30.

considered progress to ignore social mores? Moreover, there is nothing democratic about it.

The consequences of this false interpretation of freedom are all around us: abortion, euthanasia, drug use, pornography—to name just a few—are celebrations of the unencumbered self. The idea that we are answerable to no one but ourselves is dangerous to the individual, and it sets in motion damage to many others that is hard to repair.

No one understands the consequences of the Holmesian conception of law better than Arkes. The U.S. Supreme Court decision that struck down state laws against abortion, *Roe v. Wade*, was wrong, he says, not primarily because it created a right to abortion not found in the Constitution but because it violated the natural law. Human life begins at conception: all the DNA properties that make someone a unique person are present at fertilization. Intentionally to take the life of an innocent person is immoral and cannot be justified. Therefore, laws that do violence to this verity are inherently wrong. "When we move to the level of a moral judgment", Arkes writes, "we move away from statements of merely personal taste or private choice, and we begin to speak about the things that are more generally or universally right or wrong, just or unjust, for others as well as ourselves."[15]

The Founders understood right from wrong, never defending the exercise of rights that did not serve the ends as prescribed in the preamble to the Constitution. They sought the formation of "a more perfect Union", a society that allowed for a measure of pluralism in the states while remaining one nation. Justice had to be established, domestic tranquility was nonnegotiable, the common defense was a must, and the general welfare of the people

[15] Ibid., p. 34.

had to be upheld. Furthermore, the blessings of liberty had to be preserved for future generations. Achieving these lofty goals is not easy, and it is next to impossible in a society in which moral relativism flourishes.

The ends spelled out in the preamble are consistent with Catholic social teachings. Communitarian at the heart, the establishment of "a more perfect Union" is a very Catholic notion. Justice is one of the cardinal virtues, and domestic tranquility is looked upon with favor by the Church Fathers. Catholicism recognizes the legitimate right of nations to defend themselves and is strongly committed to the general welfare of the people. Free people also have a duty to ensure that their successors enjoy the same rights that they do.

Do Rights Liberate?

It may sound counterintuitive to question whether rights liberate, but just think about it. To liberate is to set free. Can it reasonably be maintained that the right to kill oneself makes one free? Suicide, with or without the assistance of a doctor, ends all use of one's liberty.

Granted, liberty cannot be exercised without rights, but it does not follow that every action results in liberation. Some actions can lead to the opposite—slavery. If someone becomes addicted to gambling and then loses his life savings after spending it in Las Vegas, hoping to hit the jackpot, he is hardly a model of freedom. He is a pathetic person, who, seduced by the lure of a false freedom, has lost control of himself.

What if freedom results in an increase in human suffering? Should we celebrate it or condemn it? Common sense drives us to choose the latter. So, too, do the teachings of the Catholic Church. What would Jesus do? He most certainly would not applaud any ideology that added to the fund of human suffering, even if the outcome was rendered in the name of liberty. That would simply make it all the more perverse.

Should we legalize dueling? What if two men voluntarily decide to duel to death in public? What if an arena agrees to host the event? What if a pay-per-view cable channel agrees to air the contest live? What if corporate advertisers jump at the chance to make money? What if everyone agrees that the winner gets to keep a hefty slice of the proceeds? What if a portion of the proceeds goes to fighting breast cancer?

If the only value that matters is freedom of choice, then the duel is on. But are the parties to the event the only thing that matters? The participants live in society, and a free society has more interests than individual rights. There is the common good, for instance. Is the common good advanced by promoting the killing of innocent persons, even if consent is granted? What cultural message is being sent by allowing the dueling to take place? If the event dehumanizes those who are party to it, is this not a concern even to those not directly involved? If attitudes toward life are cheapened, how can this be declared a victory?

In a similar vein, what is there to celebrate when freedom kills all prospects for happiness? Those who say that all exercises of freedom should be valued for what they are, independent of whether they liberate, would still find cause for celebration. James Madison knew better. Indeed, he made plain his conviction, expressed in *The Federalist Papers*, that freedom should advance happiness, not retard it.[16] Tell that to the American Civil Liberties Union.

---

[16] Alexander Hamilton, James Madison, and John Jay, *The Federalist Papers*, ed. Clinton Rossiter (New York: American Library, 1961), no. 62, p. 380.

To this day, the American Civil Liberties Union (ACLU) defends the right of the homeless to sleep on streets and sidewalks. "Public spaces and basic freedoms belong to all New Yorkers", says a senior attorney for the New York branch of the ACLU, and this means that cops should not tell the homeless to move along.[17] What about when the temperature drops below freezing? The homeless have a right to refuse city-sponsored shelters, the civil libertarians say, even in life-and-death situations.

Not too long ago, the New York Civil Liberties Union had a Project Freeze initiative whereby attorneys were dispatched to advise the homeless, many of whom were mentally ill, that they had a constitutional right to freeze to death. The result? In one week alone, three homeless men were found dead.[18] This is what happens when hardcore ideologues abandon common sense: the innocent die. It is what happens when ideology triumphs over reason, when pie-in-the-sky ideas of freedom rule the day. If this example were an anomaly, it could be treated as unfortunate. But it is the long-established policy of the nation's leading civil liberties organization, one with chapters in every major law school in the country.

Freedom that causes human suffering is not the only bastardization of liberty that is tolerated and promoted by civil libertarians. They even justify rights that literally destroy freedom. "The founding fathers sought to establish a society with unprecedented freedom of thought and expression", writes Lowenthal, "but they had no intention

---

[17] "Complaint: NYPD Unlawfully Orders Homeless People to Leave Public Spaces", American Civil Liberties Union, May 26, 2016, https://www.nyclu.org/en/press-releases/complaint-nypd-unlawfully-orders-homeless-people-leave-public-spaces.

[18] Charles Krauthammer, "How to Save the Homeless Mentally Ill", *New Republic*, February 8, 1988, p. 24.

of allowing a freedom so broad that it would destroy free society itself."[19] As Canavan put it, when a freedom that is guaranteed is abused, it ceases "to enjoy the protection of the guarantee", unless efforts to thwart the abuses result in an even greater diminution of liberty.[20]

Canavan's position is quintessentially Catholic. The Church, following Aquinas and Augustine, teaches that the natural law applies to those rights that are exercised in a way that advances liberty. This is part of Catholicism's teleology of freedom: rights can be appraised only in relation to the good they are expected to serve. Their abuse, then, is inconsistent with their creation. So, who would object to this reasoning? The ACLU would.

The ACLU defends the right of Nazis to organize according to their own objectives, but it works against the right of the Boy Scouts to do likewise (more on the Boy Scouts in chapter 5). To defend Nazis, the ACLU says, is to defend the principle of free speech. This explains why it defended the right of neo-Nazis to march in Skokie, Illinois, in the late 1970s. Interestingly, in the early 1990s, when I debated ACLU president Norman Dorsen at Harvard Law School, this issue was raised. The crowd cheered—it was the only time it did so for me the entire night—when I said, "Nazis ought to be defeated, not defended."

The ACLU's position is nonsense on two levels: (1) the same ACLU that defends Nazis is reluctant to defend the rights of pro-life Catholics—it has even sought to prosecute them under a law written to apprehend gangsters; and (2) it makes no sense to award rights to those bent on destroying the rights of others. Moreover, as David Lowenthal argues, the preamble commits us to securing

[19] Lowenthal, *No Liberty for License*, p. 103.
[20] Canavan, *Freedom of Expression*, p. 6.

liberty's blessings for ourselves and posterity.[21] If this means
anything, it means we are obliged to stop those committed
to the overthrow of republican government.

To defend those who would abolish freedom if they
were to come to power not only lacks common sense;
it also violates the central promise of the Declaration of
Independence—our rights are inalienable. Ernest van den
Haag was a keen social observer who addressed this issue
with clarity. He argued that "if our right to choose the
government freely is *inalienable*, then we are not entitled
to *give* the right away any more than the government is
entitled to *take* it away" (his italics). In other words, freedom, properly understood, does not commit us to the
proposition that we can elect a government that pledges
to eviscerate our God-given rights. "Nor", van den Haag
says, "if freedom is to be inalienable, can invitations to
alienate it be recognized as a legitimate part of the democratic process."[22]

Similarly, political philosopher Sidney Hook maintained that there is no right to a revolution in a democracy.
He reasoned that it was the faith of every person committed to democracy that all legitimate demands could be
worked out, thus making it untenable, and unprincipled,
to counsel revolution.[23] Nazis, communists, and anarchists
do not believe in liberty, and, indeed, they are its professed
enemies. It makes no sense, then, to pretend that they are
just another dissident voice. If they had it their way, there
would be no freedom for anyone, save for themselves.
There is nothing noble in the defense of those who would
destroy freedom. It is suicidal.

---

[21] Lowenthal, *No Liberty for License*, p. 20.

[22] Ernest van den Haag, "Controlling Subversive Groups", *Annals of the
American Academy of Political and Social Science* 300 (July 1955): 62–71.

[23] Hook, *Paradoxes of Freedom*, p. 113.

Alexis de Tocqueville, the astute nineteenth-century French observer of America, warned that, in a democracy, freedom of association is far more problematic than freedom of speech. The risks, he said, were palpable. To put a realistic face on this, should we defend, or stop, terrorists from organizing for the purpose of inciting riots? According to civil libertarians, and many legal scholars, we must defend their rights. Hook said it well when he wrote that such blue-sky persons "flout the common-sense propositions of ordered society".[24]

To show just how far gone the ACLU is on this issue, consider what one of its prominent attorneys told Harvard Law professor Arthur Miller. In a panel discussion, Miller asked former ACLU attorney Jeanne Baker to ponder the prospect of two violent groups, fully armed, planning to confront each other in a demonstration. Without blinking an eye, she stuck to her guns, saying that the demonstration should proceed. Miller then taunted her: "Do I have to bring in the A-bomb?" Even that did not deter her. What is needed, she said, was to show "an imminence of danger at the location of the marchers at the time of the marches".[25]

Miller wondered aloud whether she "allowed doctrine to run riot here".[26] Indeed, it had. Her stance was void of any trace of common sense. It is also at odds with the First Amendment, which protects our right to "peaceable assembly", not the right to gather for the express purpose of engaging in violence. The government's first obligation is to maintain the peace, and threats to it must be taken seriously.

[24] Ibid., p. 38.

[25] Quoted in George McKenna, *The Constitution: That Delicate Balance* (New York: Random House, 1984), p. 286. The exchange between Miller and Baker was made in the video that accompanied the text. See episode 9 of the television series that aired on the Learning Channel.

[26] Ibid.

In 2017, after white supremacists, carrying guns, held a rally in Charlottesville, Virginia, the ACLU changed its policy on demonstrations. Anthony Romero, the executive director, said that, in the future, the ACLU would decide on a case-by-case basis whether to represent a group carrying firearms.[27] There have been many extreme left-wing groups who have demonstrated with arms before, but the ACLU never had any problem defending them. It remains to be seen how even-handed it will be in applying its new policy.

Pushing the Boundaries of Free Speech

The Catholic Church's conception of freedom of speech is another example of her adept understanding of human nature. According to Peter A. Kwasniewski of the Saint Paul Center,

> The Catholic tradition has always begun in distinctive analysis from a fact of human nature, namely, that speech is a rational activity that can be done well or poorly, rightly or wrongly. Its due exercise is measured by its purpose, which is, broadly, the communication of truth—including not only speculative truths, but also advice, opinions, predictions, and the like, when one is attempting to come as near the truth as possible.[28]

---

[27] "Charlottesville Violence Prompts ACLU to Change Policy on Hate Groups Protesting with Guns", August 18, 2017, Public Broadcasting Service, https://www.pbs.org/newshour/nation/charlottesville-violence-prompts -aclu-change-policy-hate-groups-protesting-guns.

[28] Peter A. Kwasniewski, "Freedom of Speech", in *Encyclopedia of Catholic Social Thought, Social Science, and Social Policy*, ed. Michael Coulter, Stephen Krason, Richard Myers, and Joseph Varacalli (Lanham, Md.: Scarecrow Press, 2007), p. 443.

Similarly, the Catholic Church understands that any right worth treasuring must be judiciously exercised, lest it be trivialized or diminished. If the purpose of free speech is the pursuit of truth, then the mere invocation of a right, absent any purpose, is not a responsible expression of that right. In 1832, Pope Gregory XVI denounced the "freedom to publish any writings whatever", holding that an absolutist interpretation of free speech could do much harm.[29] Contrast this position with the one favored by the ACLU. In 1920, the year the ACLU was founded, it flatly stated that it "puts no limit on the principle of free speech".[30]

This mentality—that we should all be free to express ourselves any way we want—is on a collision course with the need to protect ourselves from the abuses of freedom. Our culture is in crisis largely because we are unwilling to confront those who advocate a false freedom, namely, a freedom bereft of limits and restraints. Freedom, properly understood, does not see every call for restraint as a plea to undermine it.

Fred Friendly, former CBS journalist and student of the Constitution, often said that problems occur when the First Amendment "overheats", meaning that pushing the limits of free speech can be dangerous. Yes, when the North American Man/Boy Love Association, an organization that advocates the sexual exploitation of children, seeks to meet in a public library to outline its agenda, it is a perversion of liberty to come to their defense. It also lacks elementary decency and common sense.

Most people understand the difference between speech, expression, and conduct, though in the eyes of many judges, there isn't any difference. Increasingly, they treat

[29] Ibid. Pope Gregory XVI, encyclical letter *Mirari vos* (August 15, 1832), no. 15.

[30] See ACLU's *1921 Annual Report*, p. 8.

the right to speak about public-policy issues—which is the heart of the First Amendment's free-speech provision— the same way they treat mud wrestling and dwarf-tossing. In fact, the ACLU sees mud wrestling as an expression deserving the same protections as political speech; it also defends as speech the barroom practice of tossing dwarfs from one end of the room to the other.[31] Thus does the ACLU trivialize the meaning of free speech.

There are many rights in the Bill of Rights, and several of them conflict with another. For example, the First Amendment guarantees freedom of speech, and the Sixth Amendment guarantees a fair trial. To cite one real-life example, if TV cameras are allowed in the courtroom, this free-speech exercise may alter the behavior and thinking of lawyers, judges, and the jury, thus diminishing the prospects of a fair trial. Barring the cameras protects the Sixth Amendment but at the expense of the First Amendment. Tough choices must be made. The central point is not that some rights should be honored above others; rather, it is that rights cannot be considered absolute if they sometimes conflict with another right.

Supreme Court justice Hugo Black said he was an absolutist when it came to the First Amendment. "It is my belief that there are 'absolutes' in our Bill of Rights", he said in a 1960 lecture, "and that they were put there on purpose by men who knew what the words meant, and meant their prohibitions to be 'absolutes.'"[32] Yet when the case of flag burning came before him in 1966, this same absolutist said it was not constitutionally protected. Why not? Because burning the flag was conduct, not speech.

[31] William A. Donohue, *Twilight of Liberty: The Legacy of the ACLU* (New Brunswick, N.J.: Transaction Press, 1994), p. 189.

[32] Hugo Black, "The Bill of Rights", *New York University Law Review* 35 (April 1960): 865.

This common sense understanding, however, was thrown out by the Supreme Court in 1989 although chief justice William Rehnquist dissented from the majority and argued that flag burning "is the equivalent of an inarticulate grunt or roar" and thus not worthy of protection.[33]

Catholicism has never accepted the absolutist position, and with good reason: it is an asocial interpretation of liberty. According to the *Catechism*, "The exercise of freedom does not imply a right to say or do everything. It is false to maintain that man, 'the subject of this freedom,' is 'an individual who is fully self-sufficient and whose finality is the satisfaction of his own interests in the enjoyment of earthly goods'"[34] (1740). Yes, it is precisely because we interact with others that the "no exceptions to my rights" position proves to be utterly impractical, and therefore unpersuasive.

Pope Francis gave life to the Catholic position when he observed that the "tendency to claim ever broader individual rights" suggests "a conception of the human person as detached from all social and anthropological contexts, as if the person were a 'monad', increasingly unconcerned with other surrounding 'monads'".[35] The pope is right. We are not automatons, freewheeling robotic creatures who live a solo existence. Therefore, any conception of liberty that does not correspond with the human condition is inherently flawed.

The Catholic conception of freedom is not myopic; it is not fixated on the individual. It is a sociologically realistic understanding of the natural rights of the individual and his concomitant duties to his fellow man. But to the

---

[33] Texas v. Gregory Lee Johnson, 491 U.S. 397, June 21, 1989.

[34] Congregation for the Doctrine of the Faith, instruction *Libertatis conscientia* (March 22, 1986), no. 13.

[35] Francis, address to the European Parliament (November 25, 2014).

proponents of radical individualism, anything that suggests obligations to others is considered problematic, an impediment to total freedom. Their idea of liberty is particularly attractive to narcissists; such persons are a liability to the pursuit of freedom, properly understood.

Hook saw right through the untenable idea that rights are absolute. He contended that the Bill of Rights contain "common sense presuppositions" that must be readily acknowledged. For example, he said the Framers had a common sense understanding of the phrase "Congress shall make no law" (regarding freedom of speech). This explains why, despite the absolutist language, they allowed for reasonable exceptions. To wit: those who accepted this "absolutist" language also made it a crime to engage in libel, slander, and sedition.[36]

Hook was a realist. "No one can reasonably make a demand for freedom in an unqualified sense—a freedom to do *anything* one pleases" (his italics). To those who disagree, he offered an example that even they cannot logically argue with: "My demand for freedom to speak is at the same time a demand that the freedom of those who desire to prevent me from speaking should be curbed."[37] This was one of the many "paradoxes of freedom" that he noted.

If, as radical libertarians say, we enjoy, or should enjoy, an absolute right to free speech, that would commit us to rather bizarre positions. It would mean that all laws on libel, slander, and fraud would be stricken. This would allow us to write and say malicious falsehoods about anyone, allowing no recourse to victims. Those whose reputations were intentionally ruined would just have to deal with it, even if damage was done to their marriages or to their jobs.

---

[36] Hook, *Paradoxes of Freedom*, p. 32.
[37] Ibid., p. 10.

When called by a judge to tell the truth, we must do so, lest we be found guilty of perjury. Should we do away with this law? After all, laws against perjury are limitations on our freedom of speech.

The laws against obscenity are not enforced with much regularity, but they are still on the books. Should we excise them altogether? Should it be legal to film children performing sex acts on animals? Would that make us freer?

There are laws against the deliberate incitement to riot. Are they an infringement on our freedom of speech? If they are, it should be legal for a racist leader to meet in an urban setting with his followers, and when he is challenged by a protesting member of the targeted race, he should be allowed to instruct his supporters to beat and kill that person. Is that what we want?

Similarly, the U.S. Supreme Court has upheld penalties for "fighting words". It is not constitutionally protected speech to utter words that "tend to incite an immediate breach of the peace". In a unanimous decision, the high court held that "it has been well observed that such utterances [e.g., speech that is libelous, profane, and obscene] are no essential part of any exposition of ideas, and are of such slight social value that any benefit that may be derived from them is clearly outweighed by the social interest in order and morality."[38]

Following justice Oliver Wendell Holmes Jr., it is not considered a legitimate exercise of free speech for someone falsely to shout, "Fire!", in a crowded theater. This prohibition is definitely a suppression of free speech, but it is considered acceptable because there is a captive audience—no one has the time to offer a rebuttal—and it presents a "clear

---

[38] Chaplinsky v. New Hampshire, 315 U.S. 568, March 9, 1942.

and present danger". Should we get rid of all "clear and present danger" exceptions to the First Amendment?

If someone steals another person's work (e.g., an important invention that is legally protected), he is in violation of copyright laws. Such laws impinge on the free-speech rights of the thief. Is it time to strike them?

It is illegal to put notices in mailboxes urging homeowners to sell before minorities move in. Are such laws dated? Should we now value the free-speech rights of the racist?

Should we have the right to make harassing phone calls? Are not such limitations an abridgment of our free-speech rights?

Why should there be laws against false advertising? Who is to say what is false? Moreover, are not such laws a violation of our right to say whatever we want?

When someone applies for a job and intentionally lies about his credentials, is it not his free-speech right to do so? Is it time to jettison that exception to freedom of speech?

Verbal agreements to restrain trade are not legal, but that is also a restraint on free-speech rights. Would we have a freer society if these laws were excised?

Why is a judge allowed to hold someone in contempt of court? Why is he allowed to place sanctions on speech he objects to? His right, after all, comes at the expense of the free-speech rights of others.

We have laws against treasonous speech. They are clearly a denial of free-speech rights. Should we nix these laws?

If an accountant's client says he will grease him handsomely if he agrees to make some changes in his tax return, is he simply exercising his right to free speech, or is he engaged in bribery? What should we do about it?

As a demonstration of my right to free speech, should I be allowed to solicit a crime on the Internet? It's my free speech, isn't it?

Now ask yourself this: Is there anyone who would want to live in a society where all these abuses of speech were legal?

So where do we draw the line? Aren't we on a slippery slope to censorship? Sidney Hook nails it, as usual. He concedes that abridgements to liberty "*may* result in our hurtling down the slope", but "our very *awareness* that we have stepped on a slope is a brake on our precipitous descent."[39] Of course, he is taking for granted that common sense is operative. It is not his fault that it may not be.

If it is generally conceded that extremes are to be avoided—too much good food sours the stomach—why is it so hard to understand that the same is true of liberty? "The *extreme* of liberty (which is its abstract perfection, but its real fault)", wrote Edmund Burke, "obtains nowhere, nor ought to obtain anywhere, because extremes ... are destructive both to virtue and enjoyment."[40] The father of conservatism received support from the author of the First Amendment, James Madison, when he said that "liberty may be endangered by the abuses of liberty as well as the abuses of power."[41]

Such pronouncements cannot be said enough; they are decisively countercultural, running against conventional wisdom. It is the contemporary fixation on rights and more rights, to the neglect of their corollary, namely, individual responsibilities, that accounts for our cultural crisis. The fashionable idea that we can have it all is a close cousin to the notion that there cannot be any limitations on rights.

Plato, Aristotle, and Cicero understood that moderation was a virtue that had to be diligently nourished, lest excess

[39] Hook, *Paradoxes of Freedom*, p. 47, italics in the original.

[40] Edmund Burke, *Burke's Politics*, ed. Ross J. S. Hoffman and Paul Levack (New York: Knopf, 1967), p. 109.

[41] *The Federalist Papers*, no. 63.

prevail. Plato said it best. He counseled that an "excess of liberty, whether in states or individuals, seems only to pass into excess of slavery".[42] How can this be? Because the public will never accept the extremes of liberty—citizens will demand that the government intervene before tolerating the abuses of freedom. So, if tyranny is to be avoided, calls for unlimited rights must be rejected.

Freedom Requires Virtue

We would not be in the throes of a cultural crisis if more people exercised virtue, or good habits. Instead of cultivating virtue, many have nurtured vice. That is why we hear so many people demand that their rights be respected, without any acknowledgment of their concomitant responsibilities.

Good parents instinctively know that rights are tethered to responsibilities. They expand rights when their children act responsibly and limit them when they do not. That's why they sometimes ground their children. Being grounded means that a child's right to leave the house is taken away because he has used his freedom irresponsibly. Unfortunately, this common sense way of raising children is not as common as it once was. Our intoxication with rights makes it difficult to employ sanctions for untoward behaviors.

Rights and responsibilities go together. Their relationship is the key to a free society, for without a sense of responsibility, whatever rights are granted are likely to be abused, resulting in a diminution of someone else's rights. Freedom, properly understood, must always be anchored in responsibilities.

Catholicism shares this perspective. There is no shortage of papal encyclicals that emphasize the central role

[42] Plato, *The Republic* (Mineola, N.Y.: Dover, 2008), p. 223.

that individual responsibility plays in society. This is doubly important to free societies. In his encyclical *Caritas in veritate*, Pope Benedict XVI stated that "individual rights, when detached from a framework of duties which grants them their full meaning, can run wild, leading to an escalation of demands which is effectively unlimited and indiscriminate. An overemphasis on rights leads to a disregard for duties."[43]

Saint John Paul II's *Veritatis splendor* is one of the finest expositions ever written on this subject, continuing the long tradition in Catholic social thought of conjoining rights to responsibilities. John Paul II knew what Soviet totalitarianism did to his beloved Poland, so he was fierce in his defense of individual rights. But he brooked no discussion about rights without first acknowledging responsibilities. Freedom, he taught, is not exclusively about "me"—it is also about "we".

All of us are commanded to exercise our rights in a way that serves others: freedom is best achieved when those with whom we interact, especially our loved ones, are positively affected by our decisions. The Ten Commandments place limits on our actions in order to facilitate the proper use of freedom. When Jesus made his plea "Come, follow me", it was, John Paul II noted, the greatest exaltation of freedom ever voiced.[44]

John Paul II saw freedom as inseparable from morality. True freedom, he taught, quoting Christ, is dependent on the truth: "The frank and open acceptance of truth is the condition for authentic freedom: 'You will know the truth, and the truth will set you free' (Jn 8:32)."[45] That is why he found demands for unconditional liberty so

[43] Benedict XVI, encyclical letter *Caritas in veritate* (June 29, 2009), no. 43.
[44] John Paul II, encyclical letter *Veritatis splendor* (August 6, 1993), no. 66.
[45] Ibid., no. 87.

impoverished. If liberty is not tied to the truth about what
is right and wrong, it is not worthy of the name. John Paul
II was on solid ground when he declared that the Ten
Commandments are the bedrock of freedom; they "are
the *first necessary step on the journey towards freedom*, its start-
ing point" (his emphasis). He cogently cited Saint Augustine, who wrote that to be free from "murder, adultery,
fornication, theft, fraud, sacrilege, and so forth" was "the
beginning of freedom".[46]

David Lowenthal agrees with the Catholic perspective and courageously speaks his mind on the subject. "A
nation of profligates, cheats, and cowards, of people incapable of controlling their own lust, greed, rage, and fear,
cannot, by the nature of things, use its freedom properly or
long endure."[47] Is there anyone who would disagree with
this observation? Actually, there are quite a few, many of
whom have initials after their names.

Laughlin McDonald, who once headed the ACLU's
Southern Regional Office, not only heralded loitering as
a constitutional right but saw it as ennobling. He argued
that "wanderers and loafers" have "an honored place in
our culture". He was not being facetious. "Loafing and
loitering, like privacy and many other rights we take for
granted", he said, "are not specifically mentioned in the
Constitution, but they are protected by it." On top of that,
loafing and loitering are a social good: "They give value
and meaning to life and nurture a sense of independence,
self-confidence and creativity."[48] Only a wild-eyed ideo-
logue would believe such nonsense.

[46] Ibid., no.13; cf. Augustine, *In Iohannis Evangelium Tractatus* 41, 10: *CCL*
36, 363.

[47] Lowenthal, *No Liberty for License*, p. 91.

[48] Laughlin McDonald, "A Song for Loafing", *Civil Liberties* (Spring/
Summer 1988): 7.

"Beer is proof that God loves us and wants us to be happy." The author of those words, Benjamin Franklin, was not a crazed civil libertarian. Quite the opposite. "Only a virtuous people are capable of freedom", he noted.[49] So drink up, gents, but know when to put a lid on it. John Adams was another realist. He said the Constitution was made "only for a moral and religious people".[50] That would seem to exclude the loafers and loiterers so loved by McDonald.

It is not as though the Founders were unaware of social misfits. Madison knew there was "a degree of depravity in mankind", which is why he emphasized that a republican form of government "presupposes the existence" of virtue and related characteristics.[51] Edmund Burke also understood that liberty depends on virtue and wisdom, and he even went so far as to say that, absent their existence, liberty is "the greatest of all possible evils; for it is folly, vice and madness without tuition or restraint".[52] He was advocating ordered liberty, the only liberty worthy of the name.

For many modern Americans, ordered liberty is an oxymoron: for liberty to be realized, they insist, it must be unrestrained. But that never results in more liberty, only less. Catholic social thought recognizes that liberty must be ordered if it is to be achieved and sees unbridled liberty as the oxymoron. The *Catechism* says it best: "The moral virtues are acquired by human effort. They are the fruit and

[49] Quoted in Eric Metaxas, *If You Can Keep It: The Forgotten Promise of American Liberty* (New York: Viking, 2016), p. 55.

[50] John Adams to Massachusetts Militia, October 11, 1798, Founders Online, National Archives, last modified November 26, 2017, http://founders.archives .gov/documents/Adams/99-02-02-3102.

[51] Alexander Hamilton, James Madison, and John Jay, *The Federalist Papers* (Mineola, N.Y.: Dover, 2014), no. 55, p. 275.

[52] Edmund Burke, *Reflections on the Revolution in France* (New York: Anchor, 1989), p. 263.

seed of morally good acts; they dispose all the powers of the human being for communion with divine love" (1804).

Legislating Morality

There is a popular conception that we cannot legislate morality. This is not only wrong; it is plain stupid. What else can the government legislate if not morality? From requiring seat belts to prohibiting murder, every law involves the legislation of morality. Even those who say the law has no business in our bedrooms don't mean what they say: Are they prepared to legalize spousal rape?

A more legitimate question is the scope of the law, and what behaviors it should regulate. Similarly, it is important to recognize that the law can do only so much. It cannot make an irresponsible person responsible, though it is a mistake to think it cannot abet virtue, or vice, for that matter. George Will got it right when he wrote that "statecraft is soulcraft", meaning that the proper role of government is the cultivation of good character in its citizens.[53] This is not a request for the government to assume the powers of an all-encompassing moral cop, policing our every behavior. No, it is an appeal to common sense. Government can either promote or retard virtue; it should be on the side of good behavior.

Tocqueville implored us not to set our expectations too high when considering the role of law in promoting morality. "There is no country where the law can foresee everything or where institutions should take the place of reason and mores", he wrote.[54] (Some translations

---

[53] George Will, *Statecraft as Soulcraft* (New York: Simon and Schuster, 1983).

[54] Alexis de Tocqueville, *Democracy in America*, ed. J. P. Mayer, trans. George Lawrence (New York: Harper and Row, 1966), p. 122.

substitute "common sense" for "reason.") Problems emerge when common sense is in short supply, and this is especially true when the custodians of the law are deficient in it. That is an accurate summation of our predicament.

It is not simply lawmakers who have let us down; judges have done great damage. Indeed, the lack of common sense in judicial rulings, especially as they affect sexuality, is stunning. Much of the damage is traceable to a flawed interpretation of the First Amendment.

Lowenthal cogently observes that it was after World War II that judges went into high gear proclaiming rights that were previously never recognized. The exercise of these rights often came at the expense of the common good, which the First Amendment was supposed to serve, not subvert. "Thus, the First Amendment has become a vehicle for degrading and destabilizing the republic it was meant to strengthen and preserve."[55] Indeed, it has become a "prime agent of its destruction".

Supreme Court rulings on obscenity, beginning in the late 1950s, underscore Lowenthal's point. Further decisions in the 1960s and 1970s created an environment where some pretty sick material was made widely available. Other rulings on criminality and so-called victimless crimes pushed the limits of civility. Lowenthal captures what happened with this outburst against radical libertarianism. "Profligacy, dissipation, brutality, lawlessness, and lack of rational control over the passions have all been brought into the living room, the neighborhood theater, the local drugstore, and record shop—and this not only without a struggle from educational and political authorities but with the blessing of the highest court in the land."[56] That is a severe judgment, but it is merited.

---

[55] Lowenthal, *No Liberty for License*, p. xiv.
[56] Ibid., p. 107.

When a man stands in a courthouse with a jacket that bears a vile obscenity on the back—denouncing the draft—in plain sight of women and children waiting in line, and is told by the Supreme Court that his rights are paramount, then elementary standards of civility and the common good have been plundered.[57] When legal penalties are dropped for public urination, but sanctions are employed against teachers who have Bibles on their desks, there is something twisted going on. When students can taunt their teachers—in the same schools where metal detectors screen for guns and knives—common sense has all but disappeared.

Radical libertarians respond by saying, "Where do we draw the line?" That's a fair question, but before it can be answered, we must first agree that lines must be drawn. If we cannot agree to that—if we insist that free speech is absolute and every morally depraved act must be accepted—then the conversation is over. That would commit us to the proposition that it is better to do absolutely nothing in the face of moral anarchy than to check it with the law. Only those wholly lacking in common sense are capable of drawing that conclusion.

The ACLU says there should be no limits to obscenity, contending that it cannot be defined. "No one knows what obscenity is", said Ira Glasser, former head of the ACLU, "or precisely how to define it. Like 'false speech,' obscenity often lies in the eye of the beholder."[58] This is nonsense: moral codes are not randomly chosen. For instance, we have laws against defecating in public. Should we eliminate them because some are not offended? Obscenity is always partly, but never always, in the eye of

---

[57] Cohen v. California, 403 U.S. 15 (1971).
[58] Ira Glasser, *Visions of Liberty* (New York: Arcade Publishing, 1991), p. 145.

the beholder. Moral codes are determined by consensus, not by unanimity.

The ACLU's position is also dishonest. For example, it supports the laws on sexual harassment. How can this be? How can the ACLU be sure that a sexual joke made in the workplace qualifies as sexual harassment, and not innocent banter? And if it is okay to make subjective determinations on sexual harassment, why is it not okay to make subjective determinations on obscenity? Ideology, not logic, is at work, rendering the ACLU's objections to the obscenity statutes meaningless.

The ACLU's absolutist mentality allows it to oppose all laws on child pornography. Though the Supreme Court unanimously ruled against it in 1982, it still maintains that the sale, distribution, and possession of child pornography should be legal, lest we go sliding down the slippery slope to censorship.[59] In 1991, when I debated ACLU president Norman Dorsen at Harvard, I asked him to list which free-speech rights had been banned a decade after the high court upheld the child pornography statutes. He couldn't name one.

To appreciate how thoroughly lacking in common sense, and in common decency, the ACLU is, consider what former ACLU president Nadine Strossen said when asked if she would object to NBC's showing oral sex on TV at 3:00 in the afternoon. She told family advocate Frank Russo that she would have no problem defending it.[60]

Judge Robert Bork exhibited as much common sense as anyone who ever served on the bench, and he had a ready

[59] Ibid., pp. 207–10.

[60] Quoted in William A. Donohue, *Twilight of Liberty: The Legacy of the ACLU* (New Brunswick, N.J.: Transaction Press, 2001), p. 345. Strossen and Russo debated in 1994 at the Free Library of Philadelphia.

answer to those who questioned where to draw the line on moral issues: the "common sense of the community". To those who objected, saying there is no way to make such determinations, he had a splendid rejoinder: "Almost all judgments in the law are ones of degree, and the law does not flinch from such judgments except where, as in the case of morals, it seriously doubts the community's right to define harms."[61] Take dress. There is a difference between passing a law making it a crime to dress provocatively in public (few would support it) and locking up a man who exposes his genitals as he walks down the street (few would not support it). Common sense tells us that the community has a right to defend itself against moral harms, and freedom of speech allows us to determine where the line should be drawn.

To blue-sky thinkers, nothing matters more than the right to express oneself. Moreover, these same people see the world through the distorted lens of rationalism, maintaining that moral harms are nothing but a product of our irrational fears. If we are offended by indecent exposure, they say, we should avert our eyes. Even that wouldn't be good enough: they would insist on putting quotation marks around "indecent", thus calling into question the very existence of indecent exposure.

Long before Bork, the philosophers of the Scottish Enlightenment gave a prominent role to common sense in making moral judgments. Francis Hutchinson said that distinguishing right from wrong was a natural human trait, one well suited to making moral judgments. Thomas Jefferson agreed. Thomas Reid went even further, calling this

[61] Robert H. Bork, *Tradition and Morality in Constitutional Law*, Francis Boyer Lectures on Public Policy (Washington, D.C.: American Enterprise Institute, 1984), p. 3.

natural human ability a matter of "common sense".[62] The problem today is that common sense is in short supply.

The social teachings of the Catholic Church make for a rich compendium of applied common sense, a redoubtable source for everyone, Catholic and non-Catholic alike. Those teachings provide us with a guidebook that allows us to do what Pope Francis implores us to do—namely, to "build a just and wisely ordered society".[63] Doing so requires that we turn the job over to civil society.

Family, school, church, and voluntary associations constitute the institutions of civil society; they are the true locus of liberty. Burke called them "little platoons", institutions that mediate between the state and society.[64] Though government cannot do this job, it can provide a supportive role. It can also play a destructive role, something we have become all too accustomed to in recent times.

It is in these intermediate associations that civic virtue must be nourished. Aristotle understood this well. As Gertrude Himmelfarb points out, the conventional interpretation of Aristotle's reflections on man as a "social animal" is wrong: he said "man is by nature a political animal". The difference is important. To say man is a "social animal" is to speak to his need for social bonds and social cohesion, a phenomenon shared by animals in general. To say man is a "political animal" is to acknowledge that he finds it necessary to craft "a government of laws and institutions".[65] That speaks to man's rational nature.

---

[62] Quoted in Robert Curry, *Common Sense Nation: Unlocking the Forgotten Power of the American Idea* (New York: Encounter Books, 2015), pp. 40–43.

[63] Pope Francis, address on the South Lawn of the White House (September 23, 2015).

[64] Burke, *Reflections on the Revolution in France*, p. 59.

[65] Gertrude Himmelfarb, *One Nation, Two Cultures* (New York: Knopf, 1999), pp. 80–81.

Aristotle said that the good citizen "should know how to govern as a freeman, and how to obey like a freeman—these are the virtues of a citizen."[66] To do this, we need to call on the institutions of civil society to do their job, but we also need to have a government that is supportive of these efforts. Then we will have achieved ordered liberty.

If virtue is the key to liberty—without it we are controlled by our passions—then it must be instilled in children. It does not happen by itself. Children don't need to learn self-interest, but they do need to learn individual responsibility. Those best fit to help them learn are parents, teachers, the clergy, and civic leaders. They cannot do this, however, if they are undercut by laws, court decisions, and public policies that are more interested in promoting children's rights than they are in protecting the authority of adult authority figures.

We do not allow children to drive, vote, drink alcohol, or be admitted to the theater to see any movie they want: these restrictions are testimony to their level of maturity. But we are not consistent. We treat them as near equals when it comes to their rights versus their teachers' rights. And then we wonder why school discipline is such a serious issue. No one is counseling that students should have no rights, but when teachers can be shouted down in the classroom by unruly students spouting obscenities—without appropriate punishment—we are teaching the wrong values. The inculcation of virtue takes work, and it must be consistently applied if it is to achieve desired outcomes.

Our cultural crisis is our own doing. It can be undone, but only if we commit ourselves to creating a society of ordered liberty. Otherwise, we will collapse under the weight of rights run amuck. Freedom has a lovely face, but when it is distorted, there is nothing uglier.

[66] Ibid.

2

Moral Harms

The entire world is indebted to the courageous efforts of Russian freedom fighter Alexandr Solzhenitsyn, the writer and activist who exposed the horrors of Stalinism in his home country. When he gave the commencement address at Harvard University in 1978, the crowd thought he would recount his experience. Instead, he shocked them by blasting the egregious abuses of liberty in the West. "The defense of individual rights has reached such extremes as to make society as a whole defenseless against certain individuals.... It is time, in the West, to uphold not so much human rights as human obligations."[1]

Thirty years later, Carnegie Hall hosted *Jerry Springer: The Opera*, proving Solzhenitsyn's point. Vulgar beyond belief, the play mocked the Crucifixion, trashed the Eucharist, defiled the Virgin Mary, and portrayed Jesus as a fat, effeminate character who had his genitals fondled by Eve. It was how the play ended that validated Solzhenitsyn's concerns. The audience was informed that "nothing is wrong and nothing is right" and that "there are no absolutes of good and evil."[2] Thus did the play conclude in a

---

[1] Alexandr Solzhenitsyn, "A World Split Apart", speech at Harvard University, June 8, 1978, American Rhetoric, http://www.americanrhetoric.com.

[2] *Jerry Springer: The Opera*, directed by Peter Orton (London: Pathé Distribution, 2005), DVD. The remarks are made at the end of the show.

manner that was vintage Nazi: that is exactly what Hitler's lieutenants said in their defense at Nuremberg.

The play made its way to Off Broadway in 2018, with help from the federal government. The production company that hosted the sick musical, the New Group, is an annual recipient of funds from the National Endowment for the Arts. The Catholic League pressed president Donald Trump to nominate a new NEA chairman who would no longer fund anti-Christian grantees, exhibitions, and performances.[3]

Not only did judge Robert Bork have a brilliant legal mind, but his sociological insights put him way above his peers. He was highly critical of the conventional legal perspective that holds that "the only kinds of harm that a community is entitled to suppress are physical and economic injuries." According to this view, such things as "moral harms" should never be proscribed; to do so would mean interfering with "the autonomy of the individual". But, he counseled, such a view was deficient. "That is an indefensible definition of what people are entitled to regard as harms." His explanation was sociologically sound. "The result of discounting moral harm is the privatization of morality, which requires the community to practice moral relativism."[4]

Anyone is free to disagree with the observations of Solzhenitsyn and Bork, but arguments to the contrary find no support in the real world. Wrong behaviors are counted among the human universals listed by Donald Brown. No society in history has failed to acknowledge wrong behaviors, or what might be called moral harms,

[3] Bill Donohue, "Appeal to President Trump", Catholic League, January 24, 2018, https://www.catholicleague.org/appeal-to-president-trump/.

[4] Robert Bork, *Tradition and Morality in Constitutional Law*, Francis Boyer Lectures on Public Policy (Washington, D.C.: American Enterprise Institute, 1984), p. 3.

and it matters not a whit if some disagree; social norms do not require universal assent. Similarly, no society has ever failed to employ sanctions against wrongdoers.

Therefore, the idea that a society can function in a state of moral relativism—in which people pick and choose what they regard as right and wrong—is an illusion. Unfortunately, it is a fiction widely accepted by many intellectuals.

As Donald Brown details, rape has everywhere been prohibited. Incest is regarded as unthinkable in every society; mother-and-son sexual relations are especially condemned.[5] Francis Fukuyama, a prominent student of human nature, explains why there is a universal prohibition against incest. The incest taboo "appears to have evolved spontaneously in virtually all human societies on the basis of the natural aversion people have toward incestuous acts and on the need of human groups to regulate sexual access and social exchange".[6]

Not everyone thinks that incest is unthinkable. As expected, there are intellectuals who are fine with it; unfortunately, they are not of the junior-league variety. Significantly, Sigmund Freud held that the incest taboo was "perhaps the most drastic mutilation which man's erotic life has in all time experienced".[7] Those making the case for child abuse could not do better.

Feminist Shulamith Firestone advocates for the abolition of any sanctions against incest. Only if the family and the incest taboo were destroyed, she maintains, would sexuality "be released from its straightjacket to eroticize our

[5] Donald E. Brown, *Human Universals* (New York: McGraw-Hill, 1991), p. 137.

[6] Francis Fukuyama, *The Great Disruption: Human Nature and the Reconstitution of the Social Order* (New York: Free Press, 1999), p. 160.

[7] Sigmund Freud, *Civilization and Its Discontents* (New York: W. W. Norton, 1961), p. 51.

whole culture". The goal, she explicitly says, is to promote "relations with children [that] would include as much genital sex as the child was capable of", adding that "nonsexual friendships" would be a thing of the past.[8]

It would be a mistake to think that these are just some crackpot ideas that have no consequence. No, they seriously influence the thinking of sexual deviants. They surely have had an impact on the likes of the North American Man/Boy Love Association; its members actively recruit little kids for sex. Ideas have consequences, and that includes those that are pernicious.

Given the celebrations of hedonism in the West, we might not realize it, but modesty and shame are universal attributes. Brown found that the members of every society, including those in which men and women customarily go about naked, "have standards of sexual modesty". People do not normally copulate in public, Brown says, and this is especially true of adults. "Nor do they relieve themselves without some attempt to do it modestly."[9] To this point, Walter Berns, a gifted social scientist, made an interesting observation when he concluded that shamelessness, not shame, is a culturally learned characteristic; shame is a natural impulse.[10]

Berns was correct, but these days, owing to the brilliance of our cultural elites, it is shame, not shamelessness, that is the problem. In 2017, when a teenage boy found a girl undressing beside him in the high school locker room, he complained to the principal. The young man was put in his place: the principal told him that the girl self-identifies

[8] Shulamith Firestone, *The Dialectic of Sex* (New York: Bantam Books, 1971), pp. 60, 240.

[9] Brown, *Human Universals*, p. 139.

[10] Walter Berns, "Pornography v. Democracy: The Case for Censorship", *Public Interest* (Winter 1991): 13.

as a boy and therefore can use the boys' locker room. The principal also told the boy to get over it, to "tolerate" the undressing, and to "make it as 'natural' as possible." Lawyers for the male said the school shamed him and violated his privacy.[11] We know that we have reached the height of intellectual stupidity when a lawsuit has to be filed for shaming a normal boy who objects to the shamelessness of a disturbed girl.

Modesty and shame are civilizing forces; they restrain base human appetites. We should therefore worry when they are increasingly disregarded, not when they are judiciously employed. One does not have to be a prude to understand that the sexual impulse needs to be constructively channeled, lest it express itself in a reckless manner. But from the lens of the rationalist, modesty and shame are nothing but antiquated attributes, associated with sexual repression. Their view of human beings lacks an appreciation for the emotive aspects of life that make us whole, and it is therefore incomplete and inaccurate.

Catholic Sexual Ethics

Many intellectuals fail to understand the importance of modesty and shame, but not those steeped in Catholic tradition. The *Catechism* explains, "Modesty protects the intimate center of the person" (2521). It also "encourages patience and moderation in loving relationships" (2522). Teaching modesty to young people "means awakening in them respect for the human person" (2524). In Catholic

---

[11] Todd Starnes, "School Orders Boy to 'Tolerate' Undressing with Girl and Make it 'Natural'", *Fox News*, March 22, 2017, http://www.foxnews.com/opinion/2017/03/22/school-orders-boy-to-tolerate-undressing-with-girl-and-make-it-natural.html.

moral theology, modesty is understood as central to the cardinal virtue of temperance. Regarding the latter, no society that aspires to be free can dispense with temperance as a virtue. Catholic theologian Bernard Lonergan captured its essence when he wrote, "Man is an animal for whom mere animality is indecent."[12]

Chastity plays an important role in Catholic sexual ethics and should ideally play an important role in our culture; its near absence underscores our cultural crisis. It does not help that the grand wizards who set the sexual agenda continue to promote the stereotype that Catholic ethicists have little to contribute. In fact, they have a very realistic understanding of sexuality.

Catholics who write on this subject do not underestimate the power of sexual urges; on the contrary, it is precisely because they acknowledge the force of sexual urges that they implore us to consider the virtue of chastity. The Pontifical Council for the Family took up this question in the 1990s and resoundingly concluded that "the virtue of chastity is found within temperance—a cardinal virtue enriched by grace in baptism. So chastity is not to be understood as a repressive attitude. On the contrary, chastity should be understood rather as the purity and temporary stewardship of a precious and rich gift of love, in view of the self-giving realized in each person's specific vocation."[13]

Without chastity, men, in particular, have a hard time using the brakes that God gave them, and when that happens, women lose. There is nothing to celebrate if there

[12] Quoted in Michael P. Foley, "Modesty", in *Encyclopedia of Catholic Social Thought, Social Science, and Social Policy*, ed. Michael Coulter, Stephen Krason, Richard Myers, and Joseph Varacalli (Lanham, Md.: Scarecrow Press, 2007), p. 708.

[13] Pontifical Council for the Family, *The Truth and Meaning of Human Sexuality: Guidelines for Education within the Family* (December 8, 1995), no. 4.

are no checks on the id. Therefore, if true freedom is to be achieved, limits must be observed.

The virtue of chastity takes on greater meaning when we understand that it is a vehicle of love. "Love is a gift of God", the Pontifical Council for the Family declared, "nourished by and expressed in the encounter of man and woman."[14] Saint John Paul II stressed that "chastity by no means signifies rejection of human sexuality or lack of esteem for it; rather it signifies spiritual energy capable of defending love from the perils of selfishness and aggressiveness."[15] That is what the Pontifical Council held. "To the degree that a person weakens chastity, his or her love becomes more and more selfish, that is, satisfying a desire for pleasure and no longer self-giving."[16]

True love, in the Catholic tradition, can never be about self-satisfaction or self-indulgence, and that is why chastity is such a great resource. It allows the individual to sacrifice, to cultivate a healthy restraint on the passions so that the needs of others can be met. The *Catechism* teaches that "chastity includes an *apprenticeship in self-mastery* which is a training in human freedom". Without self-mastery, the *Catechism* continues, we cannot develop our God-given abilities: it takes discipline to realize our potential. "The alternative is clear: either man governs his passions and finds peace, or he lets himself be dominated by them and becomes unhappy" (2339, italics in the original; cf. Sir 1:22).

Catholic sexual ethics stem from the Old Testament. Judaism, as Dennis Prager has said, was quite unlike the religious and secular traditions that preceded it: it placed controls on the sexual appetite. An Orthodox Jew, Prager

---

[14] Ibid.

[15] John Paul II, apostolic exhortation *Familiaris consortio* (November 22, 1981), no. 33.

[16] Pontifical Council for the Family, *The Truth and Meaning of Human Sexuality*, no. 16.

proudly explains that "Judaism's restricting of sexual
behavior was one of the essential elements that enabled
society to progress."[17] Previous societies failed to put limits on sexuality and thus failed to cultivate temperance, an
attribute tied to the development of human resources.

Christians learned from Jews how important marital sex
is and why it should be jealously safeguarded. Fornication,
homosexual acts, and adultery can only weaken marriage,
which is why they need to be checked. If marriage is a
special institution, it needs to be treated as special in law.
At a minimum, this means that competing lifestyles should
not be encouraged. This view is not widely shared these
days—thanks, in large part, to our cultural elites and their
intellectual mentors.

The New Testament expands on the Old Testament's
teachings on sexuality by warning of the need to curb
sexual desire from within. Thus, pornography and prostitution should be seen as social liabilities, not assets.
Given all that we know about these socially destructive
behaviors—the prevalence of porn on the Internet has
helped to destroy marriages—it is discouraging to note
how unreceptive appeals to chastity are. Chastity is not
some cultural chain tugging at our freedoms; rather, it is a
valuable asset that allows us to respect the rights of others.
That is why the employment of Catholic sexual ethics
is so critical to the resolution of our cultural crisis. We
should not be defensive about touting its virtues.

Sorokin's Account of the Sexual Revolution

One intellectual who fully comprehended what happens
when society lets its sexual guard down was Harvard

---

[17] Dennis Prager, "Judaism's Sexual Revolution", *Ultimate Issues* (April–June
1990): 2.

sociologist Pitirim Sorokin. His 1956 book, *The American Sex Revolution*, clearly delineated the causes and consequences of sexual libertinism.

According to Paul E. Kerry, an astute student of Sorokin's work, "*American Sex Revolution* is meant to pass on the practical wisdom and insight that Sorokin believed could be understood in its own right, through common sense, as well as through the lens of the socio-cultural theories propounded in his major works."[18]

Sexual libertinism, Sorokin observed, has historically been associated with decline, including a marked decrease in self-discipline. Ancient Greece and Rome suffered this fate in their later stages, the result being a cultural crisis: the flouting of morality spawned artistic as well as economic problems. How so? Creativity, in any field, is a function of hard work, so when a society becomes obsessed with sex, it makes it more difficult to cultivate the attributes necessary for excellence. Promiscuity, Sorokin contended, was no friend to civilization. Indeed, he maintained that societies reach their creative apex when sexual restraint is practiced.

If monogamy, not sexual experimentation, is associated with historical greatness, it is no wonder that our culture is in crisis. Sorokin lamented what he called the "sexualization of American culture", and that was before the sexual revolution.[19] Consider this: when he wrote, viewers had never seen the bedroom in Jackie Gleason's *Honeymooners*. Today even the commercials on television are laden with crude sexual images.

Sorokin was way ahead of his time. "What used to be considered morally reprehensible is now recommended as a positive value; what was once called demoralization

[18] Paul E. Kerry, " 'Confirm Thy Soul in Self-Control, Thy Liberty in Law': New Insights into Pitirim Sorokin's *American Sex Revolution*", *The Family in America* (Spring 2016): 148.

[19] Ibid., p. 153.

is now styled moral progress and a new freedom."[20] No doubt about it, traditionalism, grounded in common sense, has been upended by libertinism. The triumph of sexual stupidity is indisputable.

Intellectual Godfathers of Sexual Liberation

Perhaps no one is more responsible for discounting the existence of moral harms than John Stuart Mill. His 1859 essay *On Liberty* is the classic libertarian statement on this subject. In it, he offers his "one very simple principle", the so-called harm principle, according to which it should be legal to do whatever we want, so long as it does not harm anyone else. At face value, this sounds attractive. What constitutes harm, of course, is the crux of the matter.

Is shooting up heroin a harmless act, affecting no one but the addict? If he cannot work and is incapable of supporting his family, he becomes a drain on society. Has he not harmed the community? At what point do we stop pretending that self-destructive acts are without social consequences?

In fairness to Mill, he was no libertine. In fact, he insisted on the need for responsibility and restraint. But it is also fair to say that Judge Bork is right to contend that Mill's *On Liberty* gave "powerful impetus in our culture" to the notion that moral harms are none of the law's business.[21] The esteemed sociologist Robert Nisbet connected the dots: "From the Greenwich Village of the early twentieth century to the contemporary chaos of cultural

---

[20] Gertrude Himmelfarb, *One Nation, Two Cultures* (New York: Knopf, 1999), p. 14.

[21] Bork, *Tradition and Morality*, p. 5.

anarchy, hedonism, narcissism, and generalized flouting of idols there is a straight line best defined as Mill's one very simple principle."[22]

Mill may have had a debilitating influence on our culture, but he was certainly not alone. In fact, there are many intellectuals who have taken direct aim at the Judeo-Christian ethos that undergirds Western civilization.

In the late eighteenth century, Marquis de Sade, the French writer and pervert, spoke endlessly of the need to smash every vestige of Catholic sexual ethics. He wasn't content simply to disagree with Catholicism: his hatred was so deep that he portrayed priests and nuns fornicating, and bishops having anal sex with girls. He even created a character who had sex with nuns while saying Mass. In his personal life, he paid a prostitute to trample on a crucifix. He spent many years in an insane asylum, but not before preaching the virtues of pornography and unbridled sexual experimentation. His contribution to moral destitution was immortalized when the word "sadism" was coined after his name.[23]

Writing at the time Mill authored *On Liberty* was the American poet Walt Whitman. An angry atheist (many atheist intellectuals seem to be angry), he despised Catholicism, showing particular contempt for its teachings on sexuality. He advocated free love and no-holds-barred sexual expression. His 1855 classic, *Leaves of Grass*, no longer shocks American sensibilities, so inured to sexual deviance have we become.

In the twentieth century, the psychoanalytical writings of Wilhelm Reich savaged Catholic sexual ethics. A

[22] Robert Nisbet, *Prejudices* (Cambridge: Harvard University Press, 1982), p. 214.

[23] Bill Donohue, *Secular Sabotage: How Liberals Are Destroying Religion and Culture in America* (New York: FaithWords, 2009), p. 37.

committed Communist, Reich believed that there could
be no successful political revolution without a sexual revolution first. Called the "Father of the Sexual Revolution",
he took delight in undermining Catholic teachings on
morality and the family. He very much wanted to encourage Catholic youth to abandon the Church's strictures
on sexuality, thus paving the way toward their complete
rejection of Catholicism.[24]

It is easy to see that Sigmund Freud and Carl Jung had
a great influence on Reich. Freud admitted that his "real
enemy" was "the Roman Catholic Church".[25] Like some
other atheists, Freud knew that if Catholic teachings on
sexuality could be demolished, unbridled sexual expression
would reign. Jung went further, saying that a new religion—
the religion of psychoanalysis—had to be founded as a way
of abolishing the "sex-fixated ethics" of Catholicism.[26]

What these psychologists had in common was the habit
of projecting onto others their own foibles. The Catholic
Church isn't "sex-fixated"; her most vociferous critics are.
And, blinded by their own obsession with sexuality—in
its most perverse manifestations—they project their fixation onto those who embrace an ethic of sexual reticence.
This tendency is not confined to atheist intellectuals but
can be found among many in the arts and in the entertainment industry.

Herbert Marcuse was the intellectual superstar who
pioneered the charge that Catholicism promoted an ethic
of sexual repression. He taught in Germany and in the

[24] William Norman Grigg, "The Porn Revolution", *New American*, June 2,
2003.

[25] M. Rempel, "Understanding Freud's Philosophy of Religion", *Canadian
Journal of Psychoanalysis* 236 (Winter 1997).

[26] Quoted in "Jungian Psychology as Catholic Theology", CatholicCulture
.org, https://www.catholicculture.org/culture/library/view.cfm?recnum=545.

United States and was a member of the Frankfurt School, which consisted of neo-Marxist critics of both Soviet communism and Western capitalism. Nothing but unlimited sexual expression satisfied him, which is why he advocated "polymorphous perversity", a condition in which every conceivable sexual act—with as many partners as possible—was realized. From anthropologist Margaret Mead to author Gore Vidal, many top-flight intellectuals agreed with Marcuse; they advocated sex with those of the same sex, as well as with those of the opposite sex, alternating with regularity.[27]

James T. Jones, author of the definitive biography of Alfred Kinsey, says that the famous sexologist (he was actually a zoologist) "spent his every waking hour attempting to change the sexual mores ... of the United States". A pervert of master status, Kinsey was a voyeur and an exhibitionist. Though he was married, he was also a practicing homosexual and a masochist.

Like Reich, Freud, Jung, and Marcuse, Kinsey wanted to undermine Catholicism, seeing in it the source of much repression. It was Catholic sexual ethics, he argued, that led to the "breakdown of the modern family". A more honest analysis would admit that people like him have encouraged the normalization of sexual deviance, which has contributed to family problems. But Kinsey was a fundamentally dishonest man; he was a sexual freak who cruised the gay bars of Chicago, yet he passed himself off as a scientist. Furthermore, he argued that the mere concept of sexual deviance was a reflection of Victorian morality, a sexually repressive mind-set that had to be destroyed.

Nothing was off-limits to Kinsey. He collaborated with pedophiles, keeping "scientific" records of their sexual

[27] Donohue, *Secular Sabotage*, p. 39.

exploits with the children they masturbated and pene-trated.[28] Child abuse is what happens when there are no boundaries. Sick men stop at nothing.

Take Michel Foucault, the heralded French intellectual. He was a sexual monster who justified rape and preyed on young boys. After spending his adult life bouncing from one gay bathhouse to another, he died of AIDS, a disease he said never existed (in his warped mind, it was just a "social construction").[29]

Foucault influenced his French colleagues to eliminate all the laws forbidding sex between adults and children. From Jean-Paul Sartre to Simone de Beauvoir, many of these free-love devotees defended pedophilia. Their influence has been felt in the United States: there is a movement afoot, led by social scientists and psychiatrists, to reconcep-tualize our thinking about adult-child sex; they politely call pedophiles "minor-attracted persons". These big-sky thinkers are not unorganized—they belong to B4U-ACT, an association dedicated to ridding society of stigmatiz-ing pedophiles.[30]

Anyone is free to disagree with Catholic sexual ethics, and doing so does not make one a bigot or a deviant. But as we have seen, the intellectual godfathers of sexual lib-eration were consumed with hatred of Catholicism, and many of them were perverts or insane, or both. All of them lacked basic common sense: the sexual drive must be channeled constructively, lest it result in disease and death. In real life, libertinism, or liberty as license, does not yield more freedom—it delivers liberticide, the end of liberty.

[28] Ibid.

[29] James Miller, *The Passion of Michael Foucault* (Cambridge, Mass.: Harvard University Press, 1993), p. 21.

[30] See the website www.b4uact.org.

Cultural Challenges to Catholic Sexual Ethics

The intellectual libertines who hated Catholicism succeeded in corrupting the culture and feeding anti-Catholicism. Of course, anti-Catholics rarely admit to their bigotry; they typically defend their actions in the name of freedom of expression, even when events turn patently obscene.

For example, in 2007, an artist created a six-foot-tall anatomically correct sculpture of Jesus in milk chocolate, intending to show it in the gallery of a famous New York City hotel. The figure depicted Christ crucified and was to be displayed at street level, where children would see it. The artist chose Holy Week to offend Christians. He did not succeed—I led a media protest against it—but the fact that he won the support of the owners of the Roger Smith Hotel was disturbing enough.[31]

Colleges and universities are known for anti-Catholicism, most of it driven by antipathy to the Church's teachings on sexuality. In the late 1990s, a Penn State female student decided to do something novel when given an art assignment. On the campus, she created a huge bloody vagina with human hair, constructed in the shape of a grotto, with a statue of the Mother of Jesus placed inside.[32] In 2013, a female student dressed as the pope for Carnegie Mellon University's annual art school parade. She was naked from the waist down with her pubic hair shaved in the shape of a cross. She passed out condoms to the public.[33] Satanism,

[31] Bill Donohue, "Executive Summary", *2007 Annual Report on Anti-Catholicism*, Catholic League, https://www.catholicleague.org/category/annual-report/2007-report-on-anti-catholicism/.

[32] Bill Donohue, "Penn State Allows Catholic Bashing to Continue", Catholic League, March 11, 1997, http://archive.li/3RVDe.

[33] "CMU President Apologizes after Student Dresses as Naked Pope", May 1, 2013, KDKA 2 CBS Pittsburgh, https://pittsburgh.cbslocal.com/2013/05/01/cmu-president-apologizes-for-student-dressed-as-naked-pope/.

in the form of a Black Mass, has also been popular with some college students.[34]

Many other examples could be offered, but the point is clear: the Catholic faith is the favorite target of sexual revolutionaries. Yet Catholicism remains the most comprehensive and authoritative response to destructive sexual libertinism, and our only real hope. Yes, there are many Evangelicals, Orthodox Jews, Mormons, and Muslims who share Catholic concerns, but they need the Catholic Church to take a leadership role. The fact that the crazed sexologists focus on the teachings of Catholicism is a backhanded compliment, validating the special status of the Catholic Church.

For progress to be made, the public needs to understand what the *Catechism* teaches: "So-called *moral permissiveness* rests on an erroneous conception of human freedom; the necessary precondition for the development of true freedom is to let oneself be educated in the moral law" (2526, italics in the original).

Moral permissiveness, or libertinism, does not liberate as much as it corrupts. It corrupts our capacity to love. A society in which self-absorption is heralded as freedom necessarily undermines the psychological and social requisites of love: self-giving is predicated on sacrifice, not on selfishness. This attitude helps to explain why sexual relations are frequently untied from any expectation of procreation—children take work.

Saint John Paul II wrote, "Some ask themselves if it is a good thing to be alive or if it would be better never to have been born; they doubt therefore if it is right to bring others into life when perhaps they will curse their

[34] Francis X. Clooney, S.J., "Harvard's Black Mass and Catholicism on Campus", *America*, May 12, 2014.

existence in a cruel world with unforeseeable terrors."[35] He saw this perspective as part and parcel of the contraceptive society, where science, technology, and materialism overwhelm us. He labeled it "an anti-life mentality".

True freedom is not fostered when a contraceptive mentality takes root. To be specific, the idea that sexual expression outside of marriage is licit so long as out-of-wedlock births are checked is morally and socially deficient. It underestimates the damage done to men and women (especially women) when sexuality is randomly expressed. To be certain, marriage is limiting, but it is a liberating limitation, not a debilitating one.

A contraceptive mentality is based on a faulty idea of freedom. Narcissism and hedonism are enemies of real love and true liberty. That's because love and freedom are based on respect for others, which is not possible when "me" always supersedes "we".

The notion that sexuality confined to marriage is liberating is a hard sell in a culture that takes its cues from intellectuals who think otherwise. Their influence has percolated down from the academy to the pop culture, seeping into every social crevice. Consider *Playboy* for men and *Cosmopolitan* for women; they have both played a significant role in transforming our culture, and not for the better.

Hugh Hefner launched *Playboy* in 1953, but it was not photos of nude women that challenged Catholic sexual ethics. That would come nine years later when Hefner began his series titled *The Playboy Philosophy*.

In December 1962, Hefner made his case for sexual freedom, attacking every vestige of traditional morality. The series lasted for two and a half years, outlining all the

---

[35] John Paul II, *Familiaris consortio*, no. 30.

reasons why we should throw off the shackles of constraint. Predictably, Hefner blamed Christianity for inhibiting sexual expression, accusing it of having too many rules against nonmarital sex, homosexuality, bestiality, and the like. His reach was wide, finding a receptive home on college campuses. The men loved it. So did his friends: child rapist Roman Polanski was one of his best buddies, and serial predator Bill Cosby was a regular at the Playboy Mansion (one of his alleged victims said she was molested by Cosby at the mansion in 1974).[36] The sexual revolution, which was in its nascent stage, is unintelligible without referencing the role that Hefner's philosophy played. He died in 2017.

Helen Gurley Brown did for women what Hefner did for men—convinced them of their need of, and right to, sexual libertinism. Her book, *Sex and the Single Girl*, was published the same year that the "Playboy philosophy" began. Brown made the case that unmarried women were entitled to have all the sex they wanted, and three years later she took over *Cosmopolitan*, telling everyone how sexually free she was: "My own philosophy is if you're not having sex, you're finished."[37] She was never finished, having slept with 178 lovers, by her count, before she married at age 37.[38]

Hefner had an easier time convincing men, who are generally more promiscuous than women, of their right to sexual freedom than Brown had in making the same

[36] Shelby Grad, "Hugh Hefner's Playboy Mansion Was Hedonistic Headquarters for His Brand", *Los Angeles Times*, September 28, 2017, http://www.latimes.com/local/lanow/la-me-playboy-mansion-hugh-hefner-20170927-htmlstory.html.

[37] Rachel Hills, "Today's Sexual Dogma", *New York Times*, September 1, 2015, p. D4.

[38] Jennifer Senior, "A Self-Help Seduction Guru, Shaking Up a Prudish America", *New York Times*, July 12, 2016, p. C1.

case for women. So she made up salacious stories about women romping around—she literally told her writers to lie—hoping to make her *Cosmopolitan* readers feel inadequate if they weren't getting it on with the guys. This was her way of forging a sexual revolution.

Sue Ellen Browder worked for Brown, and she wrote about her experience in her book, *Subverted: How I Helped the Sexual Revolution Hijack the Women's Movement*. To please her boss, she betrayed everything a real journalist should be. For her *Cosmopolitan* articles, she fabricated people and created quotes out of whole cloth to make chaste women question themselves. In fact, Browder says, "The sex revolution was fabricated largely from propaganda. I know because I was one of the propagandists who helped sell single women on the notion that sex outside of marriage would set them free."[39]

To accomplish this end, Brown seized on the birth control pill, which made its commercial debut in 1960. Abortion was another option, though it would not become legal throughout the country until 1973. In Helen Gurley Brown territory, Browder recounts, separating women from children (through abortion and contraception) was required for women to be free.[40]

It is interesting to read this account from the perspective of *Humanae vitae*, the papal encyclical that warned of the dangers implicit in the distribution of contraceptives. Released in 1968, the encyclical stated that if reproduction were separated from sexual intercourse, it would abet the exploitation of women, resulting in less freedom. It strains credulity to argue that when women are separated from

---

[39] Sue Ellen Browder, *Subverted: How I Helped the Sexual Revolution Hijack the Women's Movement* (San Francisco: Ignatius Press, 2015), p. 14.

[40] Ibid., p. 36.

children, as Brown desired, they are set free. Free from their own children? In the long run, certainly, such a freedom is an empty one.

What else did the sexual revolution "free" women to do? Curse more at work. "If you hear more f-bombs dropped at your office, there's a good chance they're coming from your female co-workers." That was how one reporter summarized the findings of a 2016 study of behavior in the workplace. Millennial women took first prize.[41]

The young gals learned to be vulgar by reading women's magazines. In November 2012, *Glamour* decided to break with precedent by printing obscenities. Of course, those in charge take no responsibility. "The culture has changed, so we changed", is how the chief editor put it. "It's how our main staff, many who are under 30, talk. Certain words have gone from shocking to be neutered."[42] Yes, when people's sensibilities are relentlessly assaulted, they tend to become numb, and while *Glamour* didn't cause this to happen by itself, to say it had no role is equally untrue. What is most exasperating about this is the duplicity: the same women who utter obscenities in the workplace are told to be on high alert for any male colleague who makes a sexually suggestive comment.

The sexual revolution has long gone mainstream. Tupperware parties in suburbia still exist, but so do sex-toy parties.[43] Nightclubs are just as fashionable as they were in

[41] Scott Stump, "Who Swears More at Work, Men or Women?" *Today*, October 12, 2016, https://www.today.com/news/who-swears-more-work -men-or-women-t103819.

[42] Christine Haughney, "50 Shades of Vulgarity", *New York Times*, January 2, 2013, p. C1.

[43] Sanjay Gupta, "These Parties Go Way Beyond Tupperware", CNN, May 10, 2012, http://thechart.blogs.cnn.com/2012/05/10/these-parties-go -way-beyond-tupperware/.

more civil days, but today they include clubs that specialize in erotic, even dangerous, sex acts. In one room at Paddles in New York City, men and women can buy whips, chains, and cages. In another room, they can experience the joy of "sharing fire play, which [involves] accelerant placed on strategic points of the woman's body and set ablaze in short, dramatic bursts". Beating and bondage are routine.[44] This is *Fifty Shades of Grey* in real time.

Is this the face of emancipation or slavery? Freedom should make us happier, not more despondent. Then why are women unhappier after experiencing the culture of emancipation? Two social scientists from the University of Pennsylvania looked at the data collected over the years by the General Social Survey, the most authoritative source available, and concluded that women reported being happier than men until the 1990s.[45] It has been downhill since.

How can this be in a society in which women are "hooking up" on college campuses at record speed? Peter Wood, president of the National Association of Scholars, studied this issue and came to an interesting conclusion. "The woman who treats her sexuality as something detachable from strong mutual attachment to a single partner sooner or later discovers that men regard her as expendable."[46] Wood's observation receives support from Lisa Wade, who wrote a book on this subject. "On campuses across America, students are sounding the alarm. They are telling us that they are depressed, anxious and overwhelmed." It is the women who suffer the most. One in three who

[44] Matt Haber, "A Hush-Hush Topic No More", *New York Times*, February 28, 2013, p. E1.

[45] Quoted in Bill Donohue, *The Catholic Advantage: How Health, Happiness, and Heaven Await the Faithful* (New York: Image, 2015), pp. 134–35.

[46] Peter Wood, "The Meaning of Sex", *Weekly Standard*, May 4, 2015, p. 28.

have hooked up say their experience has been "traumatic" or "very difficult to handle". Sex on the cheap—absent commitment—yields an unhappy outcome. "In addition," Wade says, "there is persistent malaise: a deep, indefinable disappointment."[47]

As for the men, not only are they eager to "hook up" with coeds; they are the number-one supporters of a woman's "right to choose". Every survey on abortion ever taken has shown that young men are the most vociferous advocates of abortion rights. And it's not because they are closet feminists. In short, the sexual revolution gave cover to men to escape their responsibilities.

More than a half century after Hefner and Brown espoused their philosophy, following the logic of the libertine intellectuals, our culture has taken some bizarre turns. "Manners and morals once taken for granted are now derided as puritanical and hypocritical", notes the distinguished historian Gertrude Himmelfarb.[48] It's even nuttier than this: common sense has been thrown to the wind.

We don't seem to know what we want. Porn is readily available, yet in 2018 the Miss America pageant banned the swimsuit competition. *Playboy* succeeded in eroticizing the culture to such an extent that its success almost killed it, forcing Hefner to ask the girls to put their clothes back on. That was in 2016. In 2017, they took them off again. We celebrate debauchery, yet we are astonished to learn that guys regularly hit on girls in military academies and in the armed forces, some of which spins into harassment. Similarly, dropping the hammer on college boys who do not get verbal approval from their date before engaging in petting is routine.

[47] Lisa Wade, *American Hookup: The New Culture of Sex on Campus* (New York: W. W. Norton, 2017), p. 15.

[48] Himmelfarb, *One Nation, Two Cultures*, p. 118.

The objectification of women in music, television, and movies is commonplace, yet protestations against it are heard from the same people who advised women to mimic men in exploring their sexuality.

Matters climaxed in 2017 and 2018 when numerous sexual-misconduct accusations were made by women celebrities against their male colleagues and associates. For decades, Hollywood men and women wore their sexuality on their sleeves, making one raunchy movie after another. Then, after eroticizing the culture, actresses and female entertainers complained that men were acting badly. They were shocked to learn that many of those who helped to craft a libertine culture were being devoured by it. The male abusers, of course, deserved to be punished, but anyone with an ounce of common sense should know that we reap what we sow.

We are lectured on the need to be nonjudgmental, yet when Carrie Prejean, Miss California, said she did not agree with gay marriage, she was blasted by the high priests of tolerance.[49] Similarly, pro-life coeds who express their views in the college classroom are frequently treated like Barbie Doll dopes by feminist professors, thus showing the limits of being nonjudgmental. Keeping an open mind may be embraced rhetorically, but when traditional morality is defended, the minds of the "enlightened ones" shut down. If the subject is public nudity, however, keeping an open mind is a requirement.

Speaking of which, going naked in public is the source of much debate in San Francisco: Should gays be required to put a towel under their behinds while sitting in McDonald's? They tried that—it was called the "skid mark

---

[49] Victor Davis Hanson, "A Nation of Promiscuous Prudes", *Washington Times*, April 19, 2013, p. B1.

law"—but that didn't work. It failed because men continued to parade around naked in front of elementary schools. Some wore robes, flashing when they got the urge, while others charged tourists for taking pictures of them in the buff. On some occasions, men had sex in public. Finally, even some of the libertines began to push back.[50] This kind of madness is what happens when sexual reticence, as favored by Catholicism, comes under wholesale assault.

We have embraced a selective, even contradictory, morality, one that satisfies no one. We want to live the life of a libertine, but we crave the solidarity and sanity that a more traditional morality affords. We want to have it both ways, but we cannot. We must choose. If we were mature, we would embrace the common sense that inheres in Catholic sexual ethics. But that would make us parochial, so we do nothing but scratch our heads, looking endlessly for some magical third way. There isn't any.

Why Moral Harms Matter

Opposition to moral harms makes sense because it safeguards the community from behavior that undermines the moral order. Every society employs sanctions against behaviors it seeks to curb, and one important way of doing so is to stigmatize offenders. In China, there is a "wall of shame", a giant screen outside a major train station, that flashes the names and pictures of individuals and organizations that have run afoul of certain laws.[51]

---

[50] C. W. Nevius, "Castro Naked Guys Have Gone Too Far", *San Francisco Chronicle*, September 15, 2012, http://www.sfgate.com/bayarea/nevius/article/Castro-naked-guys-have-gone-too-far-3867094.php.

[51] Naomi Ng and Shen Lu, "Chinese Court Put Up 'Wall of Shame' for Overdue Fines", CNN, January 23, 2015, https://www.cnn.com/2015/01/23/world/china-wall-of-shame/index.html.

We stigmatize people as well, though the means are different. For example, we stigmatize smokers: if they light up at a house party, they will immediately be shunned or told to stop. Indeed, even admitting that one is a smoker can be risky. (Note: this applies only to those who smoke Marlboros, not marijuana.) When it comes to moral harms of a sexual nature, however, we recoil at the suggestion that some behaviors should be stigmatized. That smacks of Victorianism, and we will have none of it.

This is our dilemma. Most people do not think that out-of-wedlock births are a good idea, but most also don't want to stigmatize those who are responsible for them. Some of the objections are understandable—the stigma typically applies only to irresponsible mothers, not to irresponsible fathers. But we are still faced with a problem: If we don't employ negative sanctions to behaviors we deplore, how can we expect to curb them?

There are other objections, however, that are less persuasive. It is true that unmarried mothers used to be stigmatized, particularly in heavily Catholic nations such as Ireland. However, Irish nuns have been unfairly vilified, portrayed as evil women who punished young unwed mothers. The condemnations are unjust: the reality is much more complicated.

In more traditional times, when marriage between a man and a woman was the expected norm and the two-parent family was seen as the gold standard of child rearing, it made sense, sociologically, to reward those arrangements and shun alternatives to them. It also made sense to those who accepted Catholic sexual ethics. In practice, this meant that those who "shacked up", or lived together outside of marriage (what we call cohabitation), were stigmatized. So were adulterers and homosexuals. Having children outside of marriage was called illegitimacy, a term whose negative connotation carried considerable weight.

By today's standards, such sanctions sound harsh, even cruel. But their employment was not motivated by evil—it was done out of concern for the well-being of marriage and the welfare of children. It was hoped that stigmatizing challenges to monogamy and the two-parent family would safeguard their status. More important, this stigmatizing was done in service to children.

Today it is commonplace for the big thinkers to discuss sexuality without mentioning children. We hear a lot about women's rights, gay rights, sexual freedom, and the like, but we hear very little about the best interests of children. *New York Times* columnist Gail Collins wrote a book of nearly five hundred pages on women's achievements yet said practically nothing about children; she branded traditional women who married and had children as "breeders".[52] That stigma is spreading rapidly.

If stigmatizing alternatives to traditional marriage and the two-parent family never worked, then a rational case for condemnation could be made. But it did work. Take the 1950s. Everyone agrees it was a much more conservative time. Predictably, to this day, the strict rules governing sexuality are maligned by the deep thinkers. But it was also a time when, as family sociologist David Popenoe said, the family was very strong: "Greater family stability was achieved in the fifties than at probably any other time in history, with high marriage rates, low unwed birthrates, and low death rates not yet offset by sky-high divorce rates." Importantly, Popenoe attributes the very public and influential role played by religion as a support mechanism of the family.[53]

---

[52] Gail Collins, *When Everything Changed* (New York: Little Brown, 2009).

[53] Carol Iannone, "Family Matters: A Conversation with David Popenoe", *Academic Questions* (Winter 2008–2009): 20–21.

Now look what we have. The stigma is gone from those who cohabit, and from adulterers, homosexuals, and unwed mothers. Religion has also lost its impact. But we also have much higher rates of cohabitation, divorce, adultery, promiscuity, and out-of-wedlock births. "The more secular the culture", Popenoe observes, "the weaker the family."[54] In short, the price we pay for being "nonjudgmental" is high, and no one suffers more than innocent children. They are given short shrift by the high priests of sexual expression.

Suspending moral judgments is not without problems. When everyone is encouraged to make up his own mind about right and wrong, we are inclined not to pass moral judgments on some very serious matters. At its more extreme manifestation, it results in desensitization, the consequences of which are anything but benign.

One of the courses I taught in college was on social problems. One day, I noticed a few students smirking when I discussed the laws against obscenity. When I questioned the students, they sounded much like Mill, saying it really didn't matter what people read, said, or did, as long as no one directly interfered with their rights.

I asked them why they thought white people weren't upset about slavery. They looked puzzled. So I explained that only humans are entitled to human rights, and blacks were considered chattel, or cattle. Therefore, they weren't entitled to human rights. Whites had successfully depersonalized them. They stopped smirking.

Then I told them about Albert Speer, second in command to Hitler. When asked decades later how he was able to oversee the mass murder of Jews, he said he never hated Jews. He just depersonalized them.

[54] Ibid.

Then we discussed snuff movies. I asked my students what they thought the likely psychological effect might be on young men who watched one movie after another showing trucks running over women, smashing their skulls on the pavement, blood spilling about, their brains scattered along the road. Wouldn't it be fair to say that they would be inclined to depersonalize women?

The students started to understand my point. That is what hard-core pornography does to those who regularly consume it—it desensitizes them. No society that aspires to be free will succeed if its citizens become inured to human suffering. Common sense tells us that when we become desensitized to the plight of others, civility and community suffer, and when that happens, the prospects for freedom are diminished.

It is also true that when we become morally relaxed, children suffer. Just consider what they are exposed to these days on TV and the Internet at a very young age; it is disturbing. It used to be that weekday afternoon and prime-time evening shows were family-friendly hours, but that has long since changed. Those in Hollywood who are responsible for the increasingly vulgar fare seem not to care about the consequences of their work, so long as their own children are protected from it.

In the late 1990s, I attended a very large convention of Hollywood studio chiefs, producers, and actors. The meeting was held, in part, to answer their critics. When it was my turn to speak, I told the Tinseltown elite that they were a bunch of phonies. What I heard all day long, I said, was one Hollywood executive after another admitting that many of the TV shows they are responsible for are wholly unacceptable for children. They bragged that their children watch nothing but Nickelodeon. This raised the question, which I had to ask: "If the shows you produce are not suitable for your children, just whose kids are they good for?" Dead silence.

Does it matter what we watch? Researchers from Dartmouth studied the impact that sex on the screen has on teenagers. The study was based on nearly seven hundred popular films, all of which featured sexual content. The psychologists concluded that the more teenagers are exposed to sex on the screen, the more likely they are to be sexually active. "Adolescents who are exposed to more sexual content in movies start having sex at younger ages, have more sexual partners, and are less likely to use condoms with casual sexual partners", said the chief researcher.[55]

How much better our society would be if we were guided more by Saint John Paul II's Theology of the Body than Hollywood's hedonism. Instead of talking about all the young people who are self-indulgent, and selfish beyond belief, we would be talking about their self-giving. But to engage in self-giving, we must be able to practice self-discipline, and that is not easy to do in a culture that sees constraint as the enemy of liberty. So we slide back into a state of moral relaxation, in which standards and expectations continue to fall, benefiting no one in the long run.

Cultural Schizophrenia

Our cultural crisis manifests itself in many ways, but none more curious than in our penchant for cultural schizophrenia. The dominant culture celebrates radical individualism, "me-ism," yielding physical and psychological problems

---

[55] Andrew Hough, "Teenagers 'Can be Corrupted' by Hollywood Sex Scenes", *Telegraph*, July 18, 2012, https://www.telegraph.co.uk/news/health /news/9407978/Teenagers-can-be-corrupted-by-Hollywood-sex-scenes.html.

on a huge scale. Take, for example, the problem of sexually transmitted diseases (STDs).

No segment of the population has been hit harder with AIDS than the gay community. If restraint were practiced, there would be no AIDS, and if common sense were operative, gay leaders would have led the fight to close the bathhouses. Instead, they fought to keep them open. The intellectuals among them were particularly irresponsible.

One of the most prominent gay intellectuals to contribute to the problem is Andrew Sullivan, an English transplant. He is a bright, insightful man, though his actions often betray his words. He said he was genuinely concerned about sexual exploitation and AIDS, yet he sold his body on the Internet and participated in sex with many partners, often at the same time, doing so even after he found that he was HIV-positive.[56]

Is it wrong intentionally to give AIDS to an innocent, unsuspecting person? The ACLU says it should be legal. Many years ago, in a live radio debate I had with a gay ACLU official, I asked him if it should be illegal intentionally to put a toxic substance into a city's water supply. He knew where I was going and balked. I then told the listening audience about the ACLU's policy on AIDS transmission, which he did not refute.

The very last *Firing Line* panel debate that Bill Buckley participated in was in 1998 at Bard College in upstate New York. The topic was the ACLU. There were four speakers on each side; I was on Buckley's side. I was asked by Nadine Strossen of the ACLU why I objected to sex education. Though my views on the subject had nothing to do with the debate, I did not hesitate to answer her. I

[56] Richard Kim, "Andrew Sullivan, Overexposed", *Nation*, June 5, 2001, https://www.thenation.com/article/andrew-sullivan-overexposed/.

did not object to sex education, I said, as long as it taught the virtue of restraint. The radicals in the audience—there were many of them—laughed. Turning to them, I said that if my position were accepted, "you may not go to as many funerals." The laughter stopped immediately.

The only surefire way of stopping STDs is to change behavioral patterns, and that is the only tonic that intellectuals never support. So the death count rises. The book-wise policy advisers will recommend more money, more testing, more education, and more condoms. But they will never insist that we slam on the brakes. That would be too puritan. So they rely on funding, research, education, and technology. They have yet to figure it out: as their prescription plan has grown more widespread, STD rates have skyrocketed. We are dealing with stupidity on a grand scale.

The federal government spends tens of billions of dollars each year on AIDS, far outpacing the funds spent on a whole range of health issues. The good news is that HIV rates have declined. The bad news is that it remains an overwhelmingly gay problem: gay and bisexual men account for more than eight in ten cases. In other words, without behavioral changes, real progress will remain elusive. The need for self-restraint is not exclusive to gays. In 2017, a headline story in the *New York Times* read, "HPV [genital human papillomavirus] Infects Close to Half of U.S. Adults, Survey Finds".[57]

No one can reasonably be against spending money on testing, but when that becomes the heart of reform policies, common sense has been discarded. New York governor Andrew Cuomo is a big opponent of AIDS, but

---

[57] Nicholas Bakalar, "HPV Infects Close to Half of U.S. Adults, Survey Finds", *New York Times*, April 7, 2017, p. A22.

his goal of ending the HIV/AIDS epidemic by 2020 will never be reached. His game plan consists of thirty recommendations, and not one calls for or facilitates behavioral change. Indeed, the top two are "Make routine HIV testing truly routine" and "Expand targeted testing." Incredibly, it was suggested that an "anti-stigma media campaign" be launched.[58] It is precisely the lack of stigma that accounts for the proliferation of STDs: there wasn't much of an STD problem in the 1950s when stigma was deeply ingrained in the culture.

Cultural schizophrenia is really in evidence at private fund-raising events to combat AIDS. Videos of gay men taking "shower selfies" have been wildly popular features of these events. Since 1992, one of the biggest anti-AIDS campaigns in New York City has been run by the group Broadway Bares.[59] Naked men perform burlesque at the event, and a video of it is distributed to many venues. In 2004, *Trading Spaces* host Paige Davis did a racy routine, which caused a bit of controversy. [60] Former Spice Girl Geri Halliwell and supermodels Elle MacPherson and Kate Moss have posed nude at other AIDS-fighting fund-raisers.[61]

[58] "Governor Cuomo Receives Final Blueprint to End the HIV/AIDS Epidemic in New York State by End of 2020", New York State website, April 28, 2015, https://www.governor.ny.gov/news/governor-cuomo-receives -final-blueprint-end-hivaids-epidemic-new-york-state-end-2020.

[59] Curtis W. Wong, "Here's Your First Look at 'Broadway Bares: On Demand' ", *Huffington Post*, April 14, 2016, https://www.huffingtonpost.com /entry/broadway-bares-on-demand_us_570fc8aae4b03d8b7b9fb5d6.

[60] Wade Paulsen, " 'Trading Spaces' Host Paige Davis Strips for Charity, Then Complains about Press", *Reality TV World*, July 1, 2004, https://www .realitytvworld.com/news/trading-spaces-host-paige-davis-strips-for-charity -then-complains-about-press-2676.php.

[61] "Posh Spice Poses Nude for AIDS Charity", United Press International, May 25, 2005, https://www.upi.com/Posh-Spice-poses-nude-for -AIDS-charity/68631117040000/.

Imagine a fund-raiser to combat alcoholism featuring drunks, or an anti-smoking campaign that passes out cigarettes to the audience. Is there anyone who wouldn't conclude that the participants are not serious about their expressed health concerns? Indeed, would we not conclude that they are contributing to the very problem they claim to abhor?

Why is it that when it comes to STDs, AIDS in particular, our cultural elites promote the diseases they raise funds to combat? This schizophrenic condition can be understood only as an irrational reaction, grounded in a distorted idea of sexual restraint and sexual freedom. They are free to say no to Catholic sexual ethics, but they are not free to live without suffering the consequences.

Education is another one of those remedies favored by those who refuse to advocate behavioral changes as a means of curbing STDs, but one of the major problems with most sex education curricula is that they have less to do with education than with ideology. For example, in classes all over the nation, students at virtually every age are learning to be nonjudgmental about every conceivable sexual act, drawing no ethical distinction between sexual relations inside or outside of marriage. Indeed, they are often given explicit instructional materials that cover a range of behaviors. The Judeo-Christian ideal—sexual relations should be understood as an expression of love between married men and women—is not integrated into the sex education curriculum in most schools.

Saint John Paul II rightly criticized the contemporary approach to sex education, saying that it "reduces human sexuality to the level of something commonplace", linking it "solely with the body and with selfish pleasure". The Church, he says, "is firmly opposed to an often widespread form of imparting sex information dissociated from moral principles". He put the onus of responsibility on parents to counter the effects of the culture, teaching their children that "sexuality is an enrichment of the whole person—body, emotions and soul."[62]

Courses on sexuality in most high schools, colleges, and universities are shining examples of moral relativism—there is no such thing as a deviant sex act, they assert—but they are not as neutral as they say they are. The fact is that sides are taken: to promote a morally nonjudgmental curriculum, it is first necessary to demolish traditional conceptions of sexuality. That's a judgment. It is also where the Catholic bashing comes in.

Take, for example, what is going on at the University of Oregon. There is a "health" app for students' smartphones called SexPositive; it provides a wealth of information, all of it designed to upend traditional moral standards. "Shame" is not good—it stands in the way of "self-discovery". The goal is to depersonalize sexuality, to teach about sexual relations in a highly clinical style, void of any moral strictures. To accomplish this end, the makers of this app bring in people such as Dan Savage, a radical homosexual activist.[63] He has spent decades preaching the wonders of a no-holds-barred approach to sexuality—nothing is off-limits to this guy. He also specializes in bashing Catholicism in a manner that can only be called obscene.

Nothing is valued more by the sex education establishment than condoms. To say that we have been in the grip of condomania for the past generation is hardly an exaggeration. In New York City alone, tens of millions of condoms have been distributed, free of charge, since 1971. The goal is to decrease STDs. It is a monumental failure—STD rates continue to escalate.

---

[62] John Paul II, *Familiaris consortio*, no. 37.

[63] Mary Rice Hasson, "Your Tuition Dollars at Work: How Colleges Promote a Perverse Sexual Ideology", *The Family in America* (Winter 2014): 35–56.

Nearly 2.3 million cases of chlamydia, gonorrhea, and syphilis were diagnosed in the United States in 2017, surpassing the previous record set in 2016. The rate of chlamydia and gonorrhea among blacks is 6 times the rate among whites; the rate of gonorrhea is 8 times greater among blacks than whites. Gays are 1.6 percent of the population yet account for 80 percent of all male syphilis cases.[64]

When confronted with the evidence that condom distribution is not the answer, the sexperts say that we didn't hand out enough of them. So another round of condoms is distributed. Then comes another study showing that STD rates continue to spike.

Some condomaniacs said that too many young men don't know how to wear a condom. Their answer: we need a new round of sex education programs. Many schools followed their advice, deciding to teach students, male and female alike, how to put a condom on a cucumber. That didn't work too well either. So then the sex wizards insisted on teaching the fifteen steps of proper condom use, as outlined by the Centers for Disease Control (CDC).

I had a chance to discuss this subject on the *Today* show with Dr. Desmond Johns, director of the joint UN program on HIV/AIDS. Here is what I told him.

Did you ever read what the CDC says about the fifteen steps [of correct condom use]? Now look, we don't live in the world of the laboratory; we live in the world of the backseat of a Chevy with some fifteen-year-old kid who's drunk out of his mind—and he's going to go through the fifteen steps? The same kid who can't even do his

[64] Centers for Disease Control and Prevention, "New CDC Analysis Shows Steep and Sustained Increases in STDs in Recent Years", press release, August 28, 2018; *Sexually Transmitted Disease Surveillance 2017* (Atlanta: U.S. Department of Health and Human Services, 2018), pp. 6, 13–14, 58, 61. Both documents are available on the CDC website.

homework, who's probably illiterate, but he's going to go through the fifteen steps and say, "Is there enough air at the tip of the condom, honey? Did you make sure not to cut your fingernails this morning so you don't have another hole in the condom?" I mean, it's about time the scientific community caught up with the morality of the Catholic Church, because not only is it morally right to preach abstinence; it works.[65]

Could it be that the distribution of condoms to high school students actually accounts for an increase in teen pregnancy and a rise in STDs? In 2016, the National Bureau of Economic Research provided evidence that is worth considering: the increase in condoms, pregnancies, and STDs went hand in hand. No, correlation does not prove causation, but when the association is logical, causation cannot be discounted.

Twenty years earlier, Janet Yellen (she later became the head of the Federal Reserve) and Nobel laureate George Akerlof found that contraception makes sex cheaper and leads to an increase in out-of-wedlock births. "Although many observers expected liberalized abortion and contraception to lead to fewer out-of-wedlock births, the opposite happened—because of the erosion in the custom of shotgun marriages."[66] It could also be said that the decline in stigma associated with giving birth outside of marriage explains why rates increased for decades before finally leveling off.

To makes matters worse, the brainy ones who said that the answer to STDs was funding, testing, education, and condoms literally created a new problem—rape on college

[65] The debate took place on the *Today* show on October 10, 2003. See "Condoms and AIDS", Catholic League, November 22, 2003, https://www.catholicleague.org/condoms-and-aids/ .

[66] Naomi Schaefer Riley, "The Liberal Narrative about Free Condoms at Schools Is Debunked", *New York Post*, June 21, 2016, www.nypost.com.

campuses—and then compounded matters when they sought to remedy it by stacking the deck against men.

Every objective observer who has studied this issue knows there is no "crisis" of rape on the campuses. If anything, bogus reports of rape are commonplace. Those responsible include activists who work in the administration (especially those in student services), faculty members, and students. They have been joined by professional activists outside the campuses, many of whom have long acquired a privileged position setting their agenda. The most conspicuous, and influential, outside group to weigh in on this matter was the Obama administration.

In 2011, the Obama administration sent a "Dear Colleague Letter" to every college and university president, ordering an investigation and adjudication of sexual assault. The goal was to expand the sexual misconduct tribunals, empowering them to employ sanctions and exact punishment for wrongdoing. The letter made it clear that the presumption of innocence was not required and was indeed a hindrance to justice. The target group, of course, was men; the rights of the accused were jettisoned.

Cathy Young, who writes for *Reason* magazine, explained what happened. The Obama administration recommended that sexual assault complaints be evaluated under the "preponderance of evidence" standard. "This means that if the school believes it is even slightly more likely—as in, a 50.1 percent chance—that an assault accusation is true, it can deem the defendant guilty", she writes.[67] This set the bar much lower than the "clear and convincing evidence" standard used by most colleges, never mind the much higher threshold of "beyond a reasonable doubt" used in criminal cases.

---

[67] Cathy Young, "Betsy DeVos Is Right: Sexual Assault Policy Is Broken", *New York Times*, July 21, 2017, p. A27.

Vassar College quickly instituted safeguards against sexual violence. The definition included "using sexual names" and "insisting on dressing or not dressing in a certain way". At the University of Michigan, sexual violence meant "discounting the partner's feelings regarding sex" and "withholding sex and affection". It was open season on guys.[68]

Aside from the obvious rank injustice, and the patently absurd categories of "sexual violence", this campaign represented what Heather Mac Donald titled, "Neo-Victorianism on Campus". She cogently detailed what was happening on campus. "The new order is a bizarre hybrid of liberationist and traditionalist values. It carefully preserves the prerogative of no-strings-attached sex while cabining it with legalistic caveats that allow females at will to a stance of offended virtue."[69]

The rights of men were so slighted that between 2011 and 2017, more than three hundred students filed complaints with the Office of Civil Rights, claiming unfair treatment of their alleged sexual offenses on campus (we have no way of knowing how many others were deterred from filing a complaint).[70] In 2017, President Trump's secretary of education, Betsy DeVos, tried to do something about this by issuing guidelines that raised the standard of proof for accusers from the "preponderance of evidence" to "clear and convincing evidence". In 2018, she was sued by radical feminist groups for doing so.[71]

---

[68] Robert Carle, "Assault on the DOE", *Academic Questions* 28 (2015): 11–21.

[69] Heather Mac Donald, "Neo-Victorianism on Campus", *Weekly Standard*, October 20, 2014, pp. 25–29.

[70] K. C. Johnson, "The Campus Sex-Crime Tribunals Are Losing", *Commentary*, October 2017, p. 22.

[71] Erica L. Green, "DeVos Is Sued over Policy on Campus Sexual Assault", *New York Times*, January 26, 2018, p. A15.

This is a splendid example of cultural schizophrenia in higher education. Colleges and universities are so obsessed with the prospect of male sexual misconduct that they invent new offenses to tackle, ennobling themselves as the caring custodians of women. But that doesn't stop them from promoting sexual recklessness on the same campuses.

PART II: EQUALITY

3

Sex Inequality

The Stubbornness of Nature

The title of this chapter is deliberately countercultural: the discussion will not be about gender inequality—it will be about sex inequality. The term "gender" is currently, and deliberately, being misused. "Gender" refers to socially learned roles for males and females; "sex" refers to nature-based differences between males and females. In current usage, "gender" has replaced "sex" in the lexicon of most writers and commentators, the effect of which is to discount, if not eliminate, the role that nature plays in accounting for male-female differences. This distortion is not an accident—it is deliberate.

This change does not reflect some new anthropological findings; rather, it reflects contemporary politics. To be exact, it is a byproduct of feminist ideology and postmodernist thought. It springs from the assumption that there is no such thing as nature, or nature's God—all that exists is a social construction. Therefore, everything is subject to change, provided we have the will to reform. This is one of the most sacred beliefs of intellectuals, and they will do everything they can to achieve their utopian ideal of a sex-neutral society.

We are not talking about a few intellectuals. Fully 95 percent of sociology papers written by scholars on male-female differences deny biological differences, even though there is plenty of outstanding research to the contrary. Charlotta Stern, a sociologist at Stockholm University, however, demonstrates that gender sociologists, as they call themselves, live in "insular communities of highly dubious sacred beliefs and causes".[1]

To show how utterly lacking in common sense they are, consider the claim made by some researchers that the reason why women are shorter than men is because sexist parents unknowingly give their daughters less food than they give their sons. They argued that "new theories suggest that power imbalances and discrimination are behind height differences." One anthropologist was so taken aback that he opined, "It is incredible that we have not discovered this before."[2]

No one doubts that there are socially learned norms, values, and behaviors that are considered appropriate for males and females. What matters—and this is what is controversial—is the fact that gender roles take their cues from nature. Boys are not more aggressive than girls because they are given guns and footballs to play with, but because they are naturally more aggressive. Boys possess more testosterone than girls do, and it is testosterone—not the toys made for boys—that accounts for boys' aggressive proclivities. So it makes sense that many boys like to play with guns and footballs. Many girls, on the other hand, prefer dolls.

The push for sex equality is so strong, however, that even corporations have jumped on board. Toy companies are making products that are marketed to both girls and

---

[1] Virginia Hale, "Research: 95% Gender Sociology Papers Deny Biological Differences", October 26, 2016, *Breitbart*, https://www.breitbart.com/europe /2016/10/26/gender-sociology-deny-biological-differences/.

[2] Ibid.

boys, and major chain stores, such as Target, are creating sex-neutral and androgynous labels as well as store aisles. Disney Store no longer sells Halloween costumes for boys and girls—all outfits are labeled for "kids".

But some things never change. Mattel, the world's largest toymaker, did a survey of boys and girls, tapping their toy preferences. They found that young girls "wanted their superheroes to be authentic superheroes", which is why they balked at a gal superhero in heels. "They told us she's not going to be able to fight with heels", a Mattel official said.[3] Looks as if the kids have more common sense than the adults; they certainly have more than the average intellectual.

Mattel's marketing crew also learned something basic about boys and girls when they presented them with action figures. The director of global consumer rights, Tania Missad, got a quick lesson in sex differences. "For boys it's very much about telling a story of the good guy killing the villain. There's a winner and a loser", she said. "Girls wanted the action and the battle, but would tell us: 'Why does the good girl have to kill the villain? Can't they be friends in the end?' "[4]

Dennis Prager, who was born with an abundance of common sense, wrote a piece about the Mattel finding and offered some words of wisdom about it. Men need women, and vice versa, he said. "Men need women to soften their intrinsic aggressive nature and to help them control their predatory sexuality; and women need men to, among other things, better understand that evil people and regimes must be fought, not nurtured." He concluded,

[3] Hiroko Tabuchi, "Sweeping Away Gender-Specific Toys and Labels", *New York Times*, October 28, 2015, https://www.nytimes.com/2015/10/28/business/sweeping-away-gender-specific-toys-and-labels.html.

[4] Ibid.

"Mattel's research has told a truth that America and the world need to pay attention to."[5]

The ideological rejection of nature is so strong that it has disabled the thinking of countless intellectuals. This factor, together with a rejection of nature's God, has done more to corrupt their ability to see things clearly than any other factor.

In 1996, a physicist named Alan Sokal sought to prove just how drunk with ideology the learned ones have become; he submitted an article that was pure nonsense to the academic journal *Social Text*. In the article, he maintained that gravity was a "social construct", having nothing to do with nature. *Social Text*, considered to be "a leading North American journal of cultural studies", published it. He then blew the whistle on the corrosive effects of postmodernist thought, telling everyone about his hoax.[6] Naturally, Sokal was vilified for his stunt, but his brilliance was in showing the extent to which ideology has seduced a big segment of the academy.

In 2018, newspapers were reporting on a rash of hoax papers. Three authors—Helen Pluckrose, James A. Lindsay, and Peter Boghossian—admitted to ripping off peer-reviewed scholarly journals by submitting articles that were pure fabrications. They wrote twenty articles under a variety of pseudonyms; seven were accepted and four were published.

For instance, *Gender, Place & Culture* published a paper on canine sexual misconduct in Portland, Oregon, parks. Parks, the author claimed, were "petri dishes for canine

[5] Dennis Prager, "Feminization of America Is Bad for the World", *The Dennis Prager Show*, November 3, 2015, http://www.dennisprager.com/feminization-of-america-is-bad-for-the-world/.

[6] Quoted in John Podhoretz, "The Latest Lunatic Postmodern Target: Motherhood", *New York Post*, May 12, 2015, https://nypost.com/2015/05/12/the-latest-lunatic-postmodern-target-motherhood/.

'rape culture'", leading him to call for an "awareness into the different ways dogs are treated on the basis of gender and queering behaviors, and the chronic and perennial rape emergency dog parks pose to female dogs." The self-described "left-leaning liberals" responsible for the hoaxes said they were dismayed by "grievance studies" taking over academia.[7] "Something has gone wrong in the university—especially in certain fields within the humanities. Scholarship based less upon finding the truth and more upon attending to social grievances has become firmly established, if not fully dominant, within these fields."[8]

We can dismiss nature in our discourse, but we cannot make it vanish. It is one of those stubborn facts of life. Take age. As Donald Brown found, it is one of those human universals that is grounded in nature and socially expressed in several ways: age grades, age statuses, and age terms are found in every society. Division of labor by age is another universal characteristic. There are many nature-based classifications: age, sex, and kin are ubiquitous, as are the statuses and roles that are ascribed to each. Hierarchy is natural as well—no society is without leaders or without roles that express dominance and submission.[9]

It is sex, however, that commands the interest of postmodern ideologues. They have their work cut out for themselves. Brown details sex differences in spatial cognition and behavior; sex statuses; sexual attraction; sexual jealousy; sexual modesty; sexual regulation, including incest prevention; and a division of labor by sex. In

---

[7] Jillian Kay Melchior, "Fake News Comes to Academia", *Wall Street Journal*, October 5, 2018, https://www.wsj.com/articles/fake-news-comes-to-academia -1538520950.

[8] Jennifer Schuessler, "With Canine Sex and Hooters, Pranks Jab at Academic Papers", *New York Times*, October 5, 2018, p. A1.

[9] Donald E. Brown, *Human Universals* (New York: McGraw-Hill, 1991), p. 137.

addition, kinship terms are universal: mother, father, son, daughter.[10]

Brown's human universals also include marriage and the family. Marriage channels the sexual appetite in a socially constructive manner, and the family is the natural home for parents and children. Copulation is normally conducted in privacy, and the Oedipus complex—the attraction of boys to their mother—is another universal trait. Weaning is universal, as is the preference of mothers for their own children and close kin. To put it differently, nepotism is a natural human attribute. Children everywhere fear strangers, looking to their mothers for protection. Senior kin are expected to socialize the young, and kinship roles, statuses, and groups are universal.[11]

Women are the caregivers in every society, and men are everywhere more aggressive. In almost all instances, the biological mother and the social mother are the same person. Male and female, and adult and child, are seen as having different natures. Males dominate the public or political realms. They also engage in more violence, especially lethal violence, and are more prone to theft.[12]

It is motherhood that angers radical feminists the most. Kathleen McCartney is the president of Smith College, an elite school for women. She does not believe in nature. "Motherhood is a cultural invention", she says. "It reflects a belief adopted by society that is passed down from one generation to the next."[13] It never occurred to her why it is passed down from one generation to the next—in every society in the history of the world!

[10] Ibid., pp. 136–38.
[11] Ibid.
[12] Ibid.
[13] Quoted in Podhoretz, "Latest Lunatic Postmodern Target".

McCartney's position finds no support among serious scholars. Francis Fukuyama, citing the data, notes that motherhood is biologically determined, though it could be said that fatherhood is mostly a social construction. "It takes a great deal of effort to separate a mother from her newborn infant; by contrast, it usually takes a fair amount of effort to get a father to be involved with him", he says.[14] Steven Pinker, another astute student of human nature, agrees. "Mothers are more attached to their children, on average, than are fathers. That is true in societies all over the world and probably has been true of our lineage since the first mammals evolved some two hundred million years ago."[15]

The empirical evidence is important but is not as significant as the results of a real-life experiment. The Israeli kibbutz movement provides a great example of just how fatuous McCartney's idea of motherhood is. It shows how stubborn nature really is.

Begun in the 1950s, the kibbutz movement was a deliberate attempt to establish a truly egalitarian society. Everyone who participated did so voluntarily and with a strong commitment to the goal. The kibbutz was a collectivist society, an agricultural village, where all property was collectively owned. This meant that the trucks and tractors were owned by the kibbutz, as were the cattle they cared for, the clothes they wore, and the food they ate. All work was collectively organized, and there was no such thing as a "women's job" or a "man's job". All living arrangements were collectively adhered to, including the rearing of children.

---

[14] Francis Fukuyama, *The Great Disruption* (New York: Free Press, 1999), p. 101.

[15] Steven Pinker, *The Blank Slate: The Modern Denial of Human Nature* (New York: Penguin Books, 2002), p. 357.

But it didn't take long before some obvious problems emerged. For example, not tagging clothes (to do so would suggest individual ownership) led to a ridiculous situation when the laundry was done: tall people ended up wearing short pants, and overweight people tried to get into skinny clothes. It was the women who protested, saying this was unacceptable; before long, tagging one's clothes was restored.

Women, in fact, rebelled against most of the strict egalitarian rules. At first, men and women shared domestic responsibilities, eliminating all traditional roles. But over time, women reverted to the kitchen, cooking meals. Instead of cooking for their family, they were now cooking for four hundred people, making them wonder whether this "experiment" was worth it.

Most excruciating were the child-rearing arrangements. Child rearing was done collectively, save for late in the day. The natural parents were not permitted to be with their children, except for two hours later in the day, during "children's hour". That didn't sit too well with mothers: they found that when it came time for them to leave—to drop their kids off at their dorms—it was literally unbearable. It was these kinds of revolts that killed this utopian experiment.[16] To put it another way, common sense triumphed over ideology.

David P. Barash, an evolutionary biologist, and Judith Eve Lipton, a physician, are experts on sex differences who probed this subject. They wanted to know why the kibbutz failed. "Kibbutz women had reverted to domesticity, and men were running the affairs of the group. Contrary to the movement's hoped-for egalitarianism, boys played aggressively, imitating heroes and fierce animals, while

---

[16] Melford E. Spiro with Audrey G. Spiro, *Children of the Kibbutz*, rev. ed. (Cambridge, Mass.: Harvard University Press, 1975).

girls doted on dolls and pretended to be mothers. Women, wanting more time with their children, opted to do the bulk of the parenting."[17]

Anthropologist Melford Spiro, who chronicled what happened, concluded that this outcome showed "the triumph of nature over culture". This is not the outcome he wanted. A self-described cultural determinist, he said his decision to study the kibbutz "was to observe the influence of culture on human nature or, more accurately, to discover how a new culture produces a new human nature". Instead, he found that he was observing "the influence of human nature on culture".[18] Yonina Talmon, who also studied the kibbutz, came to a similar conclusion. "Natural relationships, based on kinship and geographical proximity, become more important than those based on ideology and shared ideas", she said.[19]

Such scholars are rare these days. Most of them just mouth the prevailing wisdom, and when they encounter evidence that undercuts their ideological preference, they ignore it. But thanks to honest men such as Spiro, these findings show the persistence of human nature.

The Catholic Perspective and Gender Ideology

There is not a single teaching of the Catholic Church that is in disharmony with Brown's findings. His categorization of sex, marriage, the family, and kinship as human universals is completely consistent with the Catholic perspective.

---

[17] David P. Barash and Judith Eve Lipton, *Gender Gap: The Biology of Male-Female Differences* (New Brunswick, N.J.: Transaction Press, 2001), p. 116.

[18] Spiro and Spiro, *Children of the Kibbutz*, p. 106.

[19] Yonina Talmon, *Family and Community in the Kibbutz* (Cambridge, Mass.: Harvard University Press, 1972), p. 37.

Men, women, and children are equal in the eyes of God, possessing the same human dignity. This basic equality between the sexes, however, does not mean that there are no fundamental differences between men and women. Those differences are a reflection of God's design and are rooted in nature. Not to acknowledge this verity is not simply wrong; it can lead to many problems.

As Brown pointed out, marriage and the family are universal institutions because they serve the purpose of constructively channeling the sex drive. This fits well with God's design. "For the Catholic Christian", writes Catholic scholar Hanna Klaus, "the genital expression of sexuality is reserved to marriage, the only human institution where both ends of the sexual act—the perfection of mutual love and the procreation of children—can be concretized." She sees in this something beautiful and quintessentially Catholic. "When spouses procreate, their love is incarnated in their child. In doing so, they reflect the Trinitarian, creative Love of God."[20]

Scripture and Tradition are rich in detail in explaining the special role of motherhood. As Saint John Paul II said, women are called by their nature to be mothers; it is part of their "feminine genius" to serve their children.[21] Furthermore, their calling is to "humanize humanity", a task that signifies their unique abilities.[22] Mary, the Mother of God, is the source and inspiration of this calling, providing all women with a role model par excellence.

In recent times, Popes John Paul II, Benedict XVI, and Francis have spoken about the complementarity of men

[20] Hanna Klaus, "Sexuality", in *Encyclopedia of Catholic Social Thought, Social Science, and Social Policy*, ed. Michael Coulter, Stephen Krason, Richard Myers, and Joseph Varacalli (Lanham, Md.: Scarecrow Press, 2007), p. 958.

[21] John Paul II, *Letter to Women* (June 29, 1995), no. 10.

[22] Philip P. Sutton, "Motherhood", *Encyclopedia of Catholic Social Thought*, p. 725.

and women. The anatomical and biological differences between men and women are only one way the sexes complement each other; there are other differences—psychological and social—that are evident. These differences deserve our attention, providing a blueprint to the way we craft our culture and build our social institutions.

In November 2014, Pope Francis stressed the complementarity of the two sexes and how "every man and every woman brings their personal contribution—personal richness, their own charisma—to the marriage and to the upbringing of their children."[23] Similarly, he said, "Children have a right to grow up in a family with a father and a mother capable of creating a suitable environment for the child's development and emotional maturity."[24]

The pope was anything but politically correct. He did not speak about "gender"; he spoke about the "sexes". He did not speak about marriage "partners" but about the contributions of each "man and woman". He did not say that children need to grow up in a family of two adults (no matter how loving); he was exact in citing the need for children to have "a father and a mother". In doing so, he gave tribute to the human universals that Brown recorded.

Ever since the U.S. Supreme Court imposed same-sex marriage on the nation in *Obergefell v. Hodges*, those who continue to believe what virtually everyone in the history of the world always believed—that two people of the same sex cannot marry—have found it increasingly difficult to espouse and act on those beliefs. "Although *Obergefell* did not compel private citizens and their private associations to change their beliefs about marriage", writes Heritage Foundation scholar Ryan T. Anderson, "in case after case,

[23] Francis, address at the International Colloquium on the Complementarity between Man and Woman (November 17, 2014), no. 1.
[24] Ibid., no. 3.

corporate and cultural pressures are mounting against those who seek to live and work consistent with their belief that marriage is the union of a man and a woman and sex is a biological reality."[25]

Anderson is right to cite corporate pressure. It is astonishing how quickly corporate America embraced the gay-rights cause. Led by Goldman Sachs, those who work on Wall Street know that if they want to get along, they had better support gay marriage, or at the very least not make an issue of it. Moreover, the Human Rights Campaign and other gay groups have succeeded in getting almost all the Fortune 500 corporations on board. Those who disagree will get nowhere by citing their religious convictions, so thoroughly in the tank with the gay agenda are many corporate leaders. Just ask Brendan Eich. He was fired as CEO of Mozilla Corporation for contributing to a California initiative that supported marriage between a man and a woman.

New York City is run by a lot of deep thinkers. In 2016, the city's Commission on Human Rights designated thirty-one "gender identities", including "genderqueer"—a "person whose gender identity is neither man nor woman, is between or beyond genders, or is some combination of genders". A "gender bender" is someone "who bends, changes, mixes, or combines society's gender conventions by expressing elements of masculinity and femininity together".[26] The gurus who determined these categories

---

[25] Ryan T. Anderson, "How to Think about Sexual Orientation and Gender Identity (SOGI) Policies and Religious Freedom", Heritage Foundation, February 13, 2017, https://www.heritage.org/marriage-and-family/report /how-think-about-sexual-orientation-and-gender-identity-sogi-policies-and.

[26] Peter Hasson, "New York City Lets You Choose from 31 Different Gender Identities", *Daily Caller*, May 24, 2016, http://dailycaller.com/2016/05/24 /new-york-city-lets-you-choose-from-31-different-gender-identities/.

did not say what someone who is beyond genders looks like, nor did they indicate what someone who is in between looks like. A photo would help.

It's not just in New York that common sense has been lost. In 2014, Facebook listed fifty-eight genders.[27] That didn't last. In 2016, the number of gender identities jumped to seventy-one, including the "Two* person". Not sure who that is, or why the asterisk.[28]

If this were just a game, it would not bear commentary. But in real life it carries weight. Ask Javier Chavez. He was fired from Macy's because he believes that men should use the men's room, and not the women's room. After a woman and her daughter found a man dressed as a woman in the women's room in a Macy's store in Queens, New York, they complained to Chavez, the senior store detective. He ordered the man to leave. But then the cross-dresser registered a complaint with Macy's officials, and Chavez was called on the carpet. He was told that he was in violation of Macy's policy: a man who identifies as a woman is permitted to use women's changing rooms and bathrooms. Chavez was unaware of the policy, but he agreed to follow it, despite his stated Catholic convictions to the contrary. That wasn't satisfactory to Macy's executives—he was fired.[29]

The policy that Macy's devised is a marvel of contemporary thought on how to deal with transgender problems

[27] Russell Goldman, "Here's a List of 58 Gender Options for Facebook Users", ABC News, February 13, 2014, https://abcnews.go.com/News/heres-a-list-of-58-gender-options-for-facebook-users/blogEntry?id=22504704.

[28] Rhiannon Williams, "Facebook's 71 Gender Options Come to UK Users", Telegraph, June 27, 2014, https://www.telegraph.co.uk/technology/facebook/10930654/Facebooks-71-gender-options-come-to-UK-users.html.

[29] Bill Donohue, "Catholic League 2016 Year in Review", https://www.catholicleague.org/catholic-league-for-religious-and-civil-rights-2016-year-in-review/.

in the workplace. Here is the advice it gives to employees who see a cross-dressing man going into the ladies' room: "If a customer presents photo identification that resembles the customer but does not represent the gender the customer presents, and if the associate believes the customer may be a transgender person, the associate will accept the document at face value, as long as the address is current and the name is correct for the account. The associate will not discuss the customer's transgender status with anyone." In other words, the customer can lie about his sex but not his address.

Furthermore, Macy's tells its employees to resist "the impulse to judge the person by his/her appearances". That's right. If a person has a beard, he may be a woman. How can this be? We need to understand that "sex and gender are not the rigid categories that we may assume them to be."[30] So, if he looks like Sam, remember that he could very well be Sally.

Macy's may be more extreme than most companies, but it accurately reflects the thinking of corporate America. Apple, Delta, and Coca-Cola are strong defenders of men using the ladies' room (provided they identify themselves as women), and those who have reservations about this had better keep their views to themselves. The sports world has jumped on the bandwagon as well, led by the NBA, the NCAA, and the NFL.

It does not help to point out the obvious: men cannot elect to become women. No matter how they dress, or what genitals they acquire, men cannot menstruate. Only women can.

---

[30] Bill Donohue, "Shoppers Beware of Macy's Sex Policy", Catholic League, January 25, 2017, https://www.catholicleague.org/shoppers-beware -of-macys-sex-policy-2/.

The push for transgender rights was fully embraced by the Obama administration. At the beginning of 2017, it came very close to forcing Catholic institutions to pay for an operation whereby a man acquires the body parts of a female, and vice versa. But a U.S. district court judge issued a preliminary injunction on New Year's Eve, stopping the Obama administration from implementing its "gender identity transition" policy.[31]

Lawyers for the Obama administration attempted to put a new spin on Title IX of the 1972 Education Amendments, which bars sex discrimination. The new regulation, Section 1557, invoked those provisions to mean that it is discriminatory to deny gender transition operations. However, in 1972, sex discrimination simply meant that it was unconstitutional to discriminate against a man or a woman, *as determined by the person's sex at birth*. It said nothing, and implied nothing, about guys switching genitals.

The Trump administration sought to undo some of Obama's transgender policies. In 2018, the Department of Education launched an investigation of a school in Decatur, Georgia, where a five-year-old girl was assaulted in a bathroom by a transgender student. The school district where the offense took place allows transgender students to use the bathroom of their choice. The Trump administration sought to learn whether the district's bathroom policy contributed to the "creation of a hostile environment for the student and other girls".[32]

Transgender activists are explicitly targeting Catholic institutions, seeking to use the power of government to

[31] Bill Donohue, "Obama Suffers Transgender Loss", Catholic League, January 3, 2017, https://www.catholicleague.org/obama-suffers-transgender-loss/.

[32] Caitlin Emma, "DeVos Investigates Whether School Transgender Bathroom Policy Led to Sexual Assault", *Politico*, October 3, 2018, www. politico .com.

force these organizations to get in line with their agenda. In 2017, a man, claiming to be a woman, filed suit against a Catholic hospital in New Jersey for refusing to allow a surgeon to perform a hysterectomy on him at the facility.[33] But men cannot have a hysterectomy—only those with a uterus can. That's just how far this sexually tortured ideology has come.

Laws that seek to secure transgender rights, Anderson notes, "send the message that traditional Judeo-Christian beliefs are not only false, but also discriminatory and rooted in animus". These laws, he argues, "are not about the freedom of LGBT people to engage in certain actions, but about coercing and penalizing people who in good conscience cannot endorse those actions".[34] Yes, in the name of tolerance, we have witnessed an onslaught of intolerance against people of faith. Yet the First Amendment protects religious liberty, and there is nothing in the Constitution about LGBT rights.

This battle is not over. Not everyone has lost his mind. In 2017, the chairmen of two U.S. bishops' committees issued a strong statement protesting any attempt on the part of the federal government to force schools to treat a student's gender identity as the student's sex. The bishops cited the "privacy and safety concerns of all students", saying such matters were best handled at the local level.[35]

Pope Francis has been an outspoken critic of gender ideology, the idea that there are identities beyond the

---

[33] Bill Donohue, "Transgender Politics Unmasked", Catholic League, January 6, 2017, https://www.catholicleague.org/transgender-politics-unmasked/.

[34] Anderson, "How to Think About Sexual Orientation", p. 4.

[35] Catholic News Service, "USCCB Committee Chairmen Applaud Decision on Transgender Directive", Catholic News Service, February 27, 2017, http://www.catholicnews.com/services/englishnews/2017/usccb-committee-chairmen-applaud-decision-on-transgender-directive.cfm.

two sexes. "Allow me to draw your attention to the value and beauty of marriage. The complementarity of man and woman, the vertex of the divine creation", he said in 2015, "is being questioned by gender ideology, in the name of a freer and more just society. The difference between a man and a woman is not meant to stand in opposition, or to subordinate, but is for the sake of communion and generation, always 'in the image and likeness of God.' "[36]

So disturbed is the Holy Father by this assault on marriage and the family that he once exclaimed, "Gender ideology is demonic." He warned against "the colonization by new ideologies", specifically mentioning how gender ideology is "out to destroy the family".[37] In 2016, he went even further, saying, "This is terrible. Today in schools they are teaching this to children—to children!" He told Poland's bishops, "We are living in a moment of annihilation of man as image of God."[38] His anthropology is as sound as his theology, posing a definitive challenge to the reigning orthodoxies.

To appreciate what is going on, consider the experience of Walt Heyer. He suffered from gender identity disorder since he was a child. He later married and, at age forty-two, underwent surgery to alter his sex. He also came to realize the source of his disorder, received help, became a Christian, and made a successful adjustment to living as a man again.

[36] Bill Donohue, "Pope Attacks Gender Ideology Again", Catholic League, June 9, 2015, https://www.catholicleague.org/pope-attacks-gender-ideology -again/.

[37] Bill Donohue, "Pope Francis and Bruce Jenner", Catholic League, June 4, 2015, https://www.catholicleague.org/pope-francis-bruce-jenner-2/.

[38] Bill Donohue, "Pope Speaks the Truth about Gender", Catholic League, August 3, 2016, https://www.catholicleague.org/pope-speaks-the -truth-about-gender-2/.

His grandmother was the source of his confusion. She
started cross-dressing him at age four, even making a chif-
fon evening dress for him. When his father found out, he
put an end to it, but that was two and a half years later, and
the seed had already been planted: Walt began to identify as a girl. Fortunately, after psychotherapy and prayer,
he came to realize that "it is a delusion to think you can
change genders. You can't. It's total nonsense."[39]

Dr. Paul McHugh, a practicing Catholic and former
chief of psychiatry at Johns Hopkins Hospital, agrees that
it is delusional to think men can become women, and vice
versa. He was among the first in the nation to pioneer sex-
change surgery, but by the 1970s he and his colleagues at
Johns Hopkins called it quits, concluding that the operation did not yield beneficial results. He also cites a classic
study in Sweden on this subject.

For over thirty years, researchers tracked sex-reassigned
people, documenting their mental disorders. "Ten to fifteen years after surgical reassignment", McHugh wrote,
"the suicide rate of those who had undergone sex-
reassignment surgery rose to twenty times that of com-
parable peers." These people need help, he instructs, not
our applause. "The treatment should strive to correct the
false, problematic nature of the assumption [that we can
change our sex] and to resolve the psychosocial conflicts
provoking it."[40]

He recently teamed up with his colleague, Dr. Lawrence S. Mayer, a psychiatrist at John Hopkins University School of Medicine, to offer the definitive account

[39] Brian Fraga, "Speaking Out about the Transgender 'Delusion'", an interview with Walt Heyer, *National Catholic Register*, May 6, 2015, http://www
.ncregister.com/daily-news/speaking-out-about-the-transgender-delusion1.

[40] Paul McHugh, "Transgenderism: A Pathogenic Meme", *Public Discourse*,
June 10, 2015, http://www.thepublicdiscourse.com/2015/06/15145/.

on transgender persons. "The hypothesis that gender identity is an innate, fixed property of human beings that is independent of biological sex—that a person might be 'a man trapped in a woman's body' or 'a woman trapped in a man's body'—is not supported by scientific evidence." They also found that those who have undergone sex-reassignment surgery "have a higher risk of experiencing poor mental health outcomes". The suicide rate of such persons is astonishing.[41]

Mayer and McHugh's work finds congruence with Catholic teachings on this subject. Men and women are different in many ways, calling us to construct social policies that respect these differences. If some cannot accept their nature-given status as a man or a woman, they should be loved and accepted as children of God, but they should also be given counseling that helps them to overcome their problems. It only complicates matters when egalitarian extremists pretend otherwise.

Male-Female Differences

On January 14, 2005, Harvard University president Lawrence Summers spoke at an off-campus conference held by the National Bureau for Economic Research. He was asked to give a provocative address, and he did not disappoint. That was an understatement—he created a furor.

Why do women constitute approximately 20 percent of science and engineering departments nationwide, holding few senior positions? Summers offered three explanations.

[41] Lawrence S. Mayer and Paul R. McHugh, "Sexuality and Gender: Findings from the Biological, Psychological, and Social Sciences", *New Atlantis* 50 (Fall 2016): 8.

Women want to have children, electing not to put in as many hours as their male peers; innate differences between men and women exist, leading men to outperform women; and discrimination against women at the undergraduate level in these fields discourages them from pursuing graduate studies.[42] It was his second contention, especially, that got him into a world of trouble.

Nancy Hopkins, a professor at Massachusetts Institute of Technology, walked out of Summers' presentation. She had to. "I would've either blacked out or thrown up", she said. "When he started talking about innate differences in aptitude between men and women, I just couldn't breathe because this kind of bias makes me physically ill."[43] Kim Gandy, president of the National Organization for Women, accused Summers of sexism, calling on him to resign. "It's time to remove the barriers [to women]", she said, "and one of them is Larry Summers."[44]

The hyperventilation was to be expected. Anyone who dares to suggest that there are innate differences between men and women is subject to punitive sanctions, so tight is the radical feminist grip in our culture. It did not matter that Summers never said, or implied, that men are better than women: his crime was saying that nature explains some of the reasons why men do better than women in certain disciplines. Radical egalitarianism allows no role for anything but nurture in explaining achievement levels.

[42] Meghan O'Rourke, "Don't Let Larry Summers Off the Hook Yet", *Slate*, January 28, 2005, http://www.slate.com/articles/news_and_politics/the _highbrow/2005/01/dont_let_larry_summers_off_the_hook_yet.html.

[43] Kate O'Beirne, *Women Who Make the World Worse* (New York: Sentinel, 2006), p. 179.

[44] National Organization for Women, "NOW Calls for Resignation of Harvard University's President", press release, January 20, 2005, http://wiseli .engr.wisc.edu/archives/NOW.pdf.

Despite the politically charged attacks on Summers, much of what he said is true. There are many biologically rooted differences between the sexes. In some areas—in verbal skills, for instance—women tend to do better than men; in other areas, such as mathematical reasoning, men tend to do better. Shooting the messenger may provide temporary relief for the aggrieved, but it is an immature way to address the human condition. Inequality occurs in every society, and in many instances its origins are rooted in nature, not nurture.

"The historical reality of male dominance of the greatest achievements in science and the arts is not open to argument." This is the conclusion of Charles Murray, a long-time student of human behavior. How much is attributable to nature, and how much is explained by nurture, is open to question, he says.[45] His views on human nature are so countercultural that in 2017, when he was to speak at Middlebury College, fifty-eight faculty members signed a petition against his visit. Worse, some students engaged in violence, leaving one professor injured. Murray was not allowed to speak.[46]

Murray notes that women are more apt than men to have their lives changed as a result of having children, a characteristic that is not confined to humans. For example, "Mammalian reproduction generally involves much higher levels of maternal than paternal investment in the raising of children."[47] He is underscoring one of the points

[45] Charles Murray, "The Inequality Taboo", *Commentary*, September 2005, https://www.commentarymagazine.com/articles/the-inequality-taboo/.

[46] Clarence Page, "The Middlebury Protest and Our World of Bubbles", *Chicago Tribune*, March 10, 2017, http://www.chicagotribune.com/news /opinion/page/ct-middlebury-murray-campus-speech-trump-page-perspec -0312-jm-20170310-story.html.

[47] Murray, "The Inequality Taboo".

made by Summers: women have their lives, and careers, interrupted by giving birth and attending to their children, putting them at a disadvantage with men in competing in the workplace.

The role that nature plays in accounting for the disparity in male–female achievement levels is real, Murray says. He notes that in the twentieth century, "women got only 2 percent of the Nobel Prizes in the sciences—a proportion constant for both halves of the century—and 10 percent of the prizes in literature." Furthermore, prestigious awards in math routinely go to men.[48]

If there is a male advantage, it manifests itself in abstract thought. "In the humanities", Murray contends, "the most abstract field is philosophy—and no woman has been a significant original thinker in any of the world's great philosophical traditions. In the sciences, the most abstract field is mathematics, where the number of great women mathematicians is approximately two (Emmy Noether definitely, Sonya Kovalevskaya maybe)."[49]

Women do much better in fields that rely more on verbal abilities and less on abstract proficiencies. Take literature. "Women have been represented among great writers virtually from the beginning of literature", Murray says, "in East Asia and South Asia as well as in the West."[50] But when it comes to musical composition, which relies heavily on abstract abilities, that is a different story.

Murray is not alone in observing that "no female composer is even close to the first rank."[51] However disconcerting it may be to some, it is nonetheless true that there are no female composers who can rival Bach, Mozart, or

[48] Ibid.
[49] Ibid.
[50] Ibid.
[51] Ibid.

Beethoven.[52] Sir Thomas Beecham, the late British conductor, was not sanguine about matters changing: "There are no women composers, never have been and possibly never will be."[53] Sounds harsh, but those who claim that the lack of female composers at the highest levels is a function of discrimination need to explain why discrimination never stopped women from becoming first-class writers, anywhere in the world. Something outside of environmental conditions must be at work.

Differences between the sexes are evident in many ways other than in scholarship, and some are noticeable within seventy-two hours after birth. Here is a sampling. Boys crawl away from their caregivers at an earlier age than girls. Typically, girls do better academically and receive better grades than boys. Women smile more than men and are more agreeable and warm. On the downside, they make up more than 90 percent of all anorexia and bulimia patients. They attempt suicide more than men, though more men succeed in killing themselves. Men are generally more assertive and more prone to take risks than women, which also accounts for their shorter life expectancy. In general, men are better at spatial relations than women, while women are better at detail; women also remember more.[54]

Recent research findings are challenging many long-held views on male-female differences. The *New York Times* examined studies on personality tests in more than

[52] Andrew Bolt, "Boy, It Makes Sense", *Herald Sun*, December 19, 2002, p. 21.

[53] Scott Cantrell, "The Rise and Rediscovery of Women Composers; They've Been There All Along, but Often Were Discouraged from Working", *Kansas City Star*, April 2, 1995, p. K1.

[54] *20/20*, season 28, episode 6, "The Difference between Men and Women", first aired September 29, 2006, on ABC; Glenn T. Stanton, "The Scientific Objectivity of Gender Differences", *The Family in America* (Winter 2016): 49–50.

sixty countries, expecting to find that the more developed nations had smaller sex differences than the developing ones. The conventional view was wrong. "It looks as if personality differences between men and women are smaller in traditional cultures like India's or Zimbabwe's than in the Netherlands or the United States." The *New York Times'* conclusion rattled many: "The more Venus and Mars have equal rights and similar jobs, the more their personalities seem to diverge."[55]

Professor Glenn T. Stanton captured the essence of what the researchers had discovered. "This led the scholars generally to favor a biological basis for gender differences over cultural construction", he said, "because when culture allowed for more freedom and opportunities, the gender distinctions became more pronounced." Indeed, they found greater male-female differences in "gender-equitable North America and Europe than across the less gender-equitable Asia and Africa".[56]

Boys are more likely than girls to engage in rough-and-tumble play. Why? Contrary to what the big thinkers say, their aggressiveness has nothing to do with socialization and everything to do with testosterone, which also explains why adults play rougher with boys than with girls. These differences, and many more, are found in every society and cannot be explained without referencing the role that nature plays. Infants are not blank slates.[57]

To some extent, male-female differences are a function of brain circuitry and powerful hormones. Dr. Louann Brizendine, a neuropsychologist and author of *The Female Brain*, says that, at birth, people's "circuitry is already

[55] Stanton, "Scientific Objectivity", pp. 50–51.
[56] Ibid., p. 51.
[57] Barash and Lipton, *Gender Gap*, pp. 139–45.

pretty much wired. They're either formed as a male brain or female brain."[58] The differences are manifest in many ways. For example, little girls play together better than boys do because of their brain wiring. According to another expert on this subject, Simon Baron-Cohen, "The female brain is predominantly hard-wired to empathy. The male brain is predominantly hard-wired for understanding and building systems."[59]

The interaction between the brain and hormones explains a lot. Testosterone explains why males think about sex every fifty-two seconds, as compared with a few times a day for teen girls. We also know that impulses and sexual thought are a function of the part of the brain called the amygdala; it is twice as large in men as in women. What causes the difference? Testosterone.[60]

"Only in the last 15 to 20 years has overwhelming evidence been amassed to show how sex differences, both large and small, exist at every level of analysis in the human animal." That observation belongs to Claire Lehmann, whose writings on the subject are a model of clarity and courageousness. Neurobiologists, for example, "have discovered that there are sex differences in how our brain hemispheres are wired, with women's being more highly connected across the left and right hemisphere, and men having more connections from front to back." Lehmann also discusses the "fundamental sex differences in basic neurochemistry". To be specific, baseline amounts of neurotransmitters such as serotonin and dopamine differ by sex.[61]

---

[58] "The Difference between Men and Women".

[59] Simon Baron-Cohen, *The Essential Difference: Male and Female Brains and the Truth about Autism* (New York: Basic Books, 2003), p. 97.

[60] "The Difference between Men and Women".

[61] Claire Lehmann, "The XX Factor", *Commentary*, April 2017, pp. 15–16.

In short, male-female differences are real. So why are these differences not more widely acknowledged? "Ideology is much more resistant to change", says Lehmann, "especially when individuals are afraid to speak out about it." She is not exaggerating: it takes guts to go against the conventional wisdom in the academy. Leading the fight to suppress the truth are not those in the hard sciences but those in the humanities and social sciences. Cordelia Fine, an Australian social psychologist, is hard to beat. She coined the term "neurosexism" to describe any research that shows the biological differences between men and women.[62] This isn't science—Fine has no expertise in this area—it is politics, pure and simple.

On the subject of male-female differences, grounded in nature, there is complete harmony between the teachings of the Catholic Church and the scientific literature. While the Church abstains from getting into the weeds— she does not pontificate on brain circuitry and hormonal interactions—she does hold that there are differences between men and women that are grounded in biology. Furthermore, the Church recognizes, as does Brown, that there are fundamental behavioral differences between the sexes that society should observe. For example, if women are better at nurturing children, why should society not accommodate this reality? Instead, we act as if such a verity is sexist.

Standing against anthropology, biology, and Church teachings are the cultural elites who believe that human behavior is best understood as a social construction. This view—it is not science—suits their ego: if all that exists is capable of being changed, then it is up to intellectuals to develop the right blueprint. They see themselves as the ultimate change agents in history. This is not simply a flawed

---

[62] Ibid., pp. 16–17.

paradigm—it reflects what happens when the mind becomes hostage to ideology; it evolves into a mental prison.

Feminists at War with Nature

The women's movement of the 1960s was shaped primarily by Betty Friedan, Kate Millett, Germaine Greer, Gloria Steinem, Simone de Beauvoir, and Shulamith Firestone. All six lived dysfunctional lives, but that didn't stop them from creating problems for millions of women.

It is telling that only Friedan had both married and borne children. But marriage and motherhood didn't work out for her: she was miserably unhappy living in suburbia, or what she called a "comfortable concentration camp".

Millett was bisexual and had to be involuntarily committed on two occasions. She was seriously depressed, bipolar, and a drug user; she attempted suicide on multiple occasions.[63]

Greer, author of *The Female Eunuch*, said marriage was outmoded; she chose to be childless. As Carolyn Graglia notes, she also committed herself to an unusual sex life: "Her preference for abstinence, anal intercourse, and *coitus interruptus* over contraceptive methods, however, suggested a lingering distaste for the womb as well as for phallic potency."[64]

Steinem had an abortion at age twenty-two and chose to be childless. She vehemently condemned any researcher who explored sex differences and was livid at the suggestion that women are better nurturers than men.[65]

[63] "Kate Millett", Wikipedia, last modified May 9, 2018, https://en.wikipedia.org/wiki/Kate_Millett.

[64] F. Carolyn Graglia, *Domestic Tranquility: A Brief against Feminism* (Dallas: Spence Publishing, 1998), pp. 13–14.

[65] O'Beirne, *Women Who Make the World Worse*, p. 181.

The French feminist de Beauvoir was bisexual, living much of her life with Jean-Paul Sartre. "Women are made, they are not born", she said.[66] She demonized housewives and fiercely opposed allowing women to choose between taking a job or working at home. "Women should not have that choice [of staying at home to raise their children]", she said, "precisely because if there is such a choice, too many women will make that one."[67] So much for being pro-choice.

Firestone railed against nature, famously saying that "pregnancy is barbaric."[68] She blamed men for every indignity women have ever experienced, including their biology. She suffered from schizophrenia and spent her last twenty-five years in asylums.[69]

These are the persons who are most responsible for shaping the way many in elite circles think about male-female differences. None believed that there are fundamental differences between men and women that are rooted in nature. They were all wrong. Unfortunately, their influence on the dominant culture has been considerable. Indeed, they helped to create our cultural crisis.

If there is one woman who is often associated with these feminists but should not be, it is the anthropologist Margaret Mead. To this day, academia cites her as having offered proof that male-female differences are wholly a cultural

[66] Andrew Heywood, *Political Ideologies: An Introduction* (New York: St. Martin's Press, 1992), p. 226.

[67] Suzanne Venker, "Should It Be Illegal to Be a Stay-at-Home Mom? Why Feminists Are So Frustrated", Fox News, March 24, 2017, http://www.foxnews.com/opinion/2017/03/24/should-it-be-illegal-to-be-stay-at-home-mom-why-feminists-are-so-frustrated.html.

[68] Bill Donohue, *The New Freedom: Individualism and Collectivism in the Social Lives of Americans* (New Brunswick, N.J.: Transaction Press, 1990), p. 60.

[69] Maureen Freely, "Where Have All the Sisters Gone?", *Ottawa Citizen*, January 23, 1999, p. B7.

phenomenon. To be sure, in her early writings Mead gave credence to that position, but she later revised her thinking: "Nowhere do I suggest that I have found any material which disproves the existence of sex differences."[70]

When asked to comment on *The Inevitability of Patriarchy*, a controversial but well-researched book by Steven Goldberg, Mead did not seek to refute the conclusions of the New York sociologist. "It is true, as Professor Goldberg points out, that all the claims so glibly made about societies ruled by women are nonsense. We have no reason to believe that they ever existed.... Men have always been the leaders in public affairs and the final authorities at home."[71]

Regarding the universality of male attainment, Mead was explicit. "Men may cook, or weave or dress dolls or hunt hummingbirds, but if such activities are appropriate behavior for men, then the whole society, men and women alike, votes them as important. When the same occupations are performed by women, they are regarded as less important."[72] While serious scholars take note of Mead's position, many ideologues and activists continue to mislead their students by putting words into her mouth, words she expressly refuted.

Politicizing Inequality

The greatest showcase of sex segregation in the world today is the Olympics: men and women compete separately. It

[70] Steven Goldberg, "Feminism against Science", *National Review*, November 18, 1991, p. 30.

[71] Ibid.

[72] Mead made her confession in her book *Male and Female* and is quoted in Steven Goldberg, "The Iroquois—An Exception to Universal Patriarchy?", The Debunker's Domain, https://www.debunker.com/texts/iroquois.html.

is a testimony to the athletic superiority of men—they are stronger and faster than women—that even radical egalitarians do not demand a unisex Olympics; if they did, there would be few women competitors. We've all become accustomed to men competing with men and women competing with women, so if this is not seen as sexism, why are all other differences between the sexes seen as problematic?

Those who see the world through the lens of radical egalitarianism see all manifestations of inequality between men and women as an expression of sexism. They cannot conceive of a society wherein the inequalities that exist are the result of choices freely made by women as well as men. For them, it is always prejudice and discrimination that account for inequalities. Moreover, they tend to blame our cultural roots, most specifically Christianity, for the perceived injustices. Catholicism gets the lion's share of the blame.

Early in Church history, Catholic leaders championed the cause of women's rights. Saint Patrick, who had been a slave, taught that all men and women were equal in the eyes of God, possessing an equal dignity that deserved to be respected. Such an idea was seen as bizarre, if not incredible, to the pagans he evangelized in Ireland. But it also explained why women in Ireland gravitated to his side. Saint Patrick was courageous in his convictions, admonishing the British tyrant Coroticus for allowing his troops to mistreat women. "They must also free their Christian women and captives", he said.[73]

Despite its historic insistence on natural law and natural rights, the Church still comes under fire from those

---

[73] Philip Freeman, *St. Patrick of Ireland: A Biography* (New York: Simon and Schuster, 2004), pp. 170–71.

who don't know any better. "The fact that the Catholic Church, for instance, prohibits women from serving as priests or even deacons gives a *kind of a permission to male people all over the world*, that well, if God thinks that women are inferior, I'll treat them as inferiors. If she is my wife, I can abuse her with impunity, or if I'm an employer, I can pay female employees less salary."[74] The author of this condemnation of the Catholic Church is Jimmy Carter. Does the former president really think that the reason why so many women have been beaten, gang raped, tortured, and murdered in Islamic nations is because the Catholic Church does not ordain women? And is the barbaric practice of female genital mutilation in Muslim nations traceable to the same source?

Carter knows a thing or two about treating women as inferiors. When he was president, he appointed 13 cabinet officers; 3 were women. He appointed 18 women to cabinet and cabinet-level positions, yet his predecessor, Gerald Ford, who was in office for only two and a half years, appointed 22 women. Of the 5 members of Carter's White House staff, 1 was a woman. He appointed 259 judges to the federal bench, 15.8 percent of whom were women.[75]

According to Carter's logic, if the Catholic Church is responsible for women being abused across the globe because it doesn't ordain women, then he is a coconspirator in these high crimes.

Those who politicize inequality would have us believe that where there is a discrepancy between men and women, it is the result of male dominance. They cannot understand why women might prefer a nominally unequal

---

[74] Bill Donohue, "Should Carter Be Jailed?", Catholic League, May 20, 2014, https://www.catholicleague.org/carter-jailed; italics added by author.
[75] Ibid.

condition to an equal one. What they don't understand is that there are some very good reasons why women have not pursued the radical egalitarian agenda.

Take the Equal Rights Amendment (ERA). The ERA was first introduced in the 1920s, soon after the Nineteenth Amendment gave women the right to vote. (It should be noted that there was nothing in the Constitution that barred women from voting. The amendment was really an addition: the words "man" or "male" are never used in the Constitution; only nonsexist language, such as "citizens" and "electors", is used.) The ERA was promoted to level the playing field in law so that there were literally no differences left between men and women. Today it is typically taught in college classrooms that men conspired to keep women in their place by opposing the ERA. Wrong. It was women who opposed it, and the opposition was led by liberal women.

Eleanor Roosevelt is regarded as one of the staunchest feminists in the first half of the twentieth century. She hated the ERA. What she hated most about it was the prospect of undoing labor laws that protected women in the factories, where jobs, she said, were hazardous and demeaning. She was hardly alone in this conviction. The American Association of Women Professors and the League of Women Voters steadfastly opposed the ERA. All of these women wanted justice, but none took the position that justice is defined in strictly egalitarian terms. In other words, they were fully aware of differences in the law that redounded to the benefit of women. They saw this as common sense.

Today, of course, any defense of laws that treat men and women differently is seen as unjust. This wouldn't be so bad if the egalitarians acknowledged that it was prominent women's groups who fought the ERA—it was not men who organized against it.

In the late 1970s, I spent a lot of time at the ACLU's headquarters in New York City combing over internal documents; I was doing research for my doctoral dissertation at New York University. When asked by some employees what I was doing, I said I was researching why the ACLU changed its policies on various issues since its inception in 1920. I gave by way of example the ACLU's opposition to the ERA. The employees got angry, telling me that I had better report that the organization no longer opposed it. In fact, it had only recently changed its mind. The ACLU fought the ERA in the 1920s, in the 1930s, in the 1940s, in the 1950s, and in the 1960s. Women led the fight. The ACLU's position did not change until September 1970.

It was judge Dorothy Kenyon, known as a radical, who used her post as the head of the ACLU's Committee on Women's Rights in the 1940s to fight the ERA (she switched positions in 1970). "Equality of rights under the law shall not be denied or abridged by the United States or by any State on account of sex." That was the language of the ERA that feminists found objectionable for a half century, calling it the "Unequal Rights Amendment". The ACLU said the wording "might well freeze mathematical equality into our Constitution and stand in the way of or overrule desirable differential legislation" and was, in any event, too broad in its scope.[76]

In the 1970s, the male-dominated Congress passed the ERA and sent it to the state legislatures for ratification. The male-dominated state legislatures moved quickly, securing thirty of the thirty-eight states needed for passage. Then came the opposition, led by women.

[76] William A. Donohue, *The Politics of the American Civil Liberties Union* (New Brunswick, N.J.: Transaction Press, 1985), pp. 89–95; Judy Klemesrud, "Assessing Eleanor Roosevelt as a Feminist", *New York Times*, November 5, 1984, p. B12.

Phyllis Schlafly took to the airwaves, making the kinds of arguments the ACLU made for decades, but had now abandoned. Indeed, she was roundly condemned by the very people who had worked so hard to stop the ERA. Women listened to both sides and lined up in support of Schlafly. In 1975, the ERA was on the ballot in two liberal states, New York and New Jersey, and it went down to a resounding defeat; it lost by a 2–1 margin. Linda Greenhouse, legal reporter for the *New York Times*, noted that it was women, not men, who killed it.[77]

Wage Gap

Today, it is considered unjust to pay women less than men for doing the same work, but in the first half of the twentieth century, it was considered unjust not to pay the family breadwinners, namely, husbands and fathers, more than women and single men. Women applauded it.

Father John Ryan was a liberal in good standing, pushing for many New Deal reforms. In his 1906 book, *A Living Wage*, he made the case for the minimum wage and an eight-hour workday. He also championed the causes of the elderly, the unemployed, and the handicapped. None of these goals are controversial today, but Ryan's advocacy of what came to be known as the "family wage" is now seen as unjust.

A century ago, the focus of social policy was not the individual; it was the family. No one, including women, considered it unjust to pay the male breadwinner more than single persons: they had multiple obligations, necessitating more pay. That the unmarried, the divorced, and

[77] Donohue, *Politics*, pp. 89–95.

widowed workers were paid less for the same job was considered fair—the family comes first.[78]

The "family wage" made common sense in a society that gave the family a privileged position. No more. Now we measure justice by equal pay for equal work, a reflection of our heightened interest in individual rights and our declining interest in the welfare of the family. We therefore greet with criticism reports of a wage gap between men and women. Every year, feminist activists decry data that indicate that a woman make seventy-seven cents for every dollar a man makes. But is this true?

Writing in *Forbes*, Shaun Gallagher noted that "common sense alone should suggest that at least some of the gap is attributable to things other than discrimination against women—for instance, differences between men's and women's career choices, work experience, salary-negotiation skills, and even the number of hours worked per week."[79] He correctly identified, unintentionally, the principal reason why the pie-in-the-sky thinkers always manage to misunderstand why there is a wage gap—they lack common sense.

Take the last common sense observation, the number of hours men and women work. Hanna Rosin is a strong proponent of women's rights; she also possesses common sense. She takes exception to those who claim that sexism alone explains the wage gap. "The official Bureau of Labor Department statistics show that the median earnings of full-time female workers is 77 percent of the median

[78] Bill Donohue, *Why Catholicism Matters* (New York: Image, 2012), pp. 112–13.

[79] Shaun Gallagher, "Mind the Male/Female Income Gap, but Don't Exaggerate It", *Forbes*, May 21, 2012, https://www.forbes.com/sites/realspin/2012/05/21/mind-the-malefemale-income-gap-but-dont-exaggerate-it/#449529602b75.

earnings of full-time male workers. But that is very different than '77 cents on the dollar for doing the same work as
men.'" As she points out, to qualify as working full-time,
workers must put in 35 hours a week, "but men work
more hours than women. That's the first problem: We
could be comparing men working 40 hours to women
working 35."[80] The data bear her out.

Women are also more likely to work part-time, and
those women who work full-time are more likely than
men to avoid working overtime. They also turn down
promotions and job transfers more than men. Why? Because many women have another set of obligations—
taking care of their children. These are rational choices
made by millions of women, having nothing to do with
workplace discrimination.

Another reason for the wage gap is the kind of work
women do. Generally speaking, they do not work in dangerous jobs; they work in low-risk occupations. Men, for
example, make up more than 90 percent of workplace
deaths. Owing to the risk factor, these jobs tend to pay
very well.[81] That they tend to be staffed by men has nothing to do with sexism—men are stronger—but it helps to
explain why there is a wage gap.

The workplace risks that men take are rarely acknowledged. Kate O'Beirne took note: "The heroes of 9/11
provided a rare opportunity to celebrate the masculine
traits that drove those firemen—not firefighters—into the
burning towers to do the dangerous, demanding, dirty

[80] Karin Agness Lips, "Don't Buy into the Gender Pay Gap Myth", *Forbes*,
April 12, 2016, https://www.forbes.com/sites/karinagness/2016/04/12/dont
-buy-into-the-gender-pay-gap-myth/#6175d4842596.

[81] Guy Bentley, "Equal Pay Day Revisited: Why the Gender Pay Gap Is
Still a Myth", *Daily Caller*, April 12, 2016, http://dailycaller.com/2016/04/12
/equal-pay-day-revisited-why-the-gender-pay-gap-is-still-a-myth/.

work of men." She further notes that "there were no feminist protests when there wasn't a pleasing gender balance among the 343 brave firemen who died on 9/11."[82] The ideologues conveniently put their bean counters away, if not for long.

It is for these reasons that attempts to mandate wage equality through law is of limited use. Yet this has not stopped the egalitarians from trying. They positively refuse to admit that there are real-life choices made by women, and real-life differences between the sexes, that account for almost all the variability in the wage gap. In fact, in 2016 it was reported that after factoring in differences in education, experience, age, location, job title, industry and even company, the adjusted gap between men and women amounts to women earning 94.6 cents per dollar compared with men.[83]

Mandating equality is, of course, exactly what excites intellectuals. The results are not auspicious, and they often come at a cost.

In 2015, Rebecca Wax became a New York firefighter, even though she repeatedly failed the physical test required by the New York City Fire Department. Her case is not an anomaly. "All over the nation", writes researcher Betsy McCaughey, "fire departments are easing physical standards." Why? Because of lawsuits. Officials have decided that it's better to lower the standards for women than to risk more costly litigation. In Chicago, McCaughey says, "two federal class-action lawsuits brought by women who flunked that city's firefighting tests claimed that the exams required more than what is actually needed to be an

---

[82] O'Beirne, *Women Who Make the World Worse*, p. 137.

[83] Robert Hohman, "This Is the Biggest Myth about the Gender Wage Gap", *Fortune*, April 12, 2016, http://fortune.com/2016/04/12/myth-gender -wage-gap/.

effective firefighter."[84] Not all women in this profession are happy about the results. "It's making us look bad", said one dissenter. "It's undermining everything we've strived for and achieved of our own accord."[85]

Much the same is true in the military. Jude Eden is a female Marine who served in Iraq in the combat zone. She is not impressed with the mandated equality that marks the armed services. "All the branches still have different standards for females and males. Why? Because most women wouldn't even qualify to be in the military if they didn't have separate standards." She points out that women can be great shooters, but they cannot run as long, or as fast, as men when carrying fifty to eighty pounds of gear. There are other, more basic, problems. She argues that "until women stop menstruating, there will always be an uphill battle for staying level and strong at all times." Then there is the fate of putting men and women together in tight quarters, and "human nature [being] what it is", certain things are bound to happen, working to the detriment of combat readiness.[86]

Professoriate Need a Reality Check

When it comes to assessing the predispositions, talents, and assorted psychological, physical, and social attributes of

[84] Betsy McCaughey, "Perils of the Push for Female Firefighters", *New York Post*, May 5, 2015, https://nypost.com/2015/05/05/fdnys-unfit-the-perils-of-pushing-women-into-firefighting/.

[85] Christine Rousselle, "FDNY Refuses to Fire Female Firefighter Who Failed Fitness Test", *Townhall*, November 11, 2013, https://townhall.com/tipsheet/christinerousselle/2013/11/11/fdny-refuses-to-fire-female-firefighter-who-failed-fitness-test-n1744523.

[86] Jude Eden, "The Problems of Women in Combat—from a Female Combat Vet", *Western Journal*, January 26, 2013, https://www.westernjournal.com/the-problems-of-women-in-combat-from-a-female-combat-vet/.

men and women, it is not the Catholic Church that needs a reality check; it's the professoriate. By steadfastly refusing to concede that many of the differences between the sexes are grounded in nature, academia continues to mislead the public, finding discrimination where there is none, and failing to come to terms with reality.

The paradigm that sees men and women competing in a series of political, economic, social, and cultural games is flawed. As the Church informs, men and women complement each other in so many ways—men are not better than women, and vice versa—that it makes no sense not to recognize this verity. Furthermore, it makes no sense not to craft norms, values, policies, and laws that reflect what nature ordains. A mature society, one guided more by common sense than by ideology, will take its cues from nature and structure society accordingly. If it does not, the cultural crisis will continue, and its outcome will benefit no one.

4

Economic Inequality

Perspectives on Equality

Nothing is more natural than inequality. Social hierarchies exist in every society, beginning with the unequal positions of power exercised by parents over their children. Economic inequality is also ubiquitous, even in those societies dedicated to its elimination. No scheme ever devised by the most ardent socialist has ever succeeded; if anything, those societies exacerbate inequality. This is not a defense of every manifestation of economic inequality—it is simply a reality check: policies designed to limit economic equality are themselves limited by some very real conditions found in nature and in society.

Donald Brown notes that prestige inequalities are universal. "Prestige is differentially distributed", he says, and the members of society "are not all economically equal."[1] These unequal economic conditions are well understood by everyone and are not, per se, deemed objectionable. Fairness, as a concept, is also universal.

This is important: there is nothing inherently unfair about inequality. For instance, no one finds it objectionable to award gold, silver, and bronze medals in the

[1] Donald E. Brown, *Human Universals* (New York: McGraw-Hill, 1991), p. 137.

Olympics to those who finished first, second, and third (and none to the other competitors). But we would object if some were allowed two votes in an election when everyone else is allowed one. So it depends. There are times when treating everyone the same (equality) is fair (equity), and there are times when it is not. Equality and equity are not identical.

Aristotle understood this distinction very well. He thought it unjust to treat unequal things equally. Tocqueville agreed and was adamant in his belief that there was little that could be done to limit inequality. In every society, he said, there were three classes, or what we would call today the upper class, the middle class, and the lower class. "The individuals in these various categories may be more or less numerous according to the state of society", he argued, "but no contrivance will prevent these classes from existing."[2]

What concerned Tocqueville the most were the unhealthy traits that democracies unleashed. "Democratic peoples always like equality", he said, "but there are times when their passion for it turns to delirium."[3] Worse was the specter of an obliging paternalistic state. Equality breeds a desire for more equality, beckoning administrative centralization as the facilitator. Unlike governmental centralization, which properly deals with the affairs of the nation, administrative centralization seeks to police and penetrate local affairs, sapping the will of the people to mind their own interests. "That power is absolute, thoughtful of detail, orderly, provident, and gentle."[4] It is a prescription for despotism.

[2] Alexis de Tocqueville, *Democracy in America*, ed. J. P. Mayer, trans. George Lawrence (New York: Harper and Row, 1966), p. 209.

[3] Ibid., p. 538.

[4] Ibid., p. 692.

The Catholic response to these issues finds total congruity with the observations made by Brown, Aristotle, and Tocqueville. Economic inequality is a natural part of life and is not necessarily a problem.

Pope Leo XIII spoke to this matter when he proclaimed the basic equality of all men yet noted the existence of legitimate inequalities. "No one doubts that all men are equal to one another, so far as regards their common origin and nature, or the last end which each has to attain, or the rights and duties which are thence derived", he said. "But, as the abilities of all men are not equal, as one differs from another in the powers of mind or body, and as there are very many dissimilarities of manner, disposition, and character, it is most repugnant to reason to extend complete equality to the institution of civil life."[5]

Pope Leo XIII's forceful condemnation of radical egalitarian policies—"it is most repugnant to reason to extend complete equality to the institution of civil life"—is totally at odds with the reigning ideology among the professoriate. But it is totally consistent with common sense: from the mentally handicapped at one extreme, to child prodigies at the other, a wide difference in abilities is obvious.

Just as evident are differences in motivation and determination, qualities that are central to a good work ethic and to economic success. Whether these differences are rooted in nature, or nurture, is important, but it is even more important that we not pretend that they do not exist. Quite frankly, the distribution of cognitive and personal attributes is not equal.

Notwithstanding these common inequalities, Catholic social teachings are not indifferent to the plight of the

[5] Leo XIII, encyclical letter *Humanum genus* (April 20, 1884), no. 26.

poor. In fact, following the commands of Jesus, the most fortunate among us are called to help the least fortunate, providing them with the resources to better themselves. As Christians, we are called to serve the common good, and that includes a preferential option for the poor. Legitimate debates can be entertained regarding the best way to ameliorate unjust economic inequalities, but there can be no debate on our moral obligation to do so. The Catholic principle of solidarity commits us to serving the dispossessed—it is nonnegotiable.

Catholic social teachings put the burden of addressing unjust economic inequalities on the institutions of civil society; they are best equipped to help the needy. With Tocqueville, who was Catholic, the Catholic tradition is one of voluntarism; it shares with him a concern for the meddling of the administrative state. The Catholic way is a one-to-one relationship between the donor and the recipient: it is not a plea for government to do what can be done at the local level.

To egalitarian-minded intellectuals, the Catholic notion of a preferential option for the poor is noble, but Catholic wariness of administrative centralization is unjustified. The blue-sky thinkers contend that only a centralized governmental apparatus is capable of rendering economic equality. Just as important, they see virtually every economic inequality as an inequitable condition, one that can be rectified by law. They seek to *order* inequality out of existence. Not only do they fail in this endeavor, but the despotism that Tocqueville warned about is its natural progeny.

No one epitomized Tocqueville's fears more than Karl Marx. His vision of a classless society never materialized—proving Tocqueville right on this score as well—and his program to eradicate inequality delivered nothing but tyranny, even mass murder. The greatest paradox of all was Marx's insistence on creating inequality as the basis for equality: "In order to establish equality, we must first establish inequality."[6]

Russell Kirk, the great twentieth-century conservative scholar, and a convert to Catholicism, called this remark by Marx the "most significant sentence" in his most famous work, *Das Kapital*. Kirk's reflection on what Marx meant is just as significant: "The clever, the strong, the industrious, the virtuous, must be compelled to serve the weak and stupid and slack and vicious; nature must submit to the socialist art, so that an Idea may be vindicated."[7]

Kirk was not being too harsh. Marx envisioned a revolution by the urban factory workers, the proletariat, who would rise against the capitalist class. But they would do so only when they developed class consciousness, that is, when they became fully aware of their oppression. They would not do this by themselves: they needed the inspiration and leadership of the intellectuals! That's right: the mavens—who had absolutely nothing in common with the working class—would promote the revolution. But before realizing the classless society, there would first be a "dictatorship of the proletariat". This would, of course, make good on what Marx preached: "In order to establish equality, we must first establish inequality."

Every society that subscribed to Marxist ideology wound up with more inequality and oppression than ever before. Worse, they all witnessed mass murder: Stalin's Russia, Mao's China, and Pol Pot's Cambodia offer positive proof that Tocqueville was right about the lust for equality and its despotic effects. That they garnered the support of

---

[6] Russell Kirk, *The Conservative Mind* (South Bend, Ind.: Gateway, 1978), p. 230.
[7] Ibid.

intellectuals—Pol Pot's advisers received their doctorates from the Sorbonne—makes the whole mess even more disturbing, though hardly surprising: if they had any common sense, they would never have entertained utopian dreams in the first place.

The quest for economic equality continues today, though its results prove to be as elusive as always. One of the most prominent egalitarians is Thomas Piketty, a senior adviser to French socialist politicians. Aghast at economic inequality, he maintains that the rich get rich as the expense of the poor and should therefore be forced to part with their earnings. He wants an 80 percent tax on the highest incomes, and so do his supporters in the United States.[8] This raises the question: Why not have a confiscatory tax and take all the money of the rich? Leaving aside the issue of government theft, the reality is that it doesn't work. If we had a 100 percent tax and redistributed all the money from those at the top to those at the bottom, it would not be enough to make the poor rich. And once the poor spend their share, what then? Whom do we fleece next?

The American people have enough common sense to know that these egalitarian measures are ineffective, which is why survey research shows that by a margin of 2 to 1 (64 percent to 33 percent), they prefer policies that expand economic growth to tax policies that narrow the gap between rich and poor.[9] Most Americans are also idealistic enough to think that even if they can't get rich, maybe their children can, which is why "getting the rich" schemes fail to enlist their support.

---

[8] Roger Scruton, "Inequality Matters", *Forbes*, October 30, 2014, https://www.forbes.com/sites/rogerscruton/2014/10/30/inequality-matters/#2a746b621dec.

[9] Ibid.

The Family as the Prime Economic Agent

Economic inequality finds its origins in the family. This is understood, if not stated explicitly, by Brown. It also finds support in the Catholic tradition.

To say that economic inequality finds its home in the family does not discount the role that schools, training programs, internships, and workplace opportunities play in determining upward social mobility; it simply means there is no substitute for the role that the family plays. It is in the home that human resources are born and bred, not elsewhere. This being the case, there is only so much that public policy and law can do to bring about economic equality.

Brown makes several observations on the role that the family and kinship groups play in determining important social outcomes. For example, they account for our ascribed identities (e.g., our race, sex, and ethnicity); they are also an important determinant of our achieved identities (e.g., our work ethic). Moreover, the roles and statuses that we share are reflective of our place in the social structure, and they, in turn, are a reflection of our family and kin relations. Those relations are never equal.[10]

There is nothing in Catholic social teachings that is contradictory to these social patterns. If anything, the Catholic understanding of the family's role in society is very much congruent with what Brown notes. For example, the *Catechism of the Catholic Church* credits marriage and the family not only with the procreation of children but with their education as well. The family, being prior to any recognized public authority, has a special responsibility to serve the best interests of children. That is why the

[10] Brown, *Human Universals*, p. 137.

Second Vatican Council proclaimed it "the first and vital cell of society".

Saint John Paul II, in *Laborem exercens*, pointed to the family as the first and most important generator of economic productivity. He saw in the family the center and purpose of all economic activity.[11] The family is also the prime agent of welfare for its members. The young, the old, the infirm, the handicapped—all find economic relief in the family. Only when family members are incapable of attending to their shared duties is there a reason for the state to intervene.

The Second Vatican Council, in *Gaudium et spes*, said that the family is charged with the educational and intellectual development of children. Furthermore, the Church teaches that families are called to reorder society, beginning with the education of children. Saint John Paul II called upon fathers and mothers to be "teachers of humanity for their own children".[12] They must do more than develop the cognitive skills of their offspring; parents are charged with the responsibility of inculcating virtue in their children, including the virtue of temperance, a loadstar attribute of economic success. They must also prepare them for citizenship, teaching them to serve the common good. This is all part of the "human ecology" that constitutes the family.

Pope Francis picked up on this theme when he implored Catholics to "foster a new human ecology". Specifically, he noted the serious social and economic problems that emerge when marriages fail and families are broken. Poverty, he notes, has increased because of a weakening of the

---

[11] Maria Sophia Aguirre, "Family and Economics", *Catholic Encyclopedia of Social Thought, Social Science, and Social Policy*, ed. Michael Coulter, Stephen Krason, Richard Myers, and Joseph Varacalli (Lanham, Md.: Scarecrow Press, 2007), p. 402.

[12] John Paul II, *Letter to Families* (February 2, 1994), no. 16.

marriage bond.[13] His observation is supported by the social science literature: the most important factor contributing to poverty is not some economic variable; rather, it is the status of marriage. There are not many two-parent families living in poverty, but there is no shortage of one-parent families who are.

An important study of social mobility was issued in 2015 by Richard Reeves of the Brookings Institution. Titled *Saving Horatio Alger*, the study showed that the likelihood that a child raised by parents born into the lowest quintile would move to the top quintile by age forty was a mere 3 percent. Fully half of those children never leave the bottom 20 percent, so devastating is their condition. But there was some good news: those children born in the lowest quintile to parents who were married and stayed married had only a 19 percent chance of remaining in the poorest quintile.[14]

Researchers from Harvard and the University of California at Berkeley found not only how important two-parent families are in accounting for upward mobility but how critical religion is in accounting for success. While they did not address Catholicism per se, it is striking how their evidence finds support in Catholic social teachings. For example, they looked at those states that experienced the greatest upward mobility and found that those areas "tended to have higher fractions of religious individuals and fewer children raised by single parents".[15] What do

[13] Pope Francis, address at International Colloquium on the Complementarity between Man and Woman (November 17, 2014), no 2.

[14] Lee Habeeb and Mike Leven, "Why Won't Liberals Talk about the Most Important Kind of 'Privilege' in America?", *National Review*, March 23, 2015, https://www.nationalreview.com/2015/03/why-arent-we-talking-about-most-important-form-privilege-america-lee-habeeb/.

[15] Mandi Woodruff, "Family and Religion Play a Critical Role in Economic Mobility", *Business Insider*, July 24, 2013, http://www.businessinsider.com/religion-family-play-pivotal-role-in-economic-mobility-2013-7.

two-parent families and a strong religious presence have in common? They value restraint and self-discipline, two key attributes for doing well in school and in the workplace.

Rutgers sociologist David Popenoe maintains that most social scientists now agree that "two married, biological parents are the gold standard for childrearing."[16] They are also the greatest engine of economic progress. That is because the much-maligned "bourgeois family" provides children with a sense of responsibility, a work ethic, and the ability to delay gratification, without which upward mobility is difficult to achieve. This is particularly true of boys: they need to develop a sense of restraint, and in this regard the role of father is key. When fathers are absent, the chances of inculcating self-discipline are dramatically weakened.

The Welfare State and Its Consequences

Economic inequality is most glaring along racial lines. There are many reasons why this income gap exists, the most important of which is the large number of black one-parent families. This cannot be explained by citing racial discrimination: when discrimination was rampant—from slavery through the worst of segregation—the black family was more intact than it is today. That is the conclusion of Herbert Gutman, considered one of the most authoritative scholars on the history of the black family. He found that family problems are a relatively recent phenomenon in the black community. Even at the outset of the Depression, he learned, the black family remained largely intact. In fact,

[16] Carol Iannone, "Family Matters: A Conversation with David Popenoe", *Academic Questions* (Winter 2008–2009): 20–21.

even as recently as the 1950s, most black families were headed by a mother and a father.[17]

To find what led to the sharp rise in female-headed households, we must look to the 1960s. While it was a period of fast political progress for blacks—from the 1964 Civil Rights Act outlawing discrimination to the Voting Rights Act of 1965—it was also a decade when the welfare state ballooned. This did not happen for economic reasons: the unemployment rate was practically nonexistent—3.5 percent nationally and 4 percent for blacks. The welfare explosion, and the dependency it induced, was a function of politics and ideology.

Charles Murray is one of the nation's foremost experts on this issue. His research led him to conclude that between 1964 and 1967 we entered a "reform period" in which policy objectives radically changed. That was when the entitlement ethic was born.[18] Policy makers in Washington and the big cities promoted what became the dominant mantra in the ghetto: "It's not your fault." Welfare was now interpreted as a right, not a privilege. William Raspberry, an influential black columnist at the time, called the "It's not your fault" attitude a disease; he dubbed it "victimism". "There is no more crippling an attitude than to think yourself primarily as a victim", he wrote.[19] It is what psychologists call inefficacy, the conviction that we are not responsible for our condition. Once this mind-set

[17] Herbert G. Gutman, *The Black Family in Slavery and Freedom, 1750–1925* (New York: Vintage Books, 1979), pp. 465–66; William A. Donohue, "Rethinking the Welfare State: A Critical Look at the Underclass", in *Leading Pennsylvania into the 21st Century: Policy Strategies for the Future*, ed. Don E. Eberly (Harrisburg, Pennsylvania: Commonwealth Foundation, 1990), p. 152.

[18] Charles Murray, *Losing Ground* (New York: Basic Books, 1984), pp. 24–25, 191.

[19] Quoted in Ken Auletta, *The Underclass* (New York: Random House, 1983), pp. 38, 60.

sinks in, it is difficult to uproot, and the damage it does is incalculable.

In 1963, just as the War on Poverty was about to begin, more than 93 percent of babies were born into two-parent families. Since that time, out-of-wedlock births have skyrocketed for both whites and blacks, especially for blacks. Nationwide, over 40 percent of all births are out-of-wedlock, and three quarters of all black births are to single parents.[20] President Barack Obama warned that "children who grow up without a father are five times more likely to live in poverty and commit crime, nine times more likely to drop out of schools and 20 times more likely to end up in prison."[21]

The results are seen on the streets of the inner city. John Blake, an astute reporter for CNN, captured the essence of what is going on by comparing living conditions in West Baltimore, where he grew up, to William Golding's *Lord of the Flies*. Black adult men, he says, have virtually disappeared. Prematurely gunned down or in prison, there are few role models in the neighborhood for young black men. Blake notes the similarities to Golding's description of what happens when affluent English schoolboys are left to themselves without adults. "The kids try to build a society of their own", he says, "but with no adult guidance, they descend into tribalism and savagery."[22]

I encountered this condition in Spanish Harlem in the 1970s. Sex segregation was everywhere. The women

---

[20] Nicholas Eberstadt, "The Tragic Failure of the War on Poverty", *Insider* (Winter 2015): 16–18.

[21] Walter E. Williams, "Challenges for Black People: Part II", CNSNews .com, July 20, 2016, https://www.cnsnews.com/commentary/walter-e-williams /challenges-black-people-part-ii.

[22] John Blake, "'Lord of the Flies' Comes to Baltimore", CNN, May 2, 2015, https://www.cnn.com/2015/05/02/us/lord-of-the-flies-baltimore/index .html.

were walking their children to school, or pushing a baby carriage, or grocery shopping with other women. On report-card night, only the mothers came. The men were "hanging out" on street corners, and the number of older men was minuscule. Violence and drugs were a way of life. Broken families break everyone—the men, the women, and the children—and when they become the norm in a neighborhood, it is not a pretty sight. It is no exaggeration to say that our cultural crisis is nowhere more apparent than in the inner city: the almost complete absence of the much-maligned bourgeois values is acutely visible in these neighborhoods.

From the mid-1960s to the mid-1990s, the welfare system encouraged men to abandon their responsibilities, and once they left, they never came back. The dependency that was created did more to set back minorities than any other factor, including institutional racism.

None of this could have happened if the policy makers, and the intellectuals who advised them, had exercised common sense. But they did not. The result was a culture of nonaccountability. Anyone with an ounce of common sense would have known that fostering dependency strips men and women of self-reliance, leaving them personally debilitated. And when it is done on a wide scale, it is socially destructive.

Had the policy makers followed the wisdom inherent in Catholic social teachings, they would not have made such bad decisions. As Catholic practitioners have shown throughout the ages, there are ways to help the needy without destroying their dignity. No private institution has pledged more, and done more, about the poor than the Catholic Church. But it does not operate on the basis of feelings. Nor does it allow compassion to be unguided by common sense. Its commitment to the poor is total, but just as important are its programs and outreach efforts.

Pope Pius XI outlined what a successful operation looks like when he issued *Quadragesimo anno* at the outset of the Depression, in 1931. He gave the Catholic principle of subsidiarity a central place in Catholic social thought. Essentially, "subsidiarity" means that any program that can be done at the local level is to be preferred to one done at a more distant level. Smaller units, those closest to the needy, are better prepared to serve the needy than are large-scale organizations. Ideally, there should be a face-to-face relationship between the giver and the recipient.

No one epitomized this principle better than Saint Teresa of Calcutta. She founded the Missionaries of Charity to care for the poorest of the poor, those abandoned and uncared for in every society. She was not opposed to the welfare state, but she believed that the best care in the world is given voluntarily by people who love the needy. What motivated her, of course, was Jesus. Everything she did for others she did for Him.

To be sure, Saint Teresa's example is not practical in every instance, and the government clearly has a significant role to play. But that is no excuse for devising policies that enfeeble the poor. When able-bodied men and women are content to be on the dole, there is something seriously wrong with the system that fosters it. All of us respond to incentives, good and bad; when they invite dependency and despair, they do a disservice to everyone.

Architects of the Welfare State

The welfare explosion that wreaked so much havoc in the inner cities did not happen by accident. It was conceived in the universities and implemented by government agencies. Had the pie-in-the-sky professors understood human nature, they would not have promoted such disastrous ideas.

New York City is a case in point. Irving Kristol understood how this ugly chapter in American history unfolded. He credited two Columbia University professors, Frances Fox Piven and Richard Cloward, with devising the blueprints. Kristol argued that "the 'welfare explosion' was the work, not of capitalism or of any other 'ism,' but of men and women like Miss Piven and Mr. Cloward—in the Welfare Rights Movement, the social work profession, the Office of Economic Opportunity, and so on."[23]

Kristol was referring to the enormously influential article by Piven and Cloward that appeared in the May 2, 1966, edition of the *Nation*, a left-wing magazine. They contended that the best way to help the poor was to bankrupt cities. Why would they want to do this? Because then the federal government would be forced to step in and establish socialism. How would this be accomplished? By convincing every person who was even remotely poor to get on the dole and by instructing welfare case workers of their duty to facilitate the process.

The strategy worked, at least in part. Welfare rolls spiked, and New York City almost went bankrupt, but socialism never materialized. It did succeed, perversely, in devastating the poor.

It cannot be said too strongly that the welfare rights movement was not a response to poor economic conditions. That was true in the 1930s—the Depression occasioned a rise in welfare rolls—but it was not true of the 1960s. Daniel Patrick Moynihan, who chronicled what

---

[23] Irving Kristol, "Welfare: The Best of Intentions, the Worst of Results", in *Social Problems: The Contemporary Debates*, 3rd ed., ed. John B. Williamson, Linda Evans, and Anne Munley (Boston: Little Brown, 1981), p. 90.

happened, was struck by the paradox. "Across the nation it had become a general rule that as poverty declined, welfare dependency increased."[24]

All of this was intentional. Piven and Cloward explicitly said that their goal was to create "a massive drive to recruit the poor *onto* the welfare rolls". They also sought to politicize the welfare establishment. "Advocacy must be supplemented", they wrote, "by organized demonstrations to create a climate of militancy that will overcome the invidious and immobilizing attitudes which many potential recipients hold toward being 'on welfare.'"[25] Given this mentality, it was not surprising that they did not seek to develop a work ethic in the able-bodied poor. "We are opposed to work-enforcing reforms", they said.[26]

If someone were to devise a program to cripple the poor, he could not improve on what Piven and Cloward did. The sight of comfortable professors sitting in their offices, sketching a plan to convince welfare recipients that they have a right to government assistance—with no stigma attached and no responsibilities expected—is nauseating. They, of course, never have to live with the consequences of their scheme. That is the fate of the poor. And for what? So that radical egalitarians get a shot at imposing their socialist agenda on the rest of us?

New York City mayor John Lindsay took the advice of Cloward, Piven, and other Columbia professors. He declared it unethical to ask the poor to prove their

---

[24] Daniel Patrick Moynihan, *The Politics of a Guaranteed Income: The Nixon Administration and the Family Assistance Plan* (New York: Vintage Books, 1973), p. 35.

[25] Richard Cloward and Frances Fox Piven, "A Strategy to End Poverty", *Nation*, May 2, 1966, pp. 510–17, italics in the original.

[26] Frances Fox Piven and Richard Cloward, *Regulating the Poor* (New York: Vintage Books, 1971), p. 347.

poverty—all they had to do was declare it. That's right: the son of a billionaire could simply walk into a welfare office, claim he was indigent, and bingo—he was immediately put on the dole. Lindsay accepted the reforms of the professors, and five years after he implemented them, the welfare rolls went from 531,000 to 1,165,000. At that point, Lindsay said enough was enough and put an end to the free rides.[27] But it was too late to change the behavioral problems of the welfare class. Moral destitution had set in, proving to be intractable.

The Welfare Reform Act of 1996

What happened in New York City may have been extreme, but something like it occurred in many parts of the nation, from the cities to the countryside. But things changed when president Bill Clinton, pushed by a Republican Congress, signed the Personal Responsibility and Work Opportunity Act, popularly known as the Welfare Reform Act of 1996. It created incentives and sanctions to exit the welfare rolls and seek employment. With lifetime limits on cash benefits, personal accountability was built into the programs. It also required welfare recipients to find a job or at least enroll in training programs; the states were given flexibility to implement their own plans.

The plan was seen as so radical at the time that even those who were critical of the dependency-inducing effects of the existing welfare system could not support it. The bishops' conference opposed it, claiming it would shortchange the poor. Moynihan predicated dire consequences, none of which happened. They allowed their compassion

[27] Moynihan, *Politics of a Guaranteed Income*, pp. 26–27.

for the poor to trump their common sense approach to the indigent.

Two decades later, the results proved that the reforms worked. According to Brookings Institution scholar Ron Haskins, welfare caseloads dropped by 60 percent. From 1993 to 2000, Haskins says, "the portion of single mothers who were employed grew from 58 percent to nearly 75 percent, an increase of almost 30 percent."[28] Moreover, Manhattan Institute expert Scott Winship found that child poverty fell and poverty among single parents hit an all-time low in 2014.[29] There is no doubting the failure of the previous welfare program, Aid to Families with Dependent Children, and the success of the new one, Temporary Assistance for Needy Families.

Not all the results are rosy. The cost of the welfare programs continues to rise, and in 2016 a Heritage Foundation report found that "the U.S. spends 16 times as much on welfare as it spent in the 1960s—about four times the amount needed to pull every poor family out of poverty—yet the federal rate remains nearly unchanged."[30] Administrative costs account for a huge chunk of the expenditures. Furthermore, in some cities, socialist-minded politicians, such as New York City mayor Bill de Blasio, have cut work requirements, allowing the rolls to swell again.[31] No matter; the Welfare Reform Act of 1996 shows that the

[28] Testimony of Ron Haskins, Senior Fellow Brookings Institution, Committee on Ways and Means, July 19, 2006, https://www.brookings.edu/wp-content/uploads/2016/06/20060719-1.pdf.

[29] Scott Winship, Poverty after Welfare Reform (New York: Manhattan Institute, 2016), p. 4, https://www.manhattan-institute.org/sites/default/files/R-SW-0816.pdf.

[30] "How to Repair Our Society", Insider (Winter 2017), http://www.insideronline.org/2016/12/how-to-repair-our-society/.

[31] Rachel L. Swarns, "De Blasio's Plan to Eliminate Workfare Lifts Hopes for Job Seekers", New York Times, November 3, 2014, p. A21.

poor respond to the right incentives just as much as anyone; conversely, when the wrong incentives are offered, negative effects follow.

Mandating Equality

Catholic social teachings respect the limits of the human condition; this explains why they advocate equal opportunity, not equal results. The difference is critical. Equal opportunity means that all persons, regardless of their class, race, ethnicity, religion, and sex, are entitled to fair treatment: they should not be impeded from upward mobility because of their demographic status. Equal results means that equal economic and social conditions should exist for everyone. Equal opportunity is possible; equal results are impossible. Worse, attempts to realize equal results not only fail but also create new problems.

Yet leftist intellectuals opt for equal results, trying to disprove Brown's observation that economic and social inequalities are found in every society. Catholicism is at one with Brown: inequality is baked into the human condition. The brainy ones also differ with Catholic thought on this matter: by showing a preference for state mandates, the bookworms see themselves as social engineers (or at least the tutors of policy makers); thus are they drawn to the reins of power. Cocksure of their intellectual prowess, they have no ethical problem mandating equal outcomes. That they always fail is without question.

Economist Thomas Sowell has observed how some racial and ethnic groups have chosen the route of education as their upward-mobility lever, while others have chosen government. The former, as demonstrated by Asians and Jews, works best. The Irish and the African Americans went the other way, and though they have both made major contributions to urban politics, their economic conditions did not improve as quickly.[32] To Sowell, who always exercises good common sense, this is not a problem, but to radical egalitarians, it is, which explains their preference for government-mandated equality.

The list of mandated strategies offered by intellectuals is endless. Beginning in the 1960s, busing was one of their big favorites for about a generation. Conveniently, it did not apply to everyone. To wit: forced integration rarely touched wealthy neighborhoods and schools. Well-educated snobs deliberately aimed it at the white working class, those men and women seen as racists and in need of reform. As with all forced-equality schemes, it bombed, producing results that even the big thinkers couldn't defend. As they found out, busing the children of the lower class to schools populated by the working class and the middle class does not stimulate academic achievement. Worse, when busing is done across racial lines, it exacerbates tensions. These outcomes are no shocker to those who possess common sense.

No amount of evidence can shake the thinking of these egalitarian wizards. The two top administrators at the college where I taught sociology and political science were convinced that we needed to establish cell groups to rid the campus of racism. They thought that if black and white students would meet regularly with a faculty member in a social setting, it would lead to better relations.

From my perspective, the degree of racism on campus was almost nonexistent to begin with. The president and the dean sharply disagreed, so I invited them to come to

[32] Thomas Sowell, *Ethnic America: A History* (New York: Basic Books, 1981), pp. 6–7.

dinner with several black students to listen to their concerns. The students had some grievances, but they were ordinary student complaints: they didn't like some of the cafeteria food, and they wanted more social functions. When none indicated there were any racial problems, I pointedly asked if they had ever experienced prejudice or discrimination. One of the females remarked that she was put off by a white student who said she didn't notice a black accent when talking to her on the phone. That was it.

Instead of expressing relief that they were wrong in their assessment, the administrators got angry. The two white feminists just assumed that many of the white students were racists. Moreover, their ideological need to discover a racial problem—so that they could solve it—was so strong that they were taken aback by learning that there were few such problem on campus. They then concluded that women, not blacks, were the most unfairly treated on campus. When I pointed out that, if that were true, that would make them the victimizers, they were livid.

Affirmative action programs are a classic example of mandating equality. Do they work? In some cases, they do—they accelerate the mobility of those who have requisite skills. But they do nothing for those who lack the fundamentals: no amount of affirmative action can help the illiterate and those who lack a work ethic. So it really amounts to a middle-class program, one that allows some blacks to move more quickly up the social ladder. The intellectuals who defend these initiatives are usually less than honest in their application of them.

I used to joke with my fellow professors that the only time they insisted on affirmative action was when they did not have a friend or a lover applying for a job. Then they became bean counters. The phoniness was too much to bear. I once told a colleague who supported affirmative action—he had recently been hired—that he had a moral obligation to resign immediately. He was puzzled. I told him that, as a white male, he had taken the job from a female or a minority. He was furious, telling me that he got the job because he was the best qualified. But that was my position, I said. All of a sudden, he believed in merit!

No president tried to mandate equality more than Barack Obama did. He launched a data-collection initiative on the basis of race that was unprecedented, all for the cause of "racial and economic justice". Hoover Institution scholar Paul Sperry explains the scope of this ambitious program. "Unbeknown to most Americans", he says, "Obama's racial bean counters are furiously mining data on their health, home loans, credit cards, places of work, neighborhoods, even how their kids are disciplined in school—all to document 'inequalities' between minorities and whites."[33]

The most far-reaching plan is the Affirmatively Furthering Fair Housing database. It is being used to monitor racial balance, neighborhood by neighborhood, all with the purpose of mandating racial integration. Racially balanced home loans are another feature: if lenders do not comply with the social engineers, sanctions are levied. Schools are being monitored as well, using databases to track student suspensions and expulsions. Any "disparate impact" is subject to penalties.

"Such databases have never before existed", wrote Sperry in 2015. "Obama is presiding over the largest consolidation of personal data in U.S. history. He is creating a diversity police state where government race cops and

---

[33] Paul Sperry, "Obama Collecting Personal Data for a Secret Race Database", *New York Post*, July 18, 2015, https://nypost.com/2015/07/18/obama-has-been-collecting-personal-data-for-a-secret-race-database/.

civil-rights lawyers will micromanage demographic out-comes in virtually every aspect of society."[34] "Orwellian" is the only term that captures the essence of this monitoring.

Not only are these efforts to mandate equality fraught with privacy issues; they never work. Equality by fiat is absurd: the causes of inequality are so complex that they defy even the most intrusive policy programs. By contrast, racially integrated neighborhoods can work, provided the races come together voluntarily and are of the same class; we have known this since sociologist Herbert J. Gans offered his account of *The Levittowners* many decades ago. But when Big Brother starts dictating integration, with scattered-site housing—building low-income units in middle-class communities—the outcome fails miserably.

The Failure of Progressive Education

Since the first half of the nineteenth century, when Horace Mann looked to the public schools as a natural venue for social reform, egalitarians have seized the schools as one of their favorite sources of experimentation. The mystique of educational reform as the great leveler is a powerful part of American tradition, though the expected results never seem to match expectations. This doesn't stop another round of educational engineering: ideology is not conquered by evidence.

According to an influential study, *The Nation's Report Card*, only 37 percent of twelfth-graders, nationwide, were proficient in reading in 2015; 25 percent were proficient in math. For black students, the situation was much worse: 17 percent were proficient in reading, and just

[34] Ibid.

7 percent in math. In some cities, such as Detroit, almost all black students cannot meet standards in reading and math. Nationwide, the average black high school graduate scores at the level of white students in the seventh and eighth grades.[35] With data such as these, how can we realistically expect to achieve economic equality?

This is not to say that there are not many excellent public schools across the nation—there are. Regrettably, there are also many that are a downright disgrace. Why? For reasons that are entirely political, it is next to impossible to terminate teachers who are unqualified or who exhibit serious behavioral problems, or both. But even in middle-tier schools, there are a lot of problems, many of which find their roots in the 1960s.

School achievement did not show signs of decline until the 1960s. In the twenty-year period from the end of World War II to the mid-1960s, SAT scores increased annually, as did other measures of academic performance. What happened to derail this success? Academics with a radical egalitarian bent hit stride in the 1960s, convinced that "new" was better. Their experiments were based not on data but on their own untested ideas. It is not hyperbole to say that they nearly destroyed the schools. Administrators who swallowed the moonshine of the intellectuals used children as guinea pigs, setting in motion problems that are still with us.

Charles Silberman was a leading progressive educator during this time. He was not happy with the state of education, noting "what grim, joyless places most American schools are, how oppressive and petty are the rules by

---

[35] Walter E. Williams, "Undermining Academic Achievement", CNSNews .com, March 1, 2017, https://www.cnsnews.com/commentary/walter-e -williams/undermining-academic-achievement.

which they are governed". He further condemned teachers for being "obsessed" with peace and quiet, saying such concerns were "unnatural".[36] Educator Jonathan Kozol agreed, charging that the schools were an "intellectual and custodial Hell".[37]

Herbert Kohl agreed with this assessment. He had a laundry list of changes. He urged teachers to do away with the practice of assigning seats to students; school kids should have the right to hang their coats wherever they want; students should not have to raise their hands to ask questions; they should be allowed to line up before class any way they want; talking in class whenever they felt like it should be honored; they should be permitted to chew gum and wear sloppy clothes.[38] This is the kind of laxity that was mainstreamed in the 1960s and the 1970s.

Neil Postman and Charles Weingartner also helped to destroy schools: they implored teachers intentionally to subvert traditional education. They argued that students should be taught by teachers not trained in the subjects they taught—English teachers should teach math, for instance, and vice versa. If a teacher used three declarative sentences per class, he should be fined. Teachers should be limited to answering questions they know nothing about (this would not be a problem for the gym teacher who teaches physics). Being good authoritarians, Postman and Weingartner recommended that we ban the use of such words as "teach", "syllabus", "IQ", "makeup

[36] Charles Silberman, *Crisis in the Classroom* (New York: Random House, 1970), pp. 10, 90.

[37] Jonathan Kozol, *Free Schools* (Boston: Houghton Mifflin, 1972), pp. 11, 118.

[38] Herbert Kohl, *The Open Classroom* (New York: Vintage Books, 1969), pp. 22–30, 111, 112.

test", "disadvantaged", "gifted", "accelerated", "course", "grade", "score", "dumb", and—my favorite—"human nature".[39]

None of the geniuses ever said that their reforms were a response to a crisis in education. That's because there was no crisis. Perversely, they created one. Just as the War on Poverty began at a time of economic affluence, the wacko educational reforms began at a time when schools were doing well. Had the social engineers left well enough alone, we would not have been beset with the problems that developed. They searched for economic and educational problems that did not exist, and then crafted solutions that proved to be a disaster.

These blue-sky thinkers exercised tremendous influence, helping to shape education for at least a generation. No, not every school adopted their prescriptions to sabotage education, but most administrators changed their thinking about traditional programs, leaving them open to experimentation. Common sense was discarded altogether.

To this list of crazy proposals we must add the rise of student rights and the decline of teacher authority. Anyone with a smidgen of common sense knows that learning cannot take place without a modicum of order in the classroom, but this comes as breaking news to the brainy ones. That is why we have metal detectors in some schools. Even in schools that are not violent, reckless students are allowed to curse out their teachers with impunity. They know their rights inside and out, but they are positively clueless about their responsibilities.

Michael Oakeshott, one of the twentieth century's most brilliant social observers, noted how these thinkers helped

---

[39] Neil Postman and Charles Weingartner, *Teaching as a Subversive Activity* (New York: Dell, 1969), pp. 137–40.

to destroy parental rights and then complained about the unruly child.[40] The same could be said about the educational wizards who subverted the rights of teachers, only to be shocked by the results.

Students who act like thugs and get off scot-free find their counterpart in delinquent teachers. In 2017, it was revealed that in New York City schools, two female teachers who romped around the classroom topless were allowed to keep their jobs. Another teacher who pressured his students to solicit dates from their mothers escaped punishment. A teacher who brought heroin to school could not be fired.

In these cases, the Department of Education, which has a long history of protecting teachers who sexually molest their students—they are given clerical work—tried to levy sanctions. It was judges who ruled in favor of the offending teachers.

James Copland, an education specialist at the Manhattan Institute, observed, "To me, this just exemplifies the lack of common sense that permeates our legal system." He added that "the legal system seems bent on protecting the rights of teachers to extraordinary degrees and leaves the students vulnerable."[41] In a just society, these judges would be removed from the bench for endangering the welfare of youth.

What Doesn't Work

Today we know a lot more about why some schools succeed and others do not, but egalitarian educators have a

[40] Michael Oakeshott, *Rationalism in Politics* (London: Methuen, 1962), p. 36.

[41] "Why Heroin and Classroom Sex Aren't Enough to Get Teachers Fired Anymore", *New York Post*, March 1, 2017, https://nypost.com/2017/03/01/why-heroin-and-classroom-sex-arent-enough-to-get-teachers-fired-anymore/.

hard time admitting what doesn't work. The numbers, however, don't lie.

Perhaps the greatest myth is the notion that good schooling can be bought. If only it could. How easy would be the task of educating students if all we had to do was to throw money at it.

We have known for decades that money doesn't buy educational success. If it did, the schools in the United States would be the best in the world, but they are not. We spend considerably more on elementary and secondary education than the rest of the developed world does—29 percent more—yet we trail in academic performance.[42]

The same is true at home. If money were controlling, students in the District of Columbia would be at the top, and students in New Hampshire and the Dakotas would be at the bottom. In fact, the reverse is true: D.C. schools are always in last place, and the schools in New Hampshire, North Dakota, and South Dakota are always near the top, notwithstanding meager funding per capita. Similarly, Alaska has one of the most well-funded school systems yet ranks near the bottom in academic achievement.[43]

Andrew J. Coulson, a researcher at the Cato Institute, studied the results of national assessment tests and correlated academic performance with state funding. He found that "there is essentially no link between state education spending (which has exploded) and the performance of students

[42] National Center for Education Statistics, *Education Expenditure by Country*, May 2018, https://nces.ed.gov/programs/coe/indicator_cmd.asp.

[43] James Marshall Crotty, "Surprise, Surprise: Higher Education Spending Doesn't Correlate with Better Academic Performance, but Low Teen Pregnancy Does", *Forbes*, February 12, 2014, https://www.forbes.com/sites/jamesmarshallcrotty/2014/02/12/infographic-higher-education-spending-does-not-correlate-with-better-academic-performance/#c8b052054d9c.

at the end of high school (which has generally stagnated or declined)." The actual correlation was 0.075.[44]

What is true at the national and state level is also true at the local level: spending money is not the answer to poor schools. In the 1980s and 1990s, a federal judge tried to mandate equality by ordering Kansas City, Missouri, to raise taxes to cover this $2 billion investment in the schools. The result? Academic performance declined! Similarly, a state judge in New Jersey ordered the state to spend more on education in Newark, and after tens of millions were spent, nothing changed.[45]

Mark Zuckerberg, founder of Facebook, has made billions, and no one questions his technical knowledge. But his egalitarian idealism allowed him to buy into the idea that money buys academic progress; his venture proved to be almost as disastrous as the judges who sought to mandate equality.

In 2010, Zuckerberg announced his plan to spend $200 million on improving the schools of Newark; he would cover half the cost and would raise the other half from donors. His fans, including Oprah Winfrey—he broached his idea on her TV show—could hardly contain themselves. Five years later, no one was cheering: it was mostly a bust.

Almost half the money, more than $89 million, was spent on the teachers' unions; before the plan could start, union chiefs demanded that $31 million be spent on "back pay", money they said they were owed for two years. Consultants lined their pockets to the tune of $21 million

[44] Andrew J. Coulson, "State Education Trends: Academic Performance over the Past 40 Years", *Policy Analysis* 746 (March 18, 2014): 4, https://object.cato.org/sites/cato.org/files/pubs/pdf/pa746_2.pdf.

[45] Joshua Dunn, "Cash for Flunkers", *Claremont Review of Books* (Summer 2016): 35.

(they were paid $1,000 a day), and another $25 million
went to various local initiatives. None of these factors
made the schools any better. The one success was in the
charter schools, which received almost $60 million.[46]

No one has failed to learn the lesson that money cannot buy academic success more than New York City
mayor Bill de Blasio. His egalitarian vision is so radical
that he declared in 2014 that he would reward the worst
schools with an unprecedented amount of money. He
also worked to kill the one success story—charter public
schools. His new program designated ninety-four of the
worst schools in New York City, and three years later,
after spending $839 million, three of them had met all of
their targets; none were "turned around".[47] By contrast,
the charter schools, despite his assault on them, continued to do well.

If money were the answer to academic success, New
York City would be the best in the nation. But it is not.
In 2018, Terry Jeffrey accessed Census Bureau data and
found that New York City is "no. 1 in per pupil spending among the nation's largest 100 public school districts
... and [saw] more than twice the nationwide per-pupil
spending in elementary and secondary schools, which was
$11,762 in fiscal 2016". The result? Jeffrey notes that "in
those same New York City public schools, 72 percent of
the eighth graders were not proficient in reading and 72
percent were not proficient in math, according to results

[46] Abby Jackson, "Mark Zuckerberg's $100 Million Donation to New-
ark Public Schools Failed Miserably—Here's Where It Went Wrong", *Business Insider*, September 25, 2015, http://www.businessinsider.com/mark
-zuckerbergs-failed-100-million-donation-to-newark-public-schools-2015-9.

[47] Jeremiah Kittredge, "Time's Up for de Blasio's Failed Plan to Fix Failed
Schools", *New York Post*, December 6, 2016, https://nypost.com/2016/12/06
/times-up-for-de-blasios-failed-plan-to-fix-failed-schools/.

of the 2017 National Assessment of Educational Progress (NAEP) test."[48]

Another education myth is that by building students' self-esteem, we can encourage them to perform better. In fact, American students, when compared with Asian students, score highly on self-esteem measures, yet their academic scores are embarrassingly lower.[49] So we now have the spectacle of poorly performing American students feeling really good about themselves. Why shouldn't they? In some school districts, there are multiple honor rolls, and in sports almost everyone walks away with a trophy. That may make them feel good, but feeling good is not a reliable index of achievement, in or out of the classroom.

One way to equalize academic scores is to kill them. The idea of replacing numeric and letter grades with progress reports, using a scale of 1 to 3 or 1 to 4, excites egalitarians; it makes it harder to tell who is not doing well. But as one critic observed, this brainy idea is likely to backfire the most on the poor. The old ways of assigning grades, writes Jennifer C. Braceras, "provide a way for bright and hardworking students from lower-income families to prove themselves and win admission to the nation's elite colleges. Without grades, class rankings and honor rolls, public-school kids who lack family or boarding-school

[48] Terence P. Jeffrey, "No. 1: Public Schools Spent $24,109 per Pupil; but 72% Not Proficient in Reading, 72% Not Proficient in Math", CNSNews.com, May 21, 2018, https://www.cnsnews.com/news/article/terence-p-jeffrey/no-1-nyc-public-schools-spent-24109-pupil-72-not-proficient-reading.

[49] William L. Krayer, "The Goals of Public Education in the 1970s Have Been Realized", *Academic Questions* 28 (2015): 339–52; Yi-Chen Hung and Pey-Yan Liou, "Examining the Relationship between Student Academic Achievement and Self-Concept in the I/E, BFLPE, and Combined Models", paper presented at the fifth IEA International Research Conference, Singapore, June 26–28, 2013, https://www.iea.nl/sites/default/files/irc/IRC-2013_Hung_Liou.pdf.

connections are likely to be left behind."[50] Braceras is right: replacing grades with progress reports is a recipe for nepotism, one that favors the affluent. It is also one more example of how those who proclaim their allegiance to the needy wind up working against them, all because they don't understand how to weigh the real-life consequences of their ideas.

Despite the increasing popularity of eliminating grades, the fact remains that every city still has high-quality public schools that have very high entrance requirements. Typically, they are not populated by African Americans and Hispanics. Egalitarian dreamers claim that this is a function of racism against people of color. They are wrong. If it were a function of racism, there would be few Asian students in these schools, but all across the nation they are disproportionately represented in elite schools. No matter; this hasn't stopped cities from forcing a more "balanced" population.

No one has declared war on elite public schools more than Mayor de Blasio. He wants to order equality into being, something that always fails. In New York City, African American and Latino students make up nearly two-thirds of the city's 1.1 million schoolchildren. Yet Asians represent the majority (51.7 percent) of the students in the most prized public schools; 26.5 percent are white, 6.3 percent are Latino, and 4.1 percent are black.[51] De Blasio's way of fixing this disparity is to reserve 25 percent of the seats in these schools for blacks and Latinos. He would also like to phase out the admission

---

[50] Jennifer C. Braceras, "The War on Grades Deserves to Fail", *Wall Street Journal*, January 30, 2018, https://www.wsj.com/articles/the-war-on-grades-deserves-to-fail-1517270391.

[51] "It's Time to Integrate New York's Best Schools", editorial, *New York Times*, June 25, 2018, p. A22.

test.[52] This "fix" does not sit well with Asians. Peter Koo, a city councilman who represents the Asian neighborhood of Flushing, Queens, says, "The test is the most unbiased way to get into a school. It doesn't require an interview. It doesn't require a résumé. It doesn't even require connections."[53]

It is not just in elementary and secondary schools that Asians are feeling the pinch of radical egalitarians. For example, they must score 140 points higher than their white peers on the SAT exam to get admitted to Harvard.[54] Under the Trump administration, the Department of Justice opened an investigation into these discriminatory practices.[55]

The quota mentality—ordering equality—is most perverse when dealing with delinquent students; they are disproportionately African American. President Obama led the fight nationally to implement a quota system on suspending problem students, and the mayors of New York City and Saint Paul, Minnesota, championed the cause at the urban level. Instead of helping to make irresponsible students become responsible—that would be the smart thing to do—they put an artificial lid on the percentage of students, decided along racial lines, who

---

[52] Cedar Attanasio, Selim Algar, and Bruce Golding, "De Blasio Calls Plan to Scrap High School Admission Tests 'Blessed' ", *New York Post*, June 3, 2018, https://nypost.com/2018/06/03/de-blasio-calls-plan-to-scrap-high-school-admission-tests-blessed/.

[53] Elizabeth A. Harris and Winnie Hu, "Plan to Diversify Elite High Schools Draws Ire of Asian Groups", *New York Times*, June 6, 2018, p. A18.

[54] Yascha Mounk, "Is Harvard Unfair to Asian-Americans?", *New York Times*, November 25, 2014, p. A27.

[55] Melissa Korn and Nicole Hong, "Harvard Faces DOJ Probe over Affirmative Action Policies", *Wall Street Journal*, November 21, 2017, https://www.wsj.com/articles/harvard-faces-doj-probe-over-affirmative-action-policies-1511260380.

could be punished for reckless behavior. The result? In Saint Paul, the cops are regularly called in to stop riots; teachers are body slammed; kids overturn chairs and desks as teachers watch helplessly; and a teacher suffered a concussion in trying to break up a fight between two fifth-grade girls.[56]

Catholic Schools Work

By any measure, Catholic schools outperform public schools, and this is especially true of schools in the inner city. Moreover, parochial schools never witnessed the sharp descent in academic achievement that their competition experienced. It is not because Catholic schools have more money: they have considerably less. It is not because they have more administrators: the fact that they can afford relatively few is actually a plus—it explains why there is less tinkering with teachers. It is not because of class size: the typical Catholic classroom is populated by many more students than the typical public-school classroom. It is not because of teacher credentials: public-school teachers easily top Catholic teachers on this scale.

It is not because, as is commonly thought, Catholic schools are selective in their student body, screening out problem boys and girls. When I taught in Spanish Harlem, I saw how absurd this myth is. If anything, St. Lucy's was the school of last resort for the most recalcitrant public-school student transfers. "Let's see if a Catholic school can straighten them out" was the unspoken assumption. They did, and we invariably straightened them out.

[56]Katherine Kersten, "Mayhem in the Classroom", *Weekly Standard*, April 18, 2016, p. 24.

Catholic schools, and charter schools, which took many of their cues from them, are the only shining stars in inner cities. The mothers of my students in Spanish Harlem told me many times that the number-one reason why they chose to pay for a Catholic school was not because of academic excellence, important though that was. A moral education, steeped in the Catholic tradition—teaching right from wrong—was critical, but it was not the primary reason why they avoided the public schools. What they wanted more than anything else was safety—they wanted the assurance that when they dropped their children off in the morning, their children would not be harmed during the day. They had no such confidence in the public schools.

Why do Catholic schools do a better job educating students, especially in poor neighborhoods? One major reason is that, unlike the public schools, they never abandoned traditional education: lots of homework, parental involvement, discipline in the classroom, and a curriculum heavy on the basics. All of this makes common sense. And all of it was scratched in the public schools in the 1960s, when the geniuses who gave us "progressive" education took over.

The basics—reading, writing, and arithmetic—are a staple of Catholic education. Partly owing to a lack of revenue, Catholic schools have rarely been tempted to explore ancillary subjects and programs, the result being that their students typically master the basics. This matters greatly in the inner city.

To a large extent, we get what we demand. Applied to education, this means that if we have high expectations for students, they are more likely to succeed than if we expect little of them. I saw this firsthand at St. Lucy's. I also encountered some part-time public-school teachers (they taught remedial math and English) who didn't press their students, saying we that we can't expect too much from underprivileged children. That stereotype has disastrous consequences. When we demand little, we get little. That's common sense.

Catholic schools excel at developing impulse control, one of the most powerful factors accounting for educational success. An integral part of learning is character development, one important feature of which is the ability to defer gratification and to keep one's impulses in check. Catholic schools insist on the primacy of restraint, a virtue much maligned in failing public schools. Of course, one does not have to be Catholic to exercise impulse control: Asian parents imbue their children with this attribute. Obviously, this is harder to do in one-parent families.

Catholic schools also have the advantage of grounding impulse control in the teachings of the Catholic Church. Temperance is one of the cardinal virtues, and its role in nurturing self-discipline is paramount. Teaching right from wrong, according to the Ten Commandments and the *Catechism of the Catholic Church*, is a natural corollary to the exercise of self-restraint: we learn not to yield to our primordial desires. Knowing that we are answerable to God is another factor that allows us to practice civility. It is also another reason why public schools are handicapped—the mere mention of God is forbidden.

The role that impulse control plays in determining academic success found new support in a 2018 study by University of California–Santa Barbara professor Michael Gottfried and doctoral student Jacob Kirksey; their work was commissioned and published by the Thomas B. Fordham Institute. The most salient findings speak volumes about the quality of Catholic schools. "First, students in Catholic schools are less likely to act out or be disruptive than those in other private or public schools. Second, students in Catholic schools exhibit more self-control than those in other private or public schools. Third, regardless of demographics, students in Catholic schools exhibit more self-discipline than students in other private schools." Regarding the role that religion plays, they concluded, "Don't underestimate the power of religion to positively influence a child's behavior. But in the absence of that, schools can adopt courses or programs that might foster self-discipline."[57]

Given the success of Catholic schools in the inner city, one obvious remedy for lousy public schools in these neighborhoods is school choice. Once again, common sense is trumped by ideological factors: the egalitarian-minded education establishment will have none of it. Competition, which is the basis of America's economic success, is feared by teachers' unions and the politicians whom they support.

Economist Milton Friedman is the father of school vouchers. He was among the first to challenge the notion that public schools suffered financially when voucher programs were instituted. He pointed out that public schools typically spend much more money per student than a voucher system could afford: for every voucher student who leaves the public school for a private school, the public-school system actually gains money. For example, if the cost of a public-school student was $15,000 a year, and the voucher covered a maximum of $11,000, the public-school system would gain $4,000.[58]

[57] Michael Gottfried and Jacob Kirksey, *Self-Discipline and Catholic Education: Evidence from Two National Cohorts* (Washington, D.C.: Thomas B. Fordham Institute, 2018).

[58] Milton Friedman, "Students Left Behind Will Benefit from Choice, Too", letter to the editor, *Wall Street Journal*, August 5, 2003, p. A9.

Opponents of school choice will not give up simply because their economic arguments implode under scrutiny; Friedman's logic is impeccable. Many are opposed to competition because it helps religious schools. To be specific, when poor parents—a large number of whom are not Catholic—are given a choice where to place their children, many choose a Catholic school. In response, critics of school choice frequently make bigoted arguments, maintaining that it is some kind of Catholic cabal. But if parents freely choose a Catholic school over the local public school, why blame the Catholic school for providing a superior service? Common sense tells us that the reason why public schools are not chosen is because they fail to satisfy. It's not very complicated.

Primacy of the Family

The key to academic achievement is not found in the schools: it is found in the family. This does not mean that schools do not matter; it means that there is a limit to what even the best schools can do to spur academic performance.

In 1966, Johns Hopkins sociologist James S. Coleman released the most comprehensive study of American public schools ever published; data on 4,000 schools, including 60,000 teachers and 570,000 elementary and secondary students were collected.[59] Known as the *Coleman Report*, it explored why students succeeded or failed. Its importance continues to this day: its central findings have never been disproven.

[59] Raymond Wolters, "Why School Reform Failed", National Policy Institute, August 26, 2015, https://nationalpolicy.institute/2015/08/26/why -school-reform-failed/.

Contrary to the conventional wisdom, the *Coleman Report* said that such characteristics as class size, teacher-student ratio, school funding, teacher training, and teacher's wages were not as important as previously thought. Schools that were predominately white and predominately black were roughly equal on these measures, though whites outperformed blacks by a wide margin. So why the inequality?

What mattered most was the quality of family life. In other words, it was the resources that a child took to school that mattered more than what he acquired in the classroom.[60] That was the *Coleman Report*'s most critical finding, and it did not sit well with egalitarian engineers. After all, if what schools can do is limited by what happens in the home, then their reach is limited.

Coleman found that the strongest single determinant of academic achievement was self-responsibility.[61] This, of course, was largely a function of the quality of family life. Students who were taught in the home by their parents to take responsibility for their actions did much better in school than those who were not. It was also found, as expected, that schools that nurtured self-responsibility did better than those that did not. Score another plus for Catholic schools.

---

[60] This was one of the most widely cited conclusions. See Elizabeth Evitts Dickinson, "Coleman Report Set the Standard for the Study of Public Education", *Johns Hopkins Magazine* (Winter 2016), https://hub.jhu.edu/magazine /2016/winter/coleman-report-public-education/. See also George Will, "What Social Science Says about Education, Family Life", *Newsmax*, July 7, 2016, https:// www.newsmax.com/georgewill/democrats-moynihan-report/2016/07/07 /id/737509/.

[61] William A. Donohue, "Why Schools Fail: Reclaiming the Moral Dimension in Education", Heritage Foundation Lectures, no. 172, June 23, 1988, https://www.heritage.org/education/report/why-schools-fail-reclaiming -the-moral-dimension-education.

Today, those parents, teachers, and students who took their cues from the *Coleman Report* are doing quite well. For example, Chicago is home to the Midtown Achievement Program, a project of the Midtown Educational Foundation; this initiative seeks to guide "low-income urban youth in Chicago along pathways to success". It also wants to "help parents understand that they are the primary educators of their children".[62]

In 2015, the Midtown Achievement Program celebrated its fiftieth anniversary and its sixteenth consecutive year achieving a 100 percent high school graduation rate and college acceptance for its students. The secret to its success is character development. According to one of its practitioners, Justin Torres, the foundation "takes the position—at once trendy and time tested—that character is at the heart of education, and that classroom learning cannot be divorced from good moral habits".[63]

In other words, virtue matters. It is the lack of virtue, and the near absence of moral education in the schools, that accounts for our cultural crisis. This is common sense to most of us, but most of us are not in command of schools. The problem lies with progressive educators, the dreamers who concoct their utopian schemes on the blackboard. They are the ones who need to be brought up to speed.

Both utopians and realists have a hard time coming to grips with one of the principal causes of economic inequality—luck. After all is said and done, luck plays a role in success. That is what Harvard sociologist Christopher Jencks concluded after combing through all the data

[62] Melodie J. Bowler, "The Midtown Educational Foundation: Changing Lives in Chicago", Capital Research Center, June 30, 2016, https://capital research.org/article/the-midtown-educational-foundation-changing-lives-in -chicago/.

[63] Ibid.

on the effects of nature, as well as nurture, on measures of economic success. His socialist and egalitarian leanings did not prepare him to accept such findings, but he is an honest man.

Like Coleman, Jencks found that what happens in the home is more important in affecting academic achievement than what happens in the school. But his aim was higher—he sought to account for inequality by weighing a multitude of variables. He recorded his findings in an important book, *Inequality: A Reassessment of the Effect of Family and Schooling in America.*

Jencks studied people with identical IQs who were raised in similar families with nearly identical educational and social backgrounds. He found that some did well economically and others did not. Taking into consideration both hereditary and social factors, he could explain roughly one-quarter of the reasons why some were "winners" and others were "losers". The residual category—75 percent of all the variables—was a matter of timing, chance, and other anomalies. He called it luck.[64]

When educator Diane Ravitch reviewed *Inequality*, she said, "Common sense alone should have told us that equal education does not produce equal income."[65]

It is important to note that Jencks, who agreed with Coleman on the primacy of the home as the most important determinant of academic success, never suggested that luck was more important than virtue and a strong work ethic. His point was that there is as much inequality within families as there is in society. To put it differently, it is a

[64] Christopher Jencks, *Inequality: A Reassessment of the Effects of Family and Schooling in America* (New York: Basic Books, 1972).

[65] Diane Ravitch, "The Limits of Schooling", *Commentary*, February 1, 1973, https://www.commentarymagazine.com/articles/inequality-by-christopher -jencks-et-al/.

rare family in which all the siblings do equally well (in terms of education and income).

Jesus told us that the poor will always be with us (see Mt 26:11). A decent society will do what it can to eradicate destitution, but no society will ever be without some measure of inequality. Hierarchy is constitutive of the human condition, and attempts to obliterate it can be dangerous as well as unproductive.

PART III: FRATERNITY

5

Tradition

Tradition as an Expression of Fraternity

No society requires liberty, as in personal autonomy, to exist, nor does it demand equality. But there can be no society without a modicum of fraternity. Absent a sense of community, society devolves into an aggregate of individuals, each out for himself. That is a prescription for anarchy, which quickly finds resolution in despotism.

Among the human universals listed by Donald Brown are groups not based on the family; they speak to man's social nature. Collective identities and a common worldview are also found in every society. We don't simply live in groups; we become possessive of them: we are socially programmed to favor our in-group, even to the point of judging others by our norms and values. Contrary to what some contend, ethnocentrism is not a mere prejudice—it is a staple of the human condition; it is natural to be biased in favor of one's in-group. That is what Brown tells us.[1] So, yes, a degree of tribalism is entirely normal.

The human animal is also territorial. Fraternity is realized in groups that claim a certain locality or territory, manifesting itself in property ownership. Social structures

[1] Donald E. Brown, *Human Universals* (New York: McGraw-Hill, 1991), chap. 6.

and institutions vary from culture to culture, but no society is without these organizing elements. Cultural variability is real, and while the content of folklore differs, no society is without it: proverbs and sayings are staples of the human condition. Similarly, rituals are universal, including rites of passage.

The end of life is also marked by rituals. Sickness and death are realities that are seen as intertwined, and the fear of death is everywhere observed. Death rituals as well as mourning are as natural as they are universally acknowledged.

All of these social characteristics are expressions of fraternity, celebrated in traditions that give meaning to life and death. Traditions matter as much today as they did in the past, perhaps more so: the binding powers of tradition are especially important in societies marked by radical individualism. The Catholic Church understands this as well as any institution.

One reason why the Catholic Church has outlasted every institution in history is the primacy of its traditions. From the Mass to the sacraments, from holy days to the celebration of saints, Catholicism is replete with the rituals, customs, and practices that pay homage to the role that tradition plays. Even the Church's theology is dependent on tradition: the oral tradition was the only normative tradition until the New Testament was completed around A.D. 150.

The Catholic Church's central expressions of fraternity are found in the two great commandments: to love God and to love our neighbor. There is no greater love than God's love for us; we are obliged to reciprocate. Loving our neighbor may be a challenge, but its quest is its own reward. We have no other choice but to try. The *Catechism* is explicit: "Love of neighbor is inseparable from love for God" (1878).

The binding power of tradition, as understood by Brown, is understood by the Church, which recognizes that all of us must live in society and that this commits us to certain realities. We are organically bound to each other, and, as such, we incur mutual responsibilities, duties tied to the common good. Furthermore, the Church encourages us to create voluntary associations, organizations that facilitate the attainment of the common good. These social mechanisms unite us, creating a sense of community.

Vital though these units are, none can replace the family as the most important social cell in society. "Authority, stability, and a life of relationships within the family constitute the foundations for freedom, security, and fraternity within society." This teaching, found in the *Catechism* (2207), cites the family as the most significant locus of fraternity. Pope Francis added weight to this truism when he said, "Perhaps we are not always aware of it, but the family itself introduces fraternity into the world! Beginning with this first experience of fraternity, nourished by affection and education at home, the style of fraternity radiates like a promise upon the whole of society and on its relations among peoples."[2]

If we reflect on Brown's observations about fraternity and tradition, and couple them with the Catholic Church's teachings, we can see why they are found wanting by those who fancy themselves as rationalists. To these learned men, anything that cannot past their litmus test of reason is not worthy of respect. Ethnocentrism is parochial; territoriality is atavistic; folklore is provincial; death rituals are absurd; mourning even more so. Furthermore, God does not exist; Christ was not divine; religion is organized superstition; saints are nonexistent; and prayer is useless.

---

[2] Francis, general audience (February 18, 2015).

Given this mind-set, it makes no sense to value tradition—it's a tangle of irrational ideas, unworthy of respecting or conserving. Yet even the rationalists will admit that fraternity is necessary to the makings of society. The challenge to them is to find a substitute for tradition and religion, one that has eluded them throughout the ages.

Reason and Tradition

There is a great divide between the followers of Plato and the disciples of Aristotle on the limits of reason. Count the Catholic tradition as reflective of the Aristotelian position. The great twentieth-century Catholic philosopher Jacques Maritain was wary of overvaluing a reliance on reason. "In modern times", he said, "an attempt was made to base the life of civilization and the earthly community on the foundation of mere reason—reason separated from religion and from the Gospel. This attempt fostered immense hopes in the last two centuries, and rapidly failed."[3] That is an understatement: the genocidal monsters of the last century were driven by fascism and communism, following the dictates of "mere reason".

The big thinkers who get everything wrong favor the rationalism employed by Plato, whereas more practical persons—exemplified by Catholics such as Maritain—are drawn to Aristotle. Sociologist Robert Nisbet captures the essence of their approaches: "We find Plato ... rich in appeal to pure reason, in intuitive boldness and in revolutionary impulse ... whereas we find Aristotle rich in

---

[3] Jacques Maritain, "The Pluralist Principle in Democracy", chap. 12 in *The Range of Reason*, Jacques Maritain Center, https://maritain.nd.edu/jmc/etext/range12.htm.

the opposite of these qualities, appealing to observation, experience, tradition, and study rather than pure insight."[4]

Plato's emphasis on pure reason and Aristotle's embrace of practical wisdom could not be more different. The rationalist does not believe he has an obligation to consult history and tradition, and that's because he knows better. Why repeat the mistakes of the past? Reason alone is capable of assessing conditions, he thinks, setting the stage for the formulation of policy prescriptions. Utopian through and through, those intellectuals who prize their own reason above everything else see themselves as social engineers, ordained by training and sheer brilliance to restructure society, if not human nature itself.

For Plato and his ideological kin, fraternity can be achieved with the collectivization of children. Plato not only wanted to deny parents the right to raise their own children; he also envisioned a society in which "no parent is to know his own child, nor any child his parent."[5] The goal was to create a society in which every child would be loved and treasured as if he were the flesh and blood of everyone.

Yet there are legions of parents who don't love their own kids, never mind their neighbors' kids. Thus, to Aristotle, Plato's ideal was seen as violating practical knowledge, the kind that is born of experience.

The celebration of reason as the font of insights into the human condition reached new heights during the Enlightenment. As one student of this period, Isaac Kramnick, put it, the intellectuals "believed that unassisted human reason, not faith or tradition, was the principal guide to human

[4] Robert Nisbet, *The Social Philosophers: Community and Conflict in Western Thought* (New York: Washington Square Press, 1973), p. 16.

[5] Plato, *The Republic* (Mineola, N.Y.: Dover, 2000), p. 124.

conduct".[6] Reacting against this view was Edmund Burke. He saw the prejudices of the people as worthy of respect. By prejudice he did not mean an invidious attitude made manifest in some unjust appraisal of an individual or group of individuals. For Burke, "prejudice" meant "latent wisdom" or the "general bank and capital of nations and of ages" on which people can rely for help in making decisions instead of resorting solely to their own limited judgment.[7]

Following Burke, it is not common sense to discard the practical wisdom found in the customs and traditions that inhere in society, replacing them with abstract ideas that have never been tested. Burke captured this idea with elegance: "I feel an insuperable reluctance in giving my hand to destroy an established institution of government, upon a theory.... I prefer the collected wisdom of the ages to the abilities of any two men living."[8] This is a good account of the Catholic perspective on this issue as well.

In the mid-twentieth century, England's Michael Oakeshott carried on the tradition of Aristotle and Burke by criticizing political reformers for their "knowledge of technique". Instead of relying on tested ideas, or what he called "practical knowledge", the grand social engineers repaired to their playbook, which was full of technical solutions to human conduct.[9]

Oakeshott's observations on the mind-set of these apostles of reason explain why they do so much damage to

---

[6] Isaac Kramnick, *The Portable Enlightenment Reader* (New York: Penguin Classics, 1995), p. xi.

[7] Edmund Burke, *Reflections on the Revolution in France*, ed. Thomas H.D. Mahoney (Indianapolis: Bobbs-Merrill, 1955), p. 99.

[8] Edmund Burke, *Selected Works*, ed. W.J. Bate (New York: Modern Library, 1960), pp. 270, 397.

[9] Michael Oakeshott, *Rationalism in Politics* (London: Methuen, 1962), pp. 10–11.

society. Speaking of the rationalist, Oakeshott says, "At bottom he stands (he always *stands*) for thought free from obligation to any authority save for the authority of 'reason.'" Furthermore, "he is the *enemy* of authority, of prejudice, of the merely traditional, customary or habitual." Similarly, "there is no opinion, no habit, no belief, nothing so firmly rooted or so widely held that he hesitates to question it and to judge it by what he calls 'reason'."[10]

This kind of hubris is so foreign to Catholic thinking that the Church labels it the sin of pride. This disposition, predominant among many intellectuals, insists that there is no need for God. Who needs God when one's own reason is all that is necessary? It is this kind of intellectual arrogance that contributes to our cultural crisis.

By trashing tradition, it becomes harder to create fraternity. That is the legacy of the intellectual celebration of reason. Émile Durkheim, the great French sociologist, knew that societies were held together by customs, traditions, rituals, and prejudices. It was not reason that bonded us together—it was the social tissue expressed in primary relationships that mattered most. "We begin to feel that all is not clear and that reason does not cure all ills", he said. "We have reasoned too much!"[11] What holds society together, Durkheim noted, were ties of love and affection, emotions that cannot and should not be taken for granted, much less vilified. The moral code, which reflects deep-rooted beliefs and practices, is absolutely necessary to the workings of society. Although moral codes should be able to hold up under scrutiny, they can never be replaced by purely rational abstractions.

---

[10] Ibid., p. 1, italics in the original.
[11] Steven Lukes, *Emile Durkheim: His Life and Work, A Historical and Critical Study* (Stanford, Calif.: Stanford University Press, 1985), p. 93.

Nisbet weighed in on this matter as well. Efforts to remake society along rationalist lines "inevitably violate the complex lines of relationship which exist and must exist in any stable society". To Nisbet, this was not just an important sociological observation; it was also an expression of common sense. Prerational attachments found in primary relationships and traditions allow us to understand the world through the lens of *sensus communis*, or common sense, he said. He was referring to the "knowledge that is *common* among individuals in a nation, not something that is the special preserve of an intellectual elite".[12]

This analysis takes on greater significance when we consider how much hatred the rationalist highbrows have for the common sense that inheres in the people. It is seen, quite correctly, as a deterrent to their supposed intellectual powers. A case in point is the development of law in the West.

Nowhere is the application of common sense more pronounced than in the common law. It was the mores of the people, the unwritten laws governing human relations, that English judges relied upon through the ages to determine the law. To the grand thinkers, the knowledge contained in common law is a reflection of irrational forces, grounded in religion.

In 1918, William Renwick Riddell published a splendid piece in the *Yale Law Journal* that sheds light on this subject. Common sense, he wrote, "consists in the application of the rules of justice and honesty to the things of this work-a-day world, so full of anomalies and of fallible, imperfect human beings". He went further, declaring that

[12] Brad Lowell Stone, *Robert Nisbet* (Wilmington, Del.: ISI Books, 2002), pp. 80–81, italics in the original.

"the common law is the perfection of human reason—in a word, that the common law is common sense."[13]

In the last century, however, much of the law that reflected the common law has been undone. Indeed, it has been the focal point in the culture war, what with rationalist lawyers and activists, leaning on their favorite intellectuals, tearing up the remains of traditionalism. That is why few law students in our elite schools are capable of making a logical case against pornography, prostitution, or gay marriage. Their moral vision has been discolored by rationalist prescriptions to moral problems, making them question the most elementary tenets of common sense.

Patriotism

It is true of all societies, but nowhere is it truer than in democracies, that their citizens pay homage to their heritage and are prepared to die, if necessary, for its survival. Dictators violate our natural rights and, from a Catholic perspective, are not entitled to our loyalty; we are not bound to obey unjust laws. But in a democracy, patriotism is a necessary condition of freedom. We should therefore nurture it with care and be prepared to challenge efforts to diminish it.

Philadelphia Archbishop Charles Chaput concedes that patriotism "can be manipulated by demagogues. But at its core, it is a good thing." It is certainly a good thing in America, the freest nation in the world. "Patriotism is a form of love", writes Chaput, "and much that's worth fighting for, in this country we call home." We owe it as

[13] William Renwick Riddell, "Common Law and Common Sense", *Yale Law Journal* 27, no. 8 (June 1918): 995–96.

Christians, he says, "to make the world a better place".[14] There are many ways this can be achieved, but all efforts are contingent on our willingness to sacrifice for our nation, laying down our lives, if called to do so.

Charles Morris is an astute student of Catholicism in America, and it is his conviction that "there are no more patriotic Americans than Catholics."[15] Whether by participation in the armed services, or through voluntary and charitable giving, Catholics have a stellar record of giving back to America. The old canard about dual loyalties—Rome first, America second—is belied by the facts.

One year after 9/11, I asked some staff members of the Catholic League to call the New York Police Department and Fire Department to see if they could find out how many of the first responders were Catholic. While no official data on religion were available, we learned from discussions with top officials from both organizations that approximately 85 to 90 percent were Catholic.[16] This confirmed what we thought. Indeed, following the tragic collapse of the Twin Towers, funeral processions in Catholic churches were featured nightly on New York television.

If there is one place in America where patriotism is not nurtured, it is on college campuses. This is especially true of elite colleges and universities, where there is a huge surplus of America-hating professors—largely found in the social sciences and humanities. Further, students of privilege are the least likely to join the armed forces. In fact, fewer than 1 percent of Ivy League graduates enlist in the

[14] Charles Chaput, *Strangers in a Strange Land: Living the Catholic Faith in a Post-Christian World* (New York: Henry Holt, 2017), p. 16.

[15] Charles Morris, *American Catholics: The Saints and Sinners Who Built America's Most Powerful Church* (New York: Random House, 1997), pp. 67–69, 135.

[16] Bill Donohue, "9-11: A Year Later", Catholic League, September 23, 2002, https://www.catholicleague.org/9-11-a-year-later/.

military.[17] Worse, until recently, the Ivies banned ROTC on campus.

The ROTC ban began during the Vietnam War, and picked up steam in the 1970s. Yale banned ROTC in 1976, but only recently did it reverse course: in 2016, eighteen students were commissioned on campus. The reasoning was not entirely noble.[18] In the 1990s and 2000s, Congress took steps to cut some federal dollars to universities that barred military recruiters; the Supreme Court upheld one such measure in 2006.[19] Though elite schools aggressively pursue minority students—even lowering admission requirements to recruit them—it is still a rare sight at any of the eight Ivies to see an army reservist on campus.

It is not just in higher education that patriotism keeps a low profile; even some very traditional organizations have succumbed to the prevailing winds of the dominant culture. In 2002, a chapter of the American Red Cross in Southern California banned high school students from singing "God Bless America" and "America the Beautiful" at one of its events; it cited its "sensitivity to religious diversity". Worse, this assault on patriotism was defended by top officials at the headquarters of the American Red Cross. After the Catholic League protested, it offered an apology, but the damage had already been done.[20]

[17] "Ivy League Should Give Preference to Veterans", editorial, *Grand Forks Herald*, January 18, 2015.

[18] Michael Cochrane, "ROTC Makes a Comeback at Ivy League Schools", *World*, May 26, 2016, https://world.wng.org/2016/05/rotc_makes_a_come back_at_ivy_league_schools.

[19] Yeganeh Torbati, "On Ivy League Campuses, Military Brass Find a Warmer Welcome", Reuters, May 23, 2016, https://www.reuters.com /article/us-usa-military-elite/on-ivy-league-campuses-military-brass-find-a -warmer-welcome-idUSKCN0YE2MJ.

[20] Bill Donohue, "Executive Summary", *2002 Annual Report on Anti-Catholicism*, Catholic League, https://www.catholicleague.org/executive -summary-6/.

Celebrities have an impact on the culture, and their influence is particularly felt by young people. In 1990, actress Roseanne Barr made history with her rendition of the national anthem sung at a San Diego Padres game. She shouted the lyrics off-key, grabbed her crotch, and spit on the pitcher's mound.[21] In 2016, San Francisco quarterback Colin Kaepernick refused to stand during the national anthem, encouraging other players to follow suit.[22] These stunts are not well received by fans, and they reveal that when unpatriotic incidents occur, the guilty parties typically come from elite circles.

The same is true of challenges to the Pledge of Allegiance: they do not emanate from the ranks of the working class. We would not expect, for instance, that a cop or a firefighter would proclaim that the essence of the Pledge of Allegiance is *not pledging*. We would expect that from an official at the ACLU, and we would be right: Gara LaMarche, former head of the Texas chapter, took that exact position when he boasted of his refusal to say the Pledge at a patriotic event.[23]

What the Pledge haters despise the most are the words "under God". Several challenges in the federal courts have been turned away, but the fact that atheists such as Dr. Michael Newdow never tire of trying again is an indication of how deep the animus is. Their efforts run against the grain of history. Allegiances to God are found in the

[21] Billboard Staff, "From Kat DeLuna to Roseanne Barr, the 5 Worst National Anthem Performances Ever", *Hollywood Reporter*, July 4, 2014, https://www.hollywoodreporter.com/earshot/video-5-worst-national-anthem-716582.

[22] Michael McCarthy, "NFL Facing New PR Disaster over Colin Kaepernick Protest", *Sporting News*, August 28, 2016, http://www.sportingnews.com/us/nfl/news/colin-kaepernick-national-anthem-protest-controversy-flag-nfl-pr-image-sponsors/6p9kxi93r1fl17rvjav2geltj.

[23] Gara LaMarche, "Why I Won't Be Pledging Today", *Austin American-Statesman*, September 16, 1987.

Declaration of Independence and in the writings and say-ings of the Founders. During World War II, Congress offi-cially adopted the Pledge of Allegiance, adding the words "under God" in 1954. President Dwight D. Eisenhower said that these words "will help us to keep constantly in our minds and hearts the spiritual and moral principles which alone give dignity to man, and upon which our way of life is founded".[24]

The big thinkers have little use for patriotism, regarding it as fodder for jingoists. They are too sophisticated to be lured into parochial celebrations of tradition and too arro-gant in their convictions to think that there is anything more important than themselves. It is we who owe them a pledge—or so they think—a pledge of fealty to their intellectual prowess. They are especially wary of, if not opposed to, organized efforts to instill patriotism in young people. This explains the war on the Boy Scouts, which has been going on for decades.

"On my honor I will do my best to do my duty to God and my country and to obey the Scout Law; to help other people at all times; to keep myself physically strong, mentally awake, and morally straight." This Scout Oath was first published in 1911, a year after the Boy Scouts of America was founded. It was never considered con-troversial until left-wing activists, led by ACLU officials, declared war on it and on the organization.

From their perspective, there is much to object to. "Duty to God and country"? Those are fighting words. And what is this business about being "morally straight"? Sounds draconian. The ACLU's big target, however, was

---

[24] Dwight D. Eisenhower to the Knights of Columbus, August 6, 1954, Knights of Columbus, http://www.kofc.org/en/columbia/detail/under-god .html.

much wider, extending to membership. Why should the Three Gs—Gays, Godless, and Girls—be excluded from joining the Boy Scouts? The ACLU reasoned that if those three constituencies were able to crash the Boy Scouts, the organization would be effectively neutered. That is precisely what the activists sought.[25]

The fight to include girls got nowhere fast, owing, obviously, to the existence of the Girl Scouts. Moreover, as one leading Boy Scout official put it, "The emotional, psychological and physical needs of young boys are very different in this age group from the needs of young girls."[26] This is just common sense.

However, common sense was jettisoned in 2017, when girls were permitted to join, and again in 2018, when the Boy Scouts dropped the "Boy" in its namesake program, welcoming older girls to earn the highest rank of Eagle Scout.[27] The Mormons immediately quit, noting that they will start a new program to "help all girls and boys, young women and young men discover their eternal identity, build character and resilience, develop life skills and fulfill their divine roles as daughters and sons of God".[28]

The effort to rid the Boy Scouts of references to God has gone on for a long time but has so far been unable to convince judges that a private, voluntary association has no right to insist on an oath that expresses duty to God.

[25] William A. Donohue, *On the Front Line of the Culture War: Recent Attacks on the Boy Scouts of America*, 2nd ed. (Claremont, Calif.: Claremont Institute, 1993), pp. 4–5.

[26] Ibid., p. 10.

[27] Maya Salam, "Boy Scouts Will Drop the 'Boy' in its Namesake Program, Welcoming Girls", *New York Times*, May 3, 2018, https://www.nytimes.com/2018/05/02/us/boy-scouts-girls.html.

[28] Brady McCombs, "Mormons Severing All Ties with Boy Scouts, Ending Long Bond", *Business Insider*, May 8, 2018, https://www.businessinsider.com/ap-mormons-severing-all-ties-with-boy-scouts-ending-long-bond-2018-5?r=UK&IR=T.

Gays succeeded where atheists failed, though it was not the courts that made the Boy Scouts include homosexuals as Scout leaders; cultural elites, as well as officers in big corporations, put the pressure on, and mounting legal fees also proved decisive.

Why the hatred of the Boy Scouts? Intellectual dreamers envision a world that is secularly oriented and sexually free, but to accomplish their goal, they need to lean on the powers of the state. They have no qualms about doing so. Indeed, their vision is one in which ideally all that exists is the state and the individual. Absent from this Rousseauian view are intermediate associations, such as families, churches, and voluntary organizations, which stand in the way of this vision. This accounts for why the social engineers have the Boy Scouts in their crosshairs: it is a voluntary group that expresses duty to God and country and harbors a traditional understanding of sexuality. It is thus the target of a perfect storm.

The anti-traditionalists in the academy received a lot of help in their war on the Boy Scouts from their friends in Hollywood and in the media—who portrayed them as regressive, if not oppressive—but what really helped was the support of the business elite. Increasingly, the cultural elite and the corporate elite have come together to challenge traditional sexual mores, and no group has felt their pinch more than the Boy Scouts. In 1992, Levi Strauss and Wells Fargo pulled their donations to the Boy Scouts, and so did some chapters of the United Way. The pressure from the corporate elite to include gays grew exponentially in the decades that followed.[29]

The loss of donors plus the costs of relentless lawsuits brought by the ACLU and other nonprofit legal groups proved to be too much for the Boy Scouts. In 2013, it

---

[29] Donohue, *On the Front Line*, p. 11.

allowed homosexual boys to join, and in 2015 it ended its ban on gay adult leaders. In 2017, it yielded again, ruling that biological girls who identify with the opposite sex can join the Boy Scouts. Not much of the original organization left after that.

Frontal Assault on Western Civilization

A free country will keep its liberties only if it has the resolve to defend itself. Those threats may come from abroad, requiring a strong national defense, or they may come from within. In the latter case, vigilance matters in terms of both monitoring domestic threats and respecting civil liberties.

Regrettably, those who are leading the assaults from within occupy elite posts in the culture. They are bent on discrediting American history, thereby undermining the resolve needed to defend our liberties. It makes no sense: those who have benefited the most are precisely the ones sabotaging American society.

America has a creed: it pledges liberty, equality, and justice for all. That is a tall order, one that we have sometimes failed to fulfill. But we have made great progress over the past two centuries, and when compared with other nations today, our record looks pretty good. If that were not true, few would want to migrate here, but that is obviously not our problem—our problem is finding ways to accommodate the masses who want to come here.

Arthur M. Schlesinger Jr. is one of America's leading historians. He is not some wild-eyed patriot who refuses to acknowledge our nation's sins, but he is disturbed by the increasingly strident, and wholly unfair, portrayals of Western civilization, many of them coming from parts of the world where liberty and prosperity are largely unknown. "There is surely no reason for Western civilization to have guilt trips laid on it by champions of cultures based on despotism, superstition, tribalism, and fanaticism", he says. What distinguishes us from the rest of the world are "those liberating ideas of individual liberty, political democracy, rule of law, human rights, and cultural freedom". That is our legacy, he notes. "These are *European* ideas, not Asian, nor African, nor Middle Eastern ideas, except by adoption."[30]

Schlesinger's account is accurate, but it is not widely shared by the intellectual elite. They continue to denigrate Western civilization, so much so that they call into question its legitimacy. When William Bennett was secretary of education under president Ronald Reagan, he addressed the source of this hostility. "It comes from those so riven with relativism that they doubt the preferability of civilization to savagery, of democracy to totalitarianism. Theirs is not an America which, despite its imperfections, its weaknesses, its sins, has served as a beacon to the world; instead, theirs is an America corrupt with a host of unholy 'Isms,' such as racism, elitism, and imperialism."[31]

Attacks on Western civilization hit their stride in the 1960s, led by Marxists such as Herbert Marcuse, known as the "Father of the New Left". His agenda was nihilistic: he sought to discredit tradition and the social order, intentionally undermining the pillars of society. One of his most destructive goals—denying free speech to those who defend Western civilization—has been achieved on many college campuses today. Indeed, there is less free speech

---

[30] Arthur M. Schlesinger Jr., *The Disuniting of America: Reflections on a Multicultural Society* (Knoxville, Tenn.: Whittle Direct Books, 1991), p. 76, italics in the original.

[31] William J. Bennett, "Why Western Civilization?", speech given at Smith College, April 16, 1987.

on the average college campus today than there is in any church or synagogue in America.

Just as bad, students are better schooled in the America-hating ideas of Howard Zinn than they are in the basic principles of democracy. Zinn's textbook, *A People's History of the United States*, has been a best seller for decades; it offers a strident and distorted picture of American history. What students are rarely taught is that Zinn was an active member of the Communist Party—he was not a dispassionate historian who sought the truth.[32]

It is impossible to hate Western civilization without hating the Judeo-Christian ethos that undergirds it. To be more specific, such a hatred leads inexorably to a loathing of Catholicism, for much of the greatness of Western civilization is a direct consequence of its teachings and practices. It was Saint Patrick's evangelizing efforts that inspired Irish monasticism, and that, in turn, was responsible for preserving the great works of the ancient world. One of the first great universities, the University of Paris, flourished because of the role Pope Gregory IX played in protecting its autonomy from those who sought to compromise it. The magnificent achievements in art, music, architecture, and astronomy during the Middle Ages and the Renaissance were made possible by the Church's sponsorship. No wonder the attacks on Western civilization are often accompanied by Catholic bashing.

Multiculturalism

America's ability to absorb immigrants from all over the world is unique. It is also a source of its greatness. This was

---

[32] Ronald Radosh, "Aside from That, He Was Also a Red", *Weekly Standard*, August 16, 2010, p. 15.

noted as far back as the eighteenth century, when a French student of the American colonies, J. Hector St. John de Crèvecoeur, wrote about it in his *Letters from an American Farmer*. He had never seen such assimilation; the ability to "melt" disparate peoples into a new man was unparalleled. The idea of America as the "melting pot" had been born. It was also heralded throughout most of American history, but that came to a screeching halt in the 1980s. That was when multiculturalism took root in universities.

Multiculturalism is not about unity—it is about separation. We no longer celebrate what unites us; we brag about what divides us. Diversity is all the rage, but it is not a healthy version of pluralism; it is an insidious emphasis on our differences. In this vision of society, there is little role for tradition, and even less for patriotism—except as objects of scorn.

Things have become so topsy-turvy that the mere mention of America as a "melting pot" can get students in a whole lot of trouble on campus. It is officially labeled as a "microaggression" by psychologist Derald Wing Sue and his associates at Columbia University; their compilation of such offenses is available in the influential paper "Racial Microaggressions in Everyday Life". Similarly, referring to America as "the land of opportunity" is regarded as taboo in all the institutions that the University of California comprises.[33]

"Hey, hey, ho, ho, Western culture's got to go!" That was the rallying cry of Reverend Jesse Jackson and students at Stanford University in the late 1980s. They were protesting a Western culture program, and they succeeded in abolishing it. They did not say what culture they preferred. Nor did the faculty at Yale, who rebelled in the

---

[33] Andrew Ferguson, "Microaggression and Macrononsense", *Weekly Standard*, March 6, 2017, pp. 26–29.

1990s against an initiative to expand the Western civilization curriculum; the university gave back a $20 million donation to this cause.[34]

These anti–Western civilization campaigns on university campuses have trickled down to primary and secondary schools, which have adopted curricula that preach the wonders of non-European cultures. "The textbooks sugarcoat practices in non-Western cultures that they would condemn if done by Europeans or Americans", writes education specialist Diane Ravitch.[35]

Walter Williams is a no-nonsense African American economist with an eye for hypocrisy. Speaking of multiculturalists, he says it is one thing to say that all people should be treated as equals before the law, but "their argument borders on idiocy when they argue that one set of cultural values cannot be judged superior to another and that to do so is Eurocentrism".[36]

I challenged multiculturalism when I gave a talk to doctoral students at Carnegie Mellon University some years ago. After speaking positively about many achievements in American history, I was cornered by some students who sarcastically questioned me about my pride in America. I asked them if they believed that all cultures were equal, and they dutifully replied in the affirmative. So I said to them, "In America, we put pizzas into ovens. In Hitler's Germany, they put Jews into ovens. Different strokes for different folks. Right?" They were tongue-tied, stuttering that these things were not the same. But I explained

[34] Jacques Steinberg, "Yale Returns $20 Million to an Unhappy Patron", *New York Times*, March 15, 1995, p. A1.

[35] Ibid., pp. 13–14.

[36] Walter Williams, "Multiculturalism: A Failed Concept", CNSNews.com, June 29, 2016, https://www.cnsnews.com/commentary/walter-e-williams /multiculturalism-failed-concept.

that according to their logic, there was no difference; that without accepting certain first principles, one could not pass judgment on Nazism.

This notion that nations that practice human sacrifice and torture are on a moral par with those that respect human rights and the rule of law is commonplace among ideologues, and they are disproportionately employed by colleges and universities. The great citadels of higher education should be cultivating pride in Western civilization, not hatred of it.

There is no more pernicious element of multiculturalism than the assault on truth. Blue-sky philosopher Richard Rorty explained the postmodernist strain in the multicultural arsenal better than anyone. He declared the need "to abandon traditional notions of rationality, objectivity, method and truth". John Searle, a philosopher with his feet on the ground, took Rorty apart when he said, "Religion, history, tradition, and morality have always been subjected to searching criticism in the name of rationality, truth, evidence, reason, and logic. Now reason, truth, rationality, and logic are themselves subject to these criticisms."[37]

If there is one institution that embraces reason, truth, rationality, and logic, it is the Catholic Church. How ironic it is to note that the Church—the favorite punching bag for certain intellectuals—is the greatest defender of the very traditions that have allowed the deep thinkers to prosper in the first place. Catholic sociologist Joseph Varacalli notes that only the Catholic Church has, "theoretically at least, the worldwide intellectual, moral, and organizational resources to provide an authentic alternative model to what

[37] Dinesh D'Souza, "The Crimes of Christopher Columbus", *First Things*, November 1995, p. 26.

it means to be modern and hence is capable of upsetting the radical multicultural apple cart".[38]

No world figure saw through the radical multicultural agenda better than Pope Benedict XVI. He denounced its most pernicious trait—the denial of objective truth. He warned us of the "dictatorship of relativism" that such a conception of reality offered, making plain the need to combat it by defending objective moral norms. There is a moral code, he insisted, and in the West that code has been informed by our Judeo-Christian heritage. The idea that each individual should be allowed to live by his own moral code is not only untenable, sociologically speaking, but also dangerous. It is a recipe for disaster, not liberty.[39]

Pope Benedict XVI also observed that multicultural-ism has led to "a peculiar Western self-hatred that is noth-ing short of pathological".[40] This is what happens when reason and truth are sacrificed on the altar of diversity and inclusion, the twin pillars of multiculturalism. Any objective assessment of how various cultures have suc-ceeded in promoting freedom and equality, for instance, would rank Western civilization at the top, yet in the mind of the multiculturalist, we have much to learn from traditional societies.

Catholic author Christopher Shannon sees the irony inherent in multiculturalism: "The irony or contradiction within this ideal of diversity lies in the historical reality that

[38] Joseph A. Varacalli, "Multiculturalism, Catholicism, and American Civi-lization," Catholic Education Resource Center, https://www.catholic education.org/en/controversy/common-misconceptions/multiculturalism -catholicism-and-american-civilization.html. Originally published in *Homiletic and Pastoral Review* 94, no. 6 (March 1994).

[39] Joseph Ratzinger and Marcello Pera, *Without Roots: The West, Relativism, Christianity, Islam* (New York: Encounter Books, 2008), p. 3.

[40] Ibid.

all of the traditional cultures celebrated in the multiculturalist literature were able to flourish and develop their
unique beauty precisely because of a degree of isolation now
judged to be the incubator of intolerance." Shannon offers
two historical examples that verify his observation: "The
peoples of the South Pacific islands developed their unique
cultures largely due to their separation from the mainland
of Southeast Asia and from each other. The Hurons and the
Iroquois of North America maintained distinct cultures in
large part because they were sworn enemies."[41]

In other words, when people mix, they rub off on each
other and become less distinctive, just as the Irish, Italian,
German, and Slavic immigrants did a century ago. Don't
all their descendants eat pizza and drink beer?

Is this a truth the multiculturalists don't understand? Or
do they understand it but deliberately deny it because they
want to sow resistance against assimilation and fuel enmity
between the various groups that inhabit America? Regardless of their motives, there are consequences to denying
the truth. At the least it leads to shoddy scholarship and the
promotion of feel-good myths. At the worst it leads to
social disintegration.

An example of a myth born of multiculturalism is the
notion that Africa is the birthplace of science, philosophy,
and medicine. "The Afrocentrist case rests largely on the
proposition that ancient Egypt was essentially a black African country", Schlesinger says. But, as he demonstrates,
the Egyptians were not a mixed population; their roots are
not those of black Americans. "The great majority of their

---

[41] Christopher Shannon, "Catholicism's Antidote to Multiculturalism",
Catholic Education Resource Center, https://www.catholiceducation.org/en
/controversy/multiculturalism/catholicism-s-antidote-to-multiculturalism
.html.

[black Americans'] ancestors came from West Africa",
Schlesinger writes, "especially the Guinea coast." Indeed,
the Egyptians were not blacks from sub-Saharan Africa.[42]

Mary Lefkowitz is the nation's most brilliant critic of
Afrocentrism. The Afrocentrist charge that Aristotle "stole"
his philosophy from Egypt is absurd. There is no evidence
that he ever traveled to Egypt or had much contact with
Alexander after he left Macedonia. And it is plain stupidity
to argue that Aristotle stole his books from the library of
Alexandria. How could he? "He died in 322 B.C.", Lefkowitz notes, "and the library was not assembled until at
least 20 years after his death." Moreover, it was not until
sometime after 300 B.C., after Aristotle and Plato died, that
the Egyptians had much influence on Greek philosophy.[43]

Lefkowitz is particularly incensed by the damage that
Afrocentrists have done to history. They "not only are
assigning credit to African peoples for achievements that
properly belong to the Greeks"; they are recreating history
"in order to praise themselves or to devalue the achievements even of those peoples whom they regarded as their
enemies".[44] Justice demands that we tell the truth, and the
truth is that the Greeks—not anyone else—were the first
to offer an objective reading of historical events.

Schlesinger is also a serious student of history; this
explains his impatience with charlatans. He regards the
wild claims of Afrocentrists as preposterous:

> The West needs no lectures on the superior virtues of
> those "sun people" who sustained slavery until West-
> ern imperialism abolished it ... who still keep women in

---

[42] Schlesinger, *The Disuniting of America*, pp. 41–44.

[43] Mary Lefkowitz, "Not Out of Africa", *Chronicles*, September 1995, p. 17.

[44] Lefkowitz, "Afrocentrism Poses a Threat to the Rationalist Tradition",
Chronicle of Higher Education, May 6, 1992, p. A52.

subjection and cut off their clitorises, who carry out racial persecutions not only against Indians and other Asians but against fellow Africans from the wrong tribes, who show themselves either incapable of operating a democracy or ideologically hostile to the democratic idea, and who in their tyrannies and massacres ... have stamped with utter brutality on human rights.[45]

By any measure, the social sciences and the humanities have moved decidedly away from the kind of objective study we rightly expect from scholars—not all of them, to be sure, but far too many of them. They have divided the world into neat categories of the oppressor and the oppressed, and no amount of evidence can shake their deeply held biases. In their world, as Warren Threadgold argues, the oppressors are "Europeans and white Americans, capitalists, 'elitists,' men, and heterosexuals". I would add Christians as well. These grand thinkers see "the works of Homer, the Greek dramatists, and Shakespeare" as "elitist", even though "their original audiences came from every level of society and were largely illiterate."[46] But facts don't matter to ideologues.

The ideological disposition that Threadgold discusses was clearly shown in the celebratory reaction to the autobiography of Rigoberta Menchú. Her story of oppression and rebellion skyrocketed her to international fame, resulting in the Nobel Peace Prize. But it was all a lie.

The first lie was the claim that *I, Rigoberta Menchú* is an autobiography: the book was written by Elisabeth Burgos-Debray, the wife of Régis Debray, a noted Marxist and left-wing activist. The French author wrote passionately about

[45] Schlesinger, *The Disuniting of America*, p. 76.
[46] Warren Threadgold, "The Roots of Campus Leftism", *Weekly Standard*, September 19, 2016, p. 27.

the Menchús, portraying them as a poor Mayan family that had been ripped off by Spanish conquistadors. Rigoberta, an illiterate, never attended school; she was forced by her father, Vicente, to work in the fields. The family was so destitute that Rigoberta's younger brother died of starvation. These experiences mobilized Vicente to wage war against the exploitative landowners, and although it was a futile effort, it succeeded in politicizing Rigoberta.

No wonder her story captured the attention of those convinced of the moral depravity of the West. In truth, Rigoberta was not some uneducated poor girl: she went to a prestigious Catholic boarding school. Her family was not impoverished, and her younger brother did not starve to death. Not only were the Menchús not oppressed by the landowners; Vicente owned more than six thousand acres of land. Most important, Rigoberta turned out to be a Communist agent who worked for terrorists, lunatics who were responsible for the death of her family. David Horowitz, who helped to expose her as a fraud, concludes that she "made a fool of the credulous defenders of Third World-ism on the Nobel Prize committee" as well as those on college campuses who touted her alleged heroics.[47]

Schlesinger's analysis of the fruits of multiculturalism leads him to question its own internal contradictions. "'Multiculturalism' arises as a reaction against Anglo- or Eurocentrism; but at what point does it pass over into an ethnocentrism of its own?"[48] In the years since he wrote this, it's fair to say that we have reached that point. We are now witnessing a kind of perverse chauvinism, one that champions a history based more on myths than on reality. It is being played out in many quarters.

[47] David Horowitz, "I, Rigoberta Menchu, Liar", *Heterodoxy* (December 1998/January 1999): 6–8.

[48] Schlesinger, *The Disuniting of America*, p. 40.

In many cities, Columbus Day is now Indigenous Peoples' Day or Native American Day, and lies about Columbus have multiplied, many of them drawn from Zinn's textbook on American history. For example, students are now being taught that Columbus and his crew were "hairy, dirty and smelly men with pale, white skin, who talked 'gibberish'; cheated the Indians; and infected them with fatal diseases".[49]

All of this is coming home to roost in many ways. Students at the University of Michigan must take a required course on how racist America is, and students at the State University of New York at Binghamton can enroll in the class Stop White People (a class called Stop Black People would be seen as racist). The colleges that the University of California comprises are resolute in their conviction that microaggressions must be stamped out, and they include such allegedly offensive expressions as "There is only one race, the human race" and "I believe the most qualified person should get the job."[50] The same rules do not apply to everyone, however.

"What's wrong with slavery and racism?" That was the question I posed in 2017 following the news that Georgetown University professor Jonathan Brown had publicly come to the defense of slavery and rape, provided they were grounded in Islam. Brown, a convert to Islam, holds

---

[49] Dona De Sanctis, "Why Save Columbus Day?", *Italian American* (Fall 2014): 22.

[50] Ashley Pratte, "University of Michigan Requires Course on America's Racism", *Breitbart*, April 1, 2014, https://www.breitbart.com/big-government/2014/04/01/learn-about-how-racist-america-is-no-seriously-its-a-requirement/; Howard Hecht, "'#StopWhitePeople2K16' Is an Official Part of Residential Assistant Training", *Binghamton Review*, http://www.binghamtonreview.com/2016/08/stopwhitepeople2k16-is-an-official-part-of-residential-assistant-training/. Walter Williams, "Academic Fascism", CNS News.com, August 11, 2015, https://www.cnsnews.com/commentary/walter-e-williams/academic-fascism.

an endowed chair in Islamic studies at Georgetown. The Jesuit-run institution has a wealthy benefactor in Saudi Arabia, a nation that bans Christianity and oppresses women. In 2005, Saudi Arabia wrote a check to Georgetown for $20 million.

Brown made his qualified defense of slavery and rape at the Institute for Islamic Thought. He informed the crowd that "there is no such thing as slavery." Indeed, he said, "I don't think you can talk about slavery in Islam until you realize that there is no such thing as slavery."[51]

It is not certain what Brown would say to slaves in Mauritania and Somalia today—they are owned by their Muslim masters. No matter; if slavery does not exist in Muslim-run nations, why the need to justify it? "Slavery cannot just be treated as a moral evil in and of itself", Brown says. "I don't think it's morally evil to own somebody because we own lots of people all around us."[52] He did not say whom he owns, though if he does, he should be reported to the police.

The Georgetown wizard also spoke in defense of "non-consensual sex," or what normal people call rape. He took aim at the Western notion of "consent", maintaining that "it's hard to have this discussion because we think of, let's say in the modern United States, the *sine qua non* of morally correct sex is consent." Continuing his defense of rape, he criticized Americans for making a big deal about individual rights. "We fetishize the idea of autonomy to the extent that we forget, again who's really free? Are we really autonomous people?"[53] In other words, since none

[51] Jonathan Brown, "Slavery and Islam—Part 1: The Problem of Slavery", Yaqeen Institute, February 7, 2017, https://yaqeeninstitute.org/timeline/the-problem-of-slavery/.

[52] Ibid.

[53] Ibid.

of us is really autonomous, the difference between us and a rape victim is more contrived than real.

This is moral relativism gone off the cliff. It is a direct consequence of multiculturalism run amuck. On campuses across the country, the Judeo-Christian ethos and heritage has been slashed and burned, the rubble of which is on display at Georgetown University.

Indians

Every attack on Western civilization has much to say about the way the Indians were treated in the Americas. Objective scholars readily admit that there is a litany of abuses that no one can deny, but they also debunk the many myths that often accompany the most hysterical accounts.

The Indians were not native to America—they migrated here like the rest of us. One theory is that they came by way of a land bridge between the two continents, crossing the Bering Sea from Siberia. Though most came from East Asia, recent archaeological evidence indicates that some Indians derive from a people related to present-day western Eurasians.[54]

Dartmouth scholar Jeffrey Hart examined the evidence as presented by the most serious experts in this area—those who have no need to romanticize the Indians—and found that the Indian encounter with white people was marked by profound cultural differences, traits that redounded to the favor of Europeans. "The Indians lost the long war because their overall culture and Stone Age tribal organization

[54] Brian Handwerk, "'Great Surprise'—Native Americans Have West Eurasian Origins", *National Geographic*, November 22, 2013, https://news.nationalgeographic.com/news/2013/11/131120-science-native-american-people-migration-siberia-genetics/.

were inferior and could not prevail." To be specific, in addition to superior weapons, the whites were better organized than Indian tribes, who found it difficult to unite. Many of the tribes hated each other. "In fact", writes Hart, "the most warlike tribes, such as the Sioux, and [the] Comanches and the Apaches, were so savage that other tribes often joined the whites against them."[55]

According to historian William D. Rubinstein, the Aztecs were so violent that they never stopped waging war on their neighbors. Moreover, they practiced cannibalism and human sacrifice on a large scale. "About 2,000 persons were sacrificed each year at Tenochtitlan (now Mexico City), the Aztecs' capital, with another eight to eighteen thousand sacrificed each year in other Mexican cities." He estimates that 1.5 million were sacrificed in a century, many with their hearts ripped out and burned as an offering to the gods.[56]

Of course, from the jaundiced perspective of the deep thinkers, this kind of straight talk is taboo. One anthropologist who hasn't been intimidated by political correctness is Robert B. Edgerton. He notes that "many anthropologists have chosen not to write about the darker side of life in folk societies, or not write very much about it. Among themselves, over coffee or a cocktail, they may talk freely about the kinds of cruelty, irrationality, and suffering they saw during their field research", but in their public remarks, they practice self-censorship. And even when they do tell the truth, they treat barbarism with kid gloves. "Thus", writes Edgerton, "it is widely thought and written that cannibalism, torture,

---

[55] Jeffrey Hart, "Idealization of American Indian Has Become Thriving Industry", *Human Events*, February 7, 1997, p. 14.

[56] William D. Rubinstein, *Genocide: A History* (Harlow, England: Pearson, Longman, 2004), pp. 55–56.

infanticide, feuding, witchcraft, painful male initiations, female genital mutilation, ceremonial rape, headhunting, and other practices that may be abhorrent to many of us must serve some useful function in the societies in which they are traditional practices."[57]

The ethnocentrism that marks multiculturalism, as Schlesinger observes, does not allow for an honest discussion of the conquest of the Americas. Take, for example, a book by Robert Whelan, published by London's Institute of Economic Affairs, which documents some aspects of pre-Columbian man that are not well received in academic circles.

For example, some tribes destroyed forests. Why? The forests were of no use to them. "The species which the Indians most wanted to hunt, like bison, moose, elk and deer, are found easily in areas of recently burnt forest, which is why they burnt the forests over and over again." They also burned the forests for fun. Lewis and Clark saw what the Indians did in the Rocky Mountains, setting trees on fire "as after-dinner entertainment; the huge trees would explode like Roman candles in the night."[58] So much for the myth that we have much to learn from the way the Indians treasured the environment.

The assault on American traditions never fails to mention how awful the Indians fared at the hands of the Puritans. Specifically, we are told how the Puritans stole Indian lands and committed genocide against them in the Pequot War. Thomas E. Woods Jr. dispels this myth in his best-selling book *The Politically Incorrect Guide to American History*.

[57] Robert B. Edgerton, *Sick Societies: Challenging the Myth of Primitive Harmony* (New York: Free Press, 1992), p. 5.

[58] Bruce Bartlett, "Native Americans Weren't Very Kind to the Environment", *Human Events*, May 12, 2000, p. 22.

The Pequots were never a large tribe, and they were never wiped out by the Puritans. Their descendants are recognized today by the federal government and are one of the recognized tribes in Connecticut. The Puritans had political rights to Indian lands, but never property rights. In fact, as Woods makes clear, "The colonial governments actually punished individuals who made unauthorized acquisitions of Indian lands." Each colony worked cooperatively with the Indians to secure land, offering metal knives and hoes as well as clothing and jewelry. "The Puritans recognized Indian hunting and fishing rights *on lands that the Indians had sold to them*", writes Woods.[59]

Another myth holds that the Puritans forced Christianity upon the Indians. John Eliot, the great seventeenth-century Puritan missionary, did just the opposite. When he came upon the Algonquians, he realized they had no written language, so he learned their spoken language and then developed a written version of it. He then translated the Bible into that language. "If Eliot and the Puritans had simply wanted to oppress the natives", says Woods, "they could have come up with an easier way."[60]

Eliot did yeoman work, but no one's efforts can compare to the heroics of Father Bartolomé de Las Casas and Father Junípero Serra, the two greatest missionaries to Indians in the New World. If the textbooks were not politically biased against the Catholic Church, and the truth were told, students would not be so prone to believe the worst about the Church, especially in its dealings with Indians.

When it comes to championing the cause of human rights for Indians, no one rivals Las Casas, a pioneering

<hr/>

[59] Thomas E. Woods, *The Politically Incorrect Guide to American History* (Washington, D.C.: Regnery, 2004), pp. 6–9, italics in the original.
[60] Ibid.

Dominican priest. Horrified by the way the Indians were treated by Spaniards in the sixteenth century, he said that their barbaric practices were anti-Christian.

Las Casas maintained that all men were originally free and that God did not want slavery. Pope Paul III formally adopted that idea in 1537. The pope's decree *Sublimis Deus* was described by Catholic scholar Gustavo Gutiérrez as "the most important papal pronouncement on the human conditions of the Indians".[61] Pope Paul III forbade slavery in the New World under penalty of excommunication, imposing penalties on those who supported slavery. The pope followed the natural law teaching that was the basis of Las Casas' reasoning: the Indians, like everyone else, were entitled to their God-given rights.

Las Casas' persistence paid off. In 1541, he met with King Charles V, and the next year the king issued the New Laws, edicts that banned the enslavement of Indians. The pope made Las Casas the bishop of Chiapas in Guatemala in 1544.[62]

The groundbreaking work of Las Casas had a great effect on Father Serra, a devout Franciscan. Born on the island of Majorca, off the coast of Spain, in 1713, he is known as the greatest missionary in American history; he died in Monterey, California, in 1784. He traveled twenty-four thousand miles, bringing the sacraments to thousands of persons, mostly Indians.

Father Serra had but one goal: to facilitate the eternal salvation of the Indians in North America. A humble man, he was nonetheless zealous in his work. A fervent preacher, he went out of his way to bring the liturgy to the Indians.

[61] Joel S. Panzer, *The Popes and Slavery* (New York: Alba House, 1997), p. 16.

[62] Ibid.

His devotion to the Stations of the Cross is legendary: during the Way of the Cross he carried a cross on his shoulders, thus uniting his sufferings with those of Christ.

Unlike the Spanish conquistadors, who sought harsh punishments for Indians who acted badly, Serra had a good relationship with the Indians. Moreover, when the soldiers attempted a land grab from the Indians, they were met with resistance, led by Serra. The Indians took note and behaved accordingly. Serra led the effort protesting the inhumane treatment of Indians and was especially vocal in denouncing the sexual exploitation of Indian women. The Franciscans practiced a benign paternalism, segregating the Indians on the basis of age and sex, hoping to protect the females from unwanted sexual advances. It was interventions such as this that convinced the Indians that Serra did not come to conquer them—he came to introduce them to Christianity and make them good Christians.

The Franciscans established twenty-one missions in California, nine of them under the tenure of Serra, who personally founded six missions. He baptized more than six thousand Indians and confirmed more than five thousand (in 1777, the Vatican authorized him to administer the sacrament of confirmation, a task usually reserved to the bishop); some hundred thousand were baptized overall during the mission period.[63]

On September 23, 2015, Pope Francis canonized Father Junípero Serra.

Slavery

Those who work tirelessly to discredit America love to seize on slavery as exhibit A in their litany of America's

---

[63] Gregory Orfalea, *Journey to the Sun: Junípero Serra's Dream and the Founding of California* (New York: Scribner, 2014). pp. 349, 359.

sins. From the vantage of a twenty-first-century American, slavery is incomprehensible. Perhaps this is overstated: as we have seen, Georgetown University has a tenured professor on the payroll who selectively justifies slavery (as well as rape). Just as important, when this story broke, none of Georgetown's elite competitors in higher education said a word.

There is not a place on the globe that has not known slavery. The ancient Hebrews, Greeks, and Romans not only tolerated slavery but saw nothing wrong with it. Neither did the Chinese or the Japanese. Slavery was outlawed in the United States in the 1860s but was not made illegal in Africa until the 1980s (it still exists there). While this is not a moral justification for slavery, it should give the high-and-mighty professoriate pause before sounding the alarms about how corrupt the West is. Indeed, by any fair measure, they should be touting the role that the West played in ending slavery.

Western civilization was the first civilization to condemn slavery, and it could not have done so without the integral role played by Christianity. To be sure, its initial reaction was not to condemn it but rather to curtail its abuses. But the objections raised by the Church regarding the mistreatment of slaves eventually led it to call for slavery's elimination. It could not have done so without relying on natural law.

The first person in history to condemn slavery publicly was Saint Patrick in the fifth century. He himself had been enslaved, and while he did not specifically invoke natural law, he spoke its language. All men were created equal in the eyes of God, he said, and therefore, the law should respect their inherent human dignity. He was way ahead of his time in applying these principles to women: he confronted the British dictator Coroticus, demanding that he stop his soldiers from abusing women. For this reason, women—who were seen as unequal to men in the pagan world—gravitated to Patrick's side.[64]

If Aristotle was the first to espouse natural law, it was the Catholic Church that perfected it. Aristotle used natural law to justify slavery. The Church, however, proclaimed that all men, regardless of birth or ability, are children of God, possessing equal human rights. In the United States, Abraham Lincoln appealed to natural law in his famous 1858 debates with Stephen Douglas. He insisted that the principles of the Declaration of Independence were foundational to the republic, and none more so than the Jeffersonian conviction that "all men are created equal." There is no way Lincoln could have beaten Douglas in the debates without citing this verity. More important, there is no way to condemn slavery today without invoking the same proposition.

Still, many intellectuals say, slavery is as American as apple pie. For example, they point to the fact that some of the Founders owned slaves. What they don't say is that these same men, realizing the contradiction between their practice of slavery and their own convictions, discovered and articulated the principles upon which the eventual abolition of slavery would be based. Yes, George Washington owned slaves, for example, but in his will he freed them.[65]

The intellectuals who deny the high ideals of the Founders do not admit that the Africans who sold slaves to the Europeans did nothing to eradicate the practice. The truth of the matter is that blacks traded in human flesh in

---

[64] Philip Freeman, *St. Patrick of Ireland: A Biography* (New York: Simon and Schuster, 2004), pp. 108–9, 129, 171.

[65] "Ten Facts about Washington and Slavery", George Washington's Mount Vernon, https://www.mountvernon.org/george-washington/slavery/ten-facts-about-washington-slavery/.

Africa, and free blacks enslaved their own people in America.[66] The Indians of North American enslaved those taken captive in war and used black slaves on their plantations in Georgia.

America bashers like to claim that the Constitution justified slavery and that it regarded blacks as three-fifths human. This is taught in classrooms across the nation, leading students to believe the worst about their country, even though the claim is false.

The Constitution makes no mention of the words "slave", "slavery", "race", "white", "black", or "color". And nowhere does it say that blacks are three-fifths human. The three-fifths language is in Article I, Section 2, which speaks to the issue of apportionment. To determine the number of representatives each state should have, the total was to be determined by "adding to the whole number of free persons, including those bound to service for a term of years, and excluding Indians not taxed, three-fifths of all other persons". In other words, count all free persons, do not count those Indians who are not taxed, and add three-fifths of the slaves. It is this last part that has been grossly distorted.

The Northern delegates did not want to count the slaves at all, and the Southern states wanted them counted as equal to free persons. According to the twisted logic offered by ideologues, this would suggest that the North was more pro-slavery than the South. This is nonsense.

If blacks weren't counted at all, it would weaken the Southern base: the slave states would have only 41 percent of the seats in the House of Representatives. If they were counted as equal to whites, the slave states would

[66] Thomas Sowell, *Ethnic America: A History* (New York: Basic Books, 1981), chap. 8.

have 50 percent of the House seats. The compromise—counting the slaves as three-fifths—meant that the slave states wound up with 47 percent of the seats. The important point is that this controversy never had anything to do with passing judgment on the inherent human worth of blacks—the three-fifths discussion was over apportionment and nothing else.[67]

Sometimes prudence dictates that we don't push for everything we want, no matter how noble. The late John Noonan, a judge and esteemed Catholic author, maintained that, had Jesus called for the abolition of slavery, it would have resulted in "an uprising like Spartacus's".[68] Similarly, had the Northern delegates insisted that the slaves be freed as a condition of establishing the Union, the Southern delegates would have walked. In other words, those pushing for emancipation got the best they could get at the time.

The really creative, and heroic, part about the Constitution is that it set in motion the eventual demise of slavery. Article I, Section 9, provided for the end of the Atlantic slave trade in 1808. True to form, the slave trade ended in 1808: Thomas Jefferson signed the statute, at the earliest constitutionally allowable date. This took courage: when Jefferson proposed the abolition of slavery, 40 percent of the nation was enslaved.[69]

To be sure, slavery still existed, and it found support in 1858 when Supreme Court chief justice Roger B. Taney

---

[67] Robert A. Goldwin, "Why Blacks, Women and Jews Are Not Mentioned in the Constitution", *Commentary*, May 1987, posted at American Enterprise Institute, http://www.aei.org/publication/why-blacks-women-and-jews-are-not-mentioned-in-the-constitution/.

[68] John T. Noonan, *The Church That Can and Cannot Change* (Notre Dame, Ind.: Notre Dame Press, 2005), p. 32.

[69] Gordon S. Wood, "Prodigy of Freedom: Thomas Jefferson, Virginian and American", *Weekly Standard*, June 12, 2017, p. 31.

ruled that it was constitutional. But to do so, he had to ignore the plain wording of the Declaration of Independence. It took a civil war to undo this injustice, but without the leadership of Lincoln, who invoked the natural law reasoning of the Declaration, slavery would not have been abolished.

Ironically, the same professors who rail against America, citing slavery as an example of its wickedness, are also the most strident critics of natural law. They tout the virtues of moral relativism, the very philosophical train of thought that justified slavery in the first place.

If there were not such an animus against Christianity in higher education, more professors would credit Christianity for making America special. The collective conscience of America is rooted in Christianity, which even nonbelievers cannot deny. It was Christ who implored us to treat others, including the least among us, as we would ourselves. That is something every American should be grateful for, independent of religious affiliation.

6

Religion

Religion and Rationalism

The universality of religion has been noted by virtually all anthropologists, and that certainly includes Donald Brown. The belief in the supernatural—of something that transcends our mundane existence on earth—may not be true of every individual, but it is true of every society: there is no society without religious beliefs and practices. Divination is also a universal trait, though belief in God is expressed in many ways. Among those religious practices found everywhere are care of the sick and reverence for the dead.[1]

From the vantage of smug intellectuals, many of whom boast of their atheism, religion does not make any sense. For committed rationalists, if something cannot be subjected to scientific inquiry or proven by empirical methods, it is not to be taken seriously. To put it another way, every idea must be capable of passing the acid test of rationalism; otherwise, it can be discarded.

This lacks common sense. Forget religion for a moment. The pie-in-the-sky deep thinkers fail to understand that

---

[1] Donald E. Brown, *Human Universals* (New York: McGraw-Hill, 1991), p. 139.

humans are not completely rational.[2] Moreover, there is
nothing wrong or deficient about it—that's the way we are.

What is rational about a funeral? What is rational about
keeping an heirloom? What is rational about collecting
autographs? What is rational about sacrificing one's life so
that others can be free? Martyrdom is similarly irrational.

Common sense tells us that grieving is part of the human
condition. That is why we look askance at those who
take a nonchalant attitude toward human tragedy. To be
human is to express emotion. It is true that the dead cannot show their gratitude to those who express their grief at
a funeral, but that doesn't matter: we need to express grief
for our own sakes.

Likewise, we treasure certain family artifacts because
they remind us of those whom we love. Some collect
autographs because the autographs make them feel closer
to persons they admire. Soldiers sacrifice their lives for liberty because they love their nation and their families, even
if it means the end of their own liberty. Martyrs for Christ
are motivated by love for the Almighty.

These examples all entail something beyond the individual. Funerals, heirlooms, autographs, sacrifices—they
bind us to others, evincing an affection that is as deep as it
is real. That's what religion does: our belief in the transcen-
dent ties us to something beyond ourselves. For Christians,
that means Jesus Christ. For Catholics, in particular, it also
means our participation in the life of the Church: without
the institutionalization of Christianity, the legacy of Jesus
cannot be sustained.

None of this makes any sense to professors who worship
at the altar of rationalism. But they have their own irratio-
nalities. Catholics believe in God, and atheists do not—we

[2] Robert B. Edgerton, *Sick Societies: Challenging the Myth of Primitive Harmony*
(New York: Free Press, 1992), p. 60.

are both believers. Catholics cannot prove that God exits, and the mighty professors cannot prove that he doesn't. Catholics participate in the rituals of the Church, and academics participate in the rituals of higher education, such as donning caps and gowns and attending ceremonies. They also have their own funerals: they believe in honoring their deceased heroes with memorials and symposia. And while they do not call a priest when their manuscript has been turned down, they believe it is entirely rational to seek the help of a therapist.

Those who are religious, as well as those who are not, find fraternity in the communities they embrace, and that is a good thing, because fraternity is a basic need of all people. But when nonreligious intellectuals try to destroy the communities of religious people, that is a bad thing.

A case in point is Abraham Maslow, one of the twentieth century's most prominent psychologists, who pioneered the technique of self-actualization. Ever the rationalist, he was intrigued by such positively human qualities as defense mechanisms, role-playing, and the like. It was his conviction that people need to liberate themselves from the shackles of socialization, social control, status groupings, social expectations, and traditional norms and values— anything that inhibits the true self from flowering.

He was not content to write a few books, however; he deliberately sought to crash an order of nuns, using them as human guinea pigs. And he succeeded. With the exception of one nun who saw through his scheme, he created doubt and confusion among the sisters at Sacred Heart College in Newton, Massachusetts. "They [the nuns] shouldn't applaud me", he wrote, "they should attack. If they were fully aware of what I was doing, they would."[3]

[3] Richard J. Lowery, ed. *The Journal of Abraham Maslow*, vol. 1 (Monterey, Calif.: Brooks/Cole Publishing), p. 157.

Like some other atheist intellectuals, Maslow had serious personal problems. His mother and father were first cousins, and he hated them both. Proving that the apple doesn't fall far from the tree, he later fell in love with his first cousin when she was a teenager. They married. He then made a career of eroding the religious convictions of his subjects; he deliberately sought to wreak havoc in their lives. His most cynical achievement came as a result of his association with Carl Rogers, a psychologist who also preyed on nuns.

In 1965 the Sisters of the Immaculate Heart of Mary (IHM) in Los Angeles invited Rogers to help them reform their rule of life, which had been called for by the Second Vatican Council. Rogers, however, was an agent not of the Holy Spirit, who was to breathe new life into the Church, but of the "live and let live" spirit of the times. For two years, he led the sisters in exercises intended to free them from "artificially induced psychological shackles". He instructed them to bare their innermost feelings and to allow their psyches to unwind. Unmooring them from Christ and his Church, he encouraged them to become arbiters of their own truth.

As a result, the sisters examined and judged every aspect of their common life against the way it made them feel; they questioned fundamental Catholic beliefs in order to discard any that seemed outdated. As the sisters emancipated themselves from everything that had guided their lives, they fell back on themselves as the only meaningful moral compass. Sexual experimentation followed, and some became lesbians. Eventually most of the women left the IHM order. The one piece of good news is that an associate of Rogers, Bill Coulson, saw the light and dropped out of these circles; he became a distinguished Catholic psychologist.[4]

---

[4] Jim Hogue, "The Perverting of Catholic Religious (Part 1)", Catholic Psychology, https://catholicpsychology.blogspot.com/search?q=religious+%28part+1%29.

In destroying this religious community, Maslow and Rogers showed their profound stupidity about the human condition. Contrary to what they thought, there is nothing artificial about subjecting ourselves to the rules and norms of a society. We embrace our social roles and the duties that go with them because we are interdependent beings. We need other people, not only to survive but to lead meaningful lives and to accomplish common goals that are important to us. To be fully human requires that we care for others with love and that we let others care for us.

For most of us, the basic community is the family, but for those who enter religious life, it is the members of their order, who make the same vows and follow the same rule of life. Without those, there can be no community, no fraternity. And thus it is no surprise that under the guidance of Maslow and Rogers the IHM order fell apart.

Self-actualization, taken to the extremes that Maslow and Rogers pushed it, is neither normal nor helpful. Attempts to actualize oneself based only on one's feelings, with no standards outside oneself for judging human behavior and no regard for one's relationships and responsibilities, do not lead to a freer and more grounded self. They are not a prescription for emancipation but rather an invitation to self-destruction and social discord.

Catholicism, Religion, and Fraternity

The Catholic Church is not alone in fostering fraternity among its members, but its long history, replete with rich customs and traditions, offers a degree of community that is hard to beat. Even critics of Catholicism—and this would include many adherents to other religions—admire the unity and the fellowship that mark the Catholic experience. Indeed, this accounts, in part, for why some convert to the Catholic faith.

Owing to the social nature of people, Catholics look to establish fraternity outside their religion as well as within it, and they succeed in doing so because they value their inclusion in civil society. In other words, they have no problem professing their allegiance to their country as well as to the Church. But there are occasions when loyalties may conflict. Larry P. Arnn and Douglas A. Jeffrey cogently observe that "when the Sadducees ordered the Apostles to stop proclaiming the Gospel, they refused, replying, 'We must obey God rather than men' (Acts 5:28–29)."[5]

Fortunately, Catholics in America have rarely had their loyalties tested, a testimony to American exceptionalism. More common has been the reaction of their opponents to the public profession of their faith. If there is one thing that unites the nativists of the nineteenth century and the secular elites of the twenty-first century, it is their determination to cabin Catholicism, that is, to narrow its public reach, keeping it quietly insulated from the dominant culture. Fortunately, there is a long tradition in the Catholic Church of not accepting a second-class role.

In 1885, Pope Leo XIII implored Catholics not to recede from public life. In his encyclical *Immortale Dei*, he urged Catholics to proclaim their religion publicly, never succumbing to those who seek to relegate their convictions to the private realm. He was not counseling an aggressive evangelization; he was calling on Catholics to stand fast against those who would exclude them from public life.

---

[5] Larry P. Arnn and Douglas A. Jeffrey, *"We Pledge Allegiance": American Christians and Patriotic Citizenship* (Claremont, Calif.: Claremont Institute, 1998), p. 1.

Pointedly, he also reminded public officials that they have a duty to respect religious liberty.[6]

We see this phenomenon played out today when public officials speak about freedom to worship instead of freedom of religion. The former is a way of saying that religious expression should be confined to church services; the latter allows for a more robust public role. The Catholic hierarchy has consistently embraced freedom of religion.

Those who use the term "freedom to worship" deny that they are hostile to religion. But what if we treated secular elements of culture this way? For example, if there were pleas to have art confined to galleries and museums—keeping it away from sidewalk exhibits—would we not resist? If there were calls to confine music to concert halls, banning it from parks, would we not object? Why, then, is it acceptable to delegitimize the public expression of religion, asking us to settle for prayer services in churches?

Pope Paul VI, in the 1965 Declaration on Religious Freedom *Dignitatis humanae*, was adamant that freedom of religion is a right that public authorities must ensure. That right comes from God, he argued, and discrimination against people of faith must not be tolerated. "No one is to be forced to act in a manner contrary to his own beliefs", he said, "whether privately or publicly, whether alone or in association with others, within due limits."[7] His reference to the public expression of religion, and to its exercise in association with others, makes plain his rejection of the notion that we should settle for freedom to worship.

No one was more specific on what constitutes freedom of religion than Saint John Paul II. For him, freedom

---

[6] Leo XIII, encyclical *Immortale Dei* (November 1, 1885).

[7] Second Vatican Council, Declaration on Religious Freedom *Dignitatis humanae* (December 7, 1965), no 2.

of conscience and freedom of religion were inseparable: together they formed the basis of "a primary and inalienable right of the human person".[8] In 1980, he sent a letter to many heads of state outlining his position with clarity.

He stressed that freedom of religion means the right to "hold a particular faith and to join the corresponding confessional community". It also means the right to pray and worship, "individually and collectively, in private or in public". It further means that families have the freedom to choose schools for their children "without having to sustain directly or indirectly extra charges which would in fact deny them this freedom".[9]

The pope maintained that the right to receive religious assistance in hospitals, military installations, and the like is critically important. Freedom of association, particularly as it affects religious entities, is necessary, he wrote, and there must be no discrimination against people of faith "in all aspects of life".[10]

At the community level, freedom of religion requires respecting the right of churches to secure the religious rights of the individual. This means that the clergy must be free to conduct their ministry without state interference. Here again the pope emphasized the *public* expression of religion: priests must be allowed to proclaim the doctrines and moral teachings of their faith "inside as well as outside places of worship".[11]

When Saint John Paul II issued this statement, he did not have to convince anyone that he meant what he said. The year before, in 1979, he proved to the world that he

---

[8] John Paul II, *Message on the Value and Content of Freedom of Conscience and of Religion* (September 1, 1980), no 5.

[9] Ibid., no. 4.

[10] Ibid.

[11] Ibid.

was prepared to stand up to Soviet Union. In June of that year, in his native Poland, he publicly proclaimed his faith in Christ. Communist leaders braced themselves for what might happen were the Holy Father to insist on human rights. Good thing they did—the pope did not mince words. He not only told the huge audience to remain resolute in their struggle for freedom; he also took dead aim at Marxism, the ideological basis of Soviet rule. In the nine days the pope spent in his homeland, he spoke to one-third of the nation, either in person or on TV, changing the fate of his people forever. Four simple words sent a chill down the spine of communist dictators: "Do not be afraid." This was the beginning of the end of totalitarianism in Poland. Solidarity, the Polish movement that challenged communism, proved to be unstoppable.

Pope Benedict XVI also experienced totalitarianism; he witnessed Nazism firsthand. Living under Hitler made him sensitive to extremist appeals, whether issued by secular zealots or religious ones. He knew there could be no true fraternity if religious leaders threw reason to the wind; similarly, a sense of community cannot be achieved when secular leaders crusade against religion.

He spoke to this issue in 2006, when he gave his much misunderstood address at Regensburg University. Muslims were up in arms—some resorted to murder—when he quoted a fourteenth-century Byzantine emperor who criticized Muhammad for commanding that Islam be spread by the sword. "The emperor, after having expressed himself so forcefully", said the pope, "goes on to explain in detail the reasons why spreading the faith through violence is something unreasonable."[12]

---

[12] Benedict XVI, lecture at meeting with representatives of science, Regensburg University, Germany (September 12, 2006).

The pope was illustrating what happens when faith becomes unhinged from reason. He was consistent in also calling attention to what happens when reason becomes unhinged from faith. "Listening to the great experiences and insights of the religious traditions of humanity, and those of the Christian faith in particular, is a source of knowledge, and to ignore it would be an unacceptable restriction of our listening and responding", he said, though the media did not give much coverage to that part of his speech. Jihad and atheistic ideologies are both inhuman—this is what the pope was getting at: the former is a manifestation of uncoupling faith from reason; the latter is an example of separating reason from faith.

Pope Benedict XVI was warning the West about losing its Christian bearings, a message he repeated when he visited Washington, D.C., in 2008. He praised America for its ability to respect separation of church and state, taking particular note of the vibrancy of religion in the United States. But he cautioned against the "subtle influence of secularism", which can "color the way people allow their faith to influence their behavior". Going to church on Sunday is not enough, he said. Catholics must be willing to practice their religion during the week by, for example, avoiding "business practices or medical procedures" that contravene the faith. Above all, he insisted, "any tendency to treat religion as a private matter must be resisted."[13]

Most of us think that peace is achieved when conflicting parties reach a compromise or when one side yields in war. One does not have to be Catholic to understand that peace also rests on religious fraternity, or the ability of people of different faiths to live in harmony with others. Pope Benedict XVI was a great teacher of this truism. On New

---

[13] Benedict XVI, address to the bishops of the United States (April 16, 2008).

Year's Day 2011, he issued a statement commemorating World Peace Day that brought this idea to light.

The pope called upon world leaders to achieve peace by respecting the religious liberties of their people. As with his predecessors, he stressed the need for the public expression of religion. "Each person must be able freely to exercise the right to profess and manifest, individually or in community, his or her own religion or faith, in public and in private, in teaching, in practice, in publications, in worship and in ritual observances."[14] Religious freedom, he instructed, is the path to peace.

Pope Francis continued this tradition when he came to the White House in 2015. He could have resorted to pleasantries, to making noncontroversial remarks, but instead he pledged his unwavering support for religious freedom.

What made his plea so dramatic was the setting: President Obama had just welcomed him, and it was the Obama administration that was at war with the American bishops over the Health and Human Services mandate. The mandate sought to force Catholic nonprofit organizations to pay for abortion-inducing drugs, contraception, and sterilization in their healthcare plans. The pope was pointed in his remarks. "As my brothers, the United States Bishops, have reminded us", he said, "all are called to be vigilant, precisely as good citizens, to preserve and defend that freedom [religious liberty] from everything that would threaten or compromise it."[15] Everyone knew what he was referring to.

Pope Francis did not yield in his comments on religious liberty while speaking to others during his American trip.

---

[14] Benedict XVI, message for World Day of Peace (January 1, 2011), no. 5.

[15] Francis, address on the South Lawn of the White House (September 23, 2015).

He told the Congress that religion was a "voice of fraternity and love", noting its reliance on liberty.[16] When he spoke to Hispanic leaders in Philadelphia, he made specific his demand for freedom of religion, saying it was insufficient to settle for freedom to worship. "Religious freedom certainly means the right to worship", he said, "individually and in community, as our conscience dictates. But religious liberty, by its nature, transcends places of worship and the private sphere of individuals and families."[17] Religion, he said, was not a subculture, but a vital part of the dominant culture.

The Status of Religion in America

The American people are somewhat conflicted about religion these days. On the one hand, they are less inclined to attend religious services than in the past, but on the other hand, they are quick to decry religion's declining influence in society. They don't seem to like the burdens and duties that religion demands, yet they long for days when America was more religious. These contradictory characteristics are not easily reconciled, and indeed they require us to make a choice. This problem is at the heart of our cultural crisis: we know what medicine to take, but we don't like the way it tastes.

In 2007, six out of ten Catholics surveyed said that "religion does not currently have enough influence" in society.[18] That was a big jump from a decade earlier, when

---

[16] Francis, address to the United States Congress (September 24, 2015).

[17] Ibid.

[18] "Church Weakened by Clergy Abuse Scandal, While Support for Leaders Strong, Poll Finds", Le Moyne College and Zogby International Poll, Abuse Tracker, http://www.bishop-accountability.org/AbuseTrackerArchive/2007/04/. The poll was taken April 4, 2007.

most Catholics seemed okay with the current state of religion. By 2014, the alarms were going off: nearly three-quarters said religion was losing it influence, and they were not happy about it.[19] In 2017, despite the onslaught of secularism—or because of it—the majority of Americans still believed that religion is the key to resolving most of our problems.[20]

Most Americans, whether they take religion seriously or not, recognize the need for a moral consensus, and they appreciate the role that religion plays in achieving it. This is particularly true of parents: few want to raise children in a state of moral anarchy, a condition we are fast approaching. Trying to achieve fraternity without anchoring the norms and values of the dominant culture in the Judeo-Christian ethos is problematic, to say the least. As a consequence of losing our moral compass, right and wrong have switched places, creating a state of massive moral confusion.

In the 1950s, even non-Catholics watched and admired Archbishop Fulton J. Sheen on TV. Today, priests are the source of obscene and bigoted monologues on talk shows. We used to ban sexually explicit material from TV, giving prominence to family shows. Now we feature soft porn and celebrate promiscuity. Rare is a "sexually free" character who is not portrayed positively or a member of the clergy who is not portrayed negatively. The same applies to movies, the arts, and the theater. Mormons are made fun of on Broadway, but no one would write, much

[19] "Public Sees Religion's Influence Waning", Pew Research Center, September 22, 2014, http://www.pewforum.org/2014/09/22/public-sees -religions-influence-waning-2/.

[20] Art Swift, "Majority in U.S. Still Say Religion Can Answer Most Problems", Gallup, June 2, 2017, https://news.gallup.com/poll/211679/majority -say-religion-answer-problems.aspx.

less accept, a script that mocked a man transitioning to
a woman.

We've changed, and what has changed the most—it
plays a big role in accounting for our cultural crisis—is the
sidelining of religion in society. To make matters worse,
even some who wish religion well are now counseling
resignation. This is music to the ears of militant secularists,
and the professoriate who counsel them.

"We are a religious people whose constitution presupposes a Supreme Being." Those words were voiced
in 1952 by Supreme Court justice William O. Douglas,
and he was no traditionalist.[21] Sixty years later, American society had changed so much that a federal judge
was deciding whether to ban churches from erecting a
Nativity scene in a Santa Monica park while lawmakers
in San Francisco were debating whether to ban men from
going naked in public. Regarding the latter, it had already
been decided that even if men can no longer sit naked in
McDonald's (they were initially asked to sit on a towel),
gay men would still be allowed to parade naked through
the streets at the annual Folsom Street Fair and at other
homosexual events.[22] We've come a long way since Justice Douglas spoke.

Intellectual critics of religion hate it when someone says
America is a Christian nation. But in 1892, that is exactly
what the Supreme Court said it was. More recently, atheist Sam Harris, who hates Christianity, wrote a little book
titled *Letter to a Christian Nation*.[23] Looks as if he got the

---

[21] David Lowenthal, *No Liberty for License: The Forgotten Logic of the First
Amendment* (Dallas: Spence Publishing, 1997), p. 203.

[22] Mac McLelland, "The Castro: San Francisco's Public Nudity Ban", *New
York*, March 19, 2014, http://nymag.com/daily/intelligencer/2014/03/castro
-san-franciscos-public-nudity-ban.html.

[23] Sam Harris, *Letter to a Christian Nation* (New York: Vintage Books, 2008).

right address. Of course, even Christians acknowledge that we are less a Christian nation today than ever before; secularists have been ascendant. The deracination of our culture was no accident: it occurred because elite thinkers succeeded in having their secular values become the norm.

Harvard's Robert Putnam and Notre Dame's David E. Campbell collaborated on a book, *American Grace: How Religion Divides and Unites Us*, that details the causes and the consequences of the change in our culture. They point out that when Cecil B. DeMille's classic *The Ten Commandments* hit the theaters in the 1950s, monuments to the Ten Commandments were donated to communities across the country by DeMille and the Fraternal Order of Eagles. No one blinked. Putnam and Campbell correctly observe that if such an undertaking were to take place today, it would be "the subject of litigation all the way to the Supreme Court".[24]

This is not healthy. If religion is one of the most basic glues that binds us together, then its loosening cannot be cause for celebration. But if the goal is to undermine religion, regardless of its social effects, then such concerns hardly matter. Many professors have sought exactly that. Stephen Carter, an African American professor at Yale, is one academic who nails it just right. "On America's elite campuses, today", he says, "it is perfectly acceptable for professors to use the classroom to attack religion, to mock it, to trivialize it, and to refer to those to whom faith truly matters as dupes, and dangerous on top of it."[25] It has only gotten worse since he wrote that in the 1990s.

[24] Robert D. Putnam and David E. Campbell, *American Grace: How Religion Divides and Unites Us* (New York: Simon and Schuster, 2012), p. 1.

[25] Stephen L. Carter, *God's Name in Vain: The Wrongs and Rights of Religion in Politics* (New York: Basic Books, 2000), p. 187.

Gertrude Himmelfarb is one of our most gifted historians, and her writings on morality have much to recommend. As she sees it, the hippie counterculture of the 1960s was so successful—it challenged virtually every aspect of traditional morality—that it became the foundation of the dominant culture. Those who oppose the dominant culture are really the counter-countercultural folks, she says: they constitute a "reaction against the increasingly prevalent and increasingly 'looser' system of morals", or what she calls the dissident culture. The dissidents are also our only saving grace. "The dissident culture is obviously not a cure for the diseases incident to a democratic society. But it is a way of containing and mitigating those diseases." Without a moral revival, led by religious leaders, our cultural crisis will continue.[26]

Catholic scholar Michael Novak cites three factors that contributed to the change in our country. First, beginning in the late nineteenth century, America looked to Germany and other European nations to emulate, seeing in them a more progressive and enlightened people. It was American intellectuals who promoted this idea, downplaying our Judeo-Christian heritage in exchange for a more secular outlook. Second, the militant secular assault on religion that took place after World War II was destructive: atheists organized to upend our religious traditions. A third factor was the influence of Hollywood and the media, two major players in the assault on traditional morality.[27] There were other factors as well, but these three were significant.

It would be a mistake to think that alienated intellectuals are at war with religion per se. No, they do not hold

[26] Gertrude Himmelfarb, *One Nation, Two Cultures* (New York, Knopf, 1999), pp. 124, 133.

[27] Michael Novak, *On Two Wings: Humble Faith and Common Sense at the American Founding* (San Francisco: Encounter Books, 2002), pp. 110–12.

Islam in contempt the way they do Christianity. Indeed, they give Islam preferential treatment.

After the Danish cartoon controversy in 2005, when Muhammad was depicted as a terrorist, those who typically line up against Christianity went out of their way to show their empathy to Muslims. Virtually no American major media outlet reproduced the cartoons. Why did European newspapers reprint them? The reason the *Washington Post* gave was "not their love of freedom but their insensitivity—or hostility—to the growing diversity of their own societies". The *Los Angeles Times* called the cartoons "insensitive images", not deserving of reprint. The *Miami Herald* boasted that it "must take great care not to offend". The *New York Times* said it was wrong to publish "gratuitous assaults on religious symbols".[28] Never have Christians seen such compassion extended to them.

To show how absurd this situation is, consider that the *New York Times* ran a lengthy article by art critic Michael Kimmelman comparing the Catholic League reaction to the Brooklyn Museum of Art exhibit that defiled a portrait of Our Blessed Mother—the portrait was adorned with elephant dung and porn cutouts—to the behavior of Muslims upset with the Danish cartoon. The Catholic League, he noted, held a peaceful demonstration, and Muslims rioted. That was a fair comparison. But to show how clueless the newspaper is, on the same page where it noted it would not reprint the Danish cartoons—out of respect for Muslims—it reprinted the offensive portrait of the Virgin Mary on display at the Brooklyn Museum of Art.[29]

---

[28] "The Uses of Cartoons", *Washington Post*, February 8, 2006, p. A18; "The Freedom to Blaspheme", *Los Angeles Times*, February 3, 2006, p. B10; "Drawing the Line on Religious Cartoons", *Miami Herald*, February 7, 2006, p. A16; "Those Danish Cartoons", *New York Times*, February 7, 2006, p. A20.

[29] Michael Kimmelman, "A Startling New Lesson in the Power of Imagery", *New York Times*, February 8, 2006, p. E1.

It's not just big-time intellectuals who show a bias in favor of Islam; rank-and-file educators are just as bad. After 9/11, Sharon High School in Sharon, Massachusetts, held its annual Halloween costume party. The faculty gave first prize to three male students: two dressed as pregnant nuns and a third as an impregnating priest. Following complaints by Catholic students at this mostly Jewish school, administrators confessed they were taken aback by what happened. They said they were particularly on alert that year to make sure that no *Muslim students* would be offended by any of the costumes. The school issued an apology, but they were so obtuse that they asked the Anti-Defamation League to do sensitivity training (they discussed the Holocaust) instead of bringing in someone from the Catholic League to address anti-Catholicism.[30]

The Positive Role of Religion

Those who take their religion seriously do not have to defend their faith by citing studies and surveys that demonstrate the personal and social utility of religion. As believers, all that matters is their faith in God. But for those who are not believers, and even for many who are, it is worth noting the many benefits that accrue to society by allowing a prominent role for religion. This is certainly true of democratic societies. Militant secularists, taking their cues from atheist intellectuals, cannot deny the positive effects of religion, making even more absurd their efforts to undermine it. They may not want to admit it, but they are benefiting by the social capital that religion affords.

[30] Andrea Estes, "Sharon; School Is Planning Apology to Catholics", *Boston Globe*, December 6, 2001, p. 1.

More than any other factor, religion provides a sense of fraternity, binding people together on the basis of shared norms and values. Houses of worship are also venues for community, providing multiple opportunities for fellowship. These associations range from voluntary work with the sick and the infirm to coaching and teaching the young. Secular organizations can do these things as well, but they typically lack the strong bonds that religious institutions offer.

The role that religion plays in building fraternity is not a matter of speculation: numerous studies demonstrate that religious Americans are far more charitable than their nonbelieving cohorts. They give not only of their money but also of their time: they volunteer more, reaching millions who need our care. They are also more likely to give blood.

We all know that the states in the Northeast are wealthier than Southern states, but less well known is how much more charitable the latter are. In fact, the *Chronicles of Philanthropy* found that the states with the highest degree of religious participation, the Southern ones, were much more generous than those states where religious participation is low, such as in New England. Similarly, when it comes to discretionary income, those who live in the South are much more likely to give to charity than are Northerners.[31]

Arthur C. Brooks is president of the American Enterprise Institute and one of the nation's experts on charitable giving. His research findings are conclusive: "Religious people are more charitable in every measurable nonreligious way—including secular donations, informal giving, and even acts of kindness and honesty—than secularists."[32]

---

[31] "How America Gives", *Chronicle of Philanthropy*, August 23, 2012, p. B6.
[32] Albert C. Brooks, *Who Really Cares* (New York: Basic Books, 2007), p. 40.

They give to the homeless far more than secularists do, and they are more likely to contribute to those affected by national emergencies.

Does this also mean that religious people are more likely to be altruistic? Yes. The definitive study on this subject was done by Samuel and Pearl Oliner, two sociologists. As a measure of altruism, they studied those who were most likely and those who were least likely to rescue Jews during the Holocaust.

Those who were rescued were more likely to credit Christianity than were the rescuers themselves. The rescuers risked their lives to save Jews because they felt duty bound; it was constitutive of their moral background. They put into practice the ethical imperatives that they learned from their parents, values that were central to their lives. Those values included a responsibility to others—a willingness to give without expecting something in return.[33]

Pearl Oliner examined more specifically the role that religion played in the lives of rescuers. She found that Catholics, as compared with Protestants, were significantly marked by a "sharing disposition". By this she meant that they showed greater empathy for the dispossessed and a stronger tendency to "identify with the poor".[34]

So what was the profile of those least likely to be rescuers? The self-absorbed. The Oliners found that "self-preoccupation" works against altruism—such persons had little time or interest in serving others. This narcissistic trait is more closely associated with secularism than with Christianity, which is one reason why it is commonplace

[33] Samuel P. Oliner and Pearl M. Oliner, *The Altruistic Personality: Rescuers of Jews in Nazi Germany* (New York: Free Press, 1988), pp. 164, 173.

[34] Pearl M. Oliner, *Saving the Forsaken: Religious Culture and the Rescue of the Jews in Nazi Germany* (New Haven, Conn.: Yale University Press, 2004), pp. 122–23.

in Hollywood. It is hardly surprising to learn that "rescuers emphasized values relating to self significantly less frequently than nonrescuers." The sociologists also acknowledged that a priest would be more likely to rescue those in need than would a lawyer, a doctor, or an artist. This carries more weight, given that neither of the Oliners is religious.[35]

Those who are not religious, which is to say a large segment of the professoriate, benefit greatly from the self-giving of their religious countrymen. But don't expect self-absorbed big thinkers to express gratitude. Lucky for all of us they find employment in colleges, and not in firehouses.

Secularists owe the faithful in other ways as well. "Despotism may be able to do without faith", Tocqueville counseled, "but freedom cannot."[36] It is true that those who live under tyranny do not have to worry about the social order disintegrating—the state insists on compliance from the top down—but in a free society, fraternity must be achieved. That is a challenge, given the fluidity of these societies.

Tocqueville knew that religion has the effect of anchoring the individual in society, providing for stability and certainty. It also takes the eyes of the individual off himself, allowing him to focus on the needs of others. Indeed, it is a healthy tonic to the changes and irregularities that freedom affords. Religion is also a necessary antidote to materialism and self-gratification, traits that are common in democratic societies.

The Founders knew all this before Tocqueville registered his observations. Most of them were professed Christians,

[35] Dennis Prager, "A Response to Richard Dawkins", *The Dennis Prager Show*, October 1, 2013, http://www.dennisprager.com/a-response-to-richard-dawkins-2/.

[36] Alexis de Tocqueville, *Democracy in America*, ed. J. P. Mayer, trans. George Lawrence (New York: Harper and Row, 1966), p. 294.

and all appreciated the vital role that religion played in the formation of the republic. This was made manifest in the Declaration of Independence, which proclaims that there are self-evident truths, and that all of us are created equal by our Creator. Our rights are inalienable: they are not given to us by government; they are God's gift. Jefferson, the author of the Declaration, explained its purpose in a letter to Henry Lee in 1825. His goal was not to write some professorial magnum opus, but to "place before mankind the common sense of the subject.... It was intended to be an expression of the American mind."[37]

What Thomas Jefferson and the Founders believed was a matter of common sense is today attacked by members of the professorial class. But whether they like it or not, they cannot change the fact that the Declaration contains four references to God. It speaks of the "laws of nature and nature's God", of the "Creator", of the "supreme judge of the world", and of "the protection of divine providence".[38] These statements are all expressions of our natural rights, the recognition that by our very God-given nature, we possess certain rights that no government can violate or take away.

The natural-rights principles of the Declaration owe much to John Locke; his effect on the Founders was critical. Locke wrote that no one can "take away" the "life, liberty, health, limb or goods of another", because every person is "the workmanship of one omnipotent and infinitely wise Maker".[39] Jefferson, in his *Notes on the State of Virginia*, took this notion further, saying "the liberties

[37] Quoted in Robert Curry, *Common Sense Nation: Unlocking the Forgotten Power of the American Idea* (New York: Encounter Books, 2015), pp. 63–64.

[38] Lowenthal, *No Liberty for License*, p. 205.

[39] John Locke, *Second Treatise of Government* (Mineola, N.Y.: Dover, 2002), p. 3.

of the nation" cannot "be thought secure when we have removed their only firm basis, a conviction in the minds of the people that these liberties are the gift of God" and that "they are not to be violated but with his wrath."[40]

The link between religion and morality was punctuated by George Washington and John Adams. In his Farewell Address, our first president noted, "Of all the dispositions and habits which lead to political prosperity, Religion and morality are indispensable supports."[41] Similarly, John Adams opined that the Constitution was made "only for a moral and a religious people".[42] Washington and Adams knew that self-government required self-governing people, and unless individuals put a harness on their base appetites, moral chaos would follow. Christianity, with its emphasis on the need to exercise restraint, was the right prescription for a free people. James Madison understood this as well. "To suppose that any form of government will secure liberty or happiness without virtue in the people", he said, "is a chimerical idea."[43]

It is often said by secular critics that Jefferson was not a believer, thus undermining the argument that a free and democratic society benefits by being anchored in Christianity. To be sure, Jefferson was skeptical of organized religion, but he deeply appreciated its social utility.

[40] Thomas Jefferson, *Notes on the State of Virginia* (New York: Penguin Classics, 1998), p. 169.

[41] George Washington, Farewell Address (September 19, 1796), Washington Papers, University of Virginia, http://gwpapers.virginia.edu/documents/washingtons-farewell-address/.

[42] John Adams to Massachusetts Militia, October 11, 1798, Founders Online, National Archives, last modified November 26, 2017, https://founders.archives.gov/documents/Adams/99-02-02-3102.

[43] Jonathan Elliot, ed., *The Debates in the Several State Conventions, on the Adoption of the Federal Constitution*, vol. 3 (Philadelphia: J.B. Lippincott, 1907), pp. 536–37.

When heading out to church one Sunday morning, with a red prayer book in hand, he was stopped by a friend who questioned what he was doing. "You going to church, Mr. J.? You don't believe a word of it." Jefferson responded by saying, "No nation has ever existed or been governed without religion. None can be. The Christian religion is the best religion that has been given to man and I as chief Magistrate of this nation am bound to give it the sanction of my example."[44]

Not only does it not help the secularist cause to invoke Jefferson as their hero, but his presidential decisions work against their thesis. Today, atheist zealots seek to stop the government from spending a dime to assist faith-based institutions. They will find no support from Jefferson in their quest. In 1803, he signed a treaty awarding $300 to the Kaskaskia Indians for the purpose of building a Catholic church. He authorized spending $100 a year for seven years to support a Catholic priest. He also authorized government lands to be set aside for the sole purpose of religious activities, allowing Moravian missionaries to promote Christianity.[45] If any president in modern times were to state his intention to do the same, an ACLU lawsuit would be readied immediately.

Jefferson was comfortable with the expectation that, as president, he had a moral obligation to promote Christianity. If freedom depends on Christianity for support, then common sense suggests that it be given top priority. In his writings on the American founding, Michael Novak focuses on this idea.

---

[44] Nicholas Von Hoffman, "God Was Present at the Founding", *Civilization* (April–May 1998): 39.

[45] "The Founders and Public Religious Expression", WallBuilders, December 31, 2016, https://wallbuilders.com/founders-public-religious-expressions/.

The two wings of the American eagle, Novak says, are reason and faith. To our detriment, he adds, we have neglected faith. It is his comments on reason, however, that are central to my thesis. Novak intentionally chose the term "common sense" rather than "reason" in the subtitle of his book *On Two Wings: Humble Faith and Common Sense at the American Founding*. He made this choice to show that the Founders were not blue-sky Enlightenment philosophers, but practical men of affairs. "For this", he said, "'common sense' seems the better name." It was also a tribute to the "common sense philosophy" of the Founders.[46]

Novak's choice of words was influenced by Bernard Lonergan, a Canadian Jesuit priest. Lonergan's use of "common sense", he says, was meant to convey "the kind of knowledge most often employed by ordinary people and persons of practical affairs. In politics and law, as well, common sense is indispensable." People who rely on common sense, Novak writes, "do not look for a theory [to resolve issues], but for a ray of practical wisdom helpful just now."[47]

The role that religion plays in citizen formation is not confined to the political arena: virtue is also important to a market economy. Saint John Paul II analyzed the moral foundations of a market economy. He saw how socialism destroyed liberty and prosperity, but that did not make him a proponent of laissez-faire capitalism. Although it is entirely defensible to base a market economy on self-interest, he said, it is important not to allow celebrations of self-interest to conquer the common good. If capitalism were to survive, he stressed, it needed to respect the role

[46] Novak, *On Two Wings*, pp. 106–8.
[47] Ibid.

that religion plays in taming radical individualism and providing for the general welfare of society.

Saint John Paul II's concerns about the negative effects of a market economy were shared by Joseph Schumpeter, Daniel Bell, and Irving Kristol. They were well aware of the cultural challenges that a market economy posed, releasing forces that undermined its achievements. Like John Paul II, Schumpeter and Kristol were highly critical of socialism and its effects, but they were not naïve about capitalism's faults. Bell was a socialist, though his cultural conservatism allowed him to share many of the concerns voiced by Schumpeter and Kristol. Of the three, however, only Kristol saw religion as the answer to capitalism's excesses.

Schumpeter was a Harvard economist whose greatest influence was in the 1940s. Bell, a Harvard sociologist, and Kristol, a wide-ranging writer, were influential in the second half of the twentieth century. What united the three of them was their concern that capitalism's success came at the expense of undermining its cultural basis. The bourgeois ethic, with its emphasis on self-discipline and a strong work ethic, was functional to the workings of a market economy, but the values that prosperity promoted were self-gratification and self-absorption. Bell aptly dubbed this the "cultural contradictions of capitalism". Earlier, Schumpeter blamed the intellectual class for abetting this condition. In fact, the Austrian American economist predicted that the intellectuals would help to destroy capitalism.[48]

Kristol came closer to the Catholic analysis of capitalism than Schumpeter or Bell did. The idea that a market economy could not survive without the stabilizing force of religion struck him as common sense. It also made him unhappy that many of his fellow Jews failed to grasp how

[48] Himmelfarb, *One Nation, Two Cultures*, pp. 11–16, 45–46.

important religion is in the makings of a free and prosperous society. He wrote about this in the article "On the Political Stupidity of the Jews". A more accurate title, I would suggest, would be "On the Political, Economic, Social, and Cultural Stupidity of Intellectuals".[49] Why exclude stupid Catholic intellectuals as well as others?

For capitalism to survive, Kristol warned, it had to stave off the forces of nihilism and narcissism, twin byproducts of the economic order. Without self-restraint, the primordial interest in self-gratification will dominate, the result being the erosion of the kinds of virtues that a market economy needs. Only the Judeo-Christian ethos is powerful enough to keep radical individualism in check; if it were not, social and economic decay would follow, threatening to undo the good that a market economy fosters.

Atheist Intellectuals and Atheist Organizations

Most nonbelievers are harmless folks who, for whatever reason, find belief in God hard to accept. I have met some famous persons whom this description fits, and I always tell them—not in a condescending way—that I will pray for them, hoping they may someday believe. At the other end of the atheist spectrum are the militant secularists, the ones given to activism. They are not content to go their own way, leaving believers alone. No, they seek to relegate religion to a purely private status, if not eliminate it altogether. As with other activists, they look to intellectuals as their mentors, providing them with ideological ammunition.

[49] Quoted in Tom Wilson, "Irving Kristol's God", *First Things*, February 2015, p. 21.

Many intellectuals boast that they are too smart to believe in God. They wear their pride on their sleeves, letting everyone know how gifted and comfortable they are in their atheism. But what exactly is their gift? To deny that life has meaning? That would mean that life is just a crapshoot. Everything that exists, from wind and wallpaper to sports and spiders, has a purpose. So why should it be considered brilliant to say that human life is purposeless? Moreover, if they were comfortable in their atheism, they wouldn't be so busy trying to convince the rest of us. They would just relax, confident that they are right.

To understand the politics of today's atheist intellectuals, we need to consult Karl Marx in the nineteenth century and Herbert Marcuse in the twentieth. What unites them, more than anything, is their statist ideology: the state should have the final word on everything that matters. That means that the state must eclipse the authority that rests in civil society, attenuating the influence of parents, teachers, the clergy, and community leaders. For religion, this is devastating: once the autonomy of religious institutions is compromised, their public role is squashed.

Atheist intellectuals continue this legacy by whittling away at the public role of religion. But unlike nonbelievers in the past, today's brand of atheist intellectuals is characterized by meanness and a preference for nihilism. Marx, in particular, had a blueprint for reform, which is more than can be said of today's atheist savants. Flawed though Marx's prescription was, he sought to change the social order, not simply to break it down. Today's atheist intellectuals have no game plan—they simply want to annihilate the sacred. It is this pathological condition that led University of Minnesota professor P. Z. Myers to drive a rusty nail through a stolen consecrated Host. He did this to protest my criticism of a Florida college student who walked out of Mass with an unconsumed Host (the student was showing his anger at some school policy).[50]

Sam Harris is a popular atheist thinker, and his writings are a prime example of the current state of atheist thought. "The Catholic Church is more concerned about preventing contraception than protecting child rape", he says. "It's more concerned about preventing gay marriage than genocide."[51] Harris is certainly not a Marxist: Marx attributed to religion many positive contributions to society, and although he sought its undoing, he did so because he believed that the advance of socialism, and then communism, would yield a more just society. Harris prefers to mock and insult the faithful.

To show the depth of Harris' intellectual acumen, consider his writings. We would expect him not to believe in the Bible, but his stated reasons are astounding. He criticizes the Bible for not having a chapter on mathematics. No one can argue with that. He also notes that the good book fails to discuss electricity, DNA, or a cure for cancer. Right again.[52] It also doesn't have a section on the stupidity of intellectuals.

Perhaps the most famous living atheist is Richard Dawkins. He is a splendid representative of the new atheism. "I'm all for offending people's religion", he told his friends in the English media. "I think it should be offended at every opportunity."[53] Does he believe that Christians, for

[50] Bill Donohue, "Militant Atheism Unleashed", Catholic League, September 24, 2008, https://www.catholicleague.org/militant-atheism-unleashed-2/.

[51] Sam Harris on *The Daily Show with Jon Stewart*, Comedy Central, October 4, 2010.

[52] Harris, *Letter to a Christian Nation*, p. 60.

[53] Maya Oppenheim, "Richard Dawkins: Atheist Academic Calls for Religion 'To Be Offended at Every Opportunity'", *Independent*, May 23, 2016, https://www.independent.co.uk/news/people/richard-dawkins-atheist-academic-calls-for-religion-to-be-offended-at-every-opportunity-a7043226.html.

example, are an evil people who deserve to be offended? No. In fact, he says that "the vast majority" of believers do not commit evil acts.[54] This raises the question: Why, if religion is evil, are so few of its adherents evil?

No one doubts that some Christians have committed evil acts, but the real question is whether they were following the teachings of Christianity or violating them. Christians believe in sin, so to acknowledge that some Christians have done evil things is not news. This is another problem for Dawkins.

He believes that sin is "one of the nastiest aspects of Christianity".[55] But is it nasty to say that some acts are intrinsically evil? He would concede that point, but he is still bothered by the concept that certain acts are against God's will and are therefore sinful. There's the rub: to admit to sin is to admit to God, and Dawkins will have none of it.

England also gave us Christopher Hitchens, an atheist contrarian whom I debated many times. We fought hard, though we did find common ground on abortion and radical Islam, seeing both as evil. Like Dawkins, Hitchens readily admitted to bashing people of faith and took particular glee in ripping Catholics. He opened our storied 2000 debate at New York's Union League Club by saying, "I might have to admit for debate purposes that when religion is attacked in this country ... the Catholic Church comes in for a little more than its fair share." He did not find this regrettable—just the opposite. "I may say

[54] Richard Dawkins, interview on BBC's *Sunday Morning Live*, June 19, 2016, YouTube video, 6:07, posted by Firebrand Atheist, June 30, 2016, https://www.youtube.com/watch?v=mr4MVdzS-1Q.

[55] Richard Dawkins, *An Appetite for Wonder: The Making of a Scientist, A Memoir* (New York: Ecco, 2013), pp. 139–40.

that I probably contributed somewhat to that and I am not ashamed of my part in it."[56]

Anyone who thinks that there is a public price to be paid for openly admitting to bigotry needs to explain why Hitchens was celebrated in elite circles for admissions such as this. Bigotry is not a universal taboo—some expressions are seen as commendable. So, when Hitchens wrote a book arguing that "religion poisons everything", he was not chided for promoting invidious stereotypes—he was acclaimed by the literati and rewarded at the cash register.[57] Similarly, he was rarely criticized by intellectuals for his ad hominem attacks on Mother Teresa. Not content to disagree with Mother Teresa's mission, Hitchens made several vicious remarks about her looks, her virginity, and her faith.

Not all atheist intellectuals share this tendency to attack people of faith. Paul Kurtz was a prominent atheist who died in 2012 at age eighty-six. He was not religion-friendly, but he was no hater. Indeed, he hated what he called "angry atheists", referencing people such as Dawkins and Hitchens.[58] For instance, he objected to International Blasphemy Rights Day and the events associated with it. He certainly approved of promoting secular humanism, but he insisted on abiding by ethical guidelines. So, when he saw that priests were being mocked as sexual perverts, he took exception to the bigotry. It was due to his outspoken condemnation of International Blasphemy Rights Day that he was driven off the board of directors of the Center

[56] Donohue-Hitchens debate, March 23, 2000, Union League Club, New York City, YouTube video, 1:01:18, posted by Great Debates, December 12, 2015, https://www.youtube.com/watch?v=MJJQuZbtA04.

[57] Christopher Hitchens, *God Is Not Great: How Religion Poisons Everything* (New York: Twelve, 2007).

[58] Mark Oppenheimer, "Closer Look at Rift between Humanists Reveals Deeper Divisions", *New York Times*, October 2, 2010, p. A12.

for Inquiry, the organization he founded and the sponsor of the celebration.[59]

Kurtz, unfortunately, was one of the lone voices in atheist intellectual circles to denounce the bashing of religious people. So it is not surprising to learn that militant atheist organizations take their talking points more from firebrands than from sober critics of religion.

There is no tolerance today among organized atheists for the reasoned appeals of Catholic theologians such as Jacques Maritain. He appreciated separation of church and state—he challenged the thinking of Catholics who were more skeptical—but he was not an absolutist who sought to scrutinize every intersection. He saw the value to society of publicly proclaiming our allegiance to God and country.[60]

Angry atheists disagree. They are alarmed over religious invocations to open Congress and the Supreme Court, and they resent presidential addresses that pay tribute to God. They do more than pout—they sue. In 2016, two radical secularist organizations filed a federal lawsuit requesting that they be permitted to deliver opening invocations before the House of Representatives.[61]

Chief justice William Rehnquist cut to the quick in 2005 when he wrote for the majority in a landmark case. At stake was the right of a private group to donate a monument bearing the Ten Commandments to be placed outside the Texas capitol in Austin. Were the Ten

[59] Bill Donohue, "Blasphemy Rights Day Is a Farce", CNSNews.com, October 2, 2016, https://www.cnsnews.com/commentary/bill-donohue/blasphemy-rights-day-farce.

[60] James P. Kelly, *Christianity, Democracy, and the American Ideal* (Sophia Institute Press: Manchester, N.H., 2004), pp. 13–20.

[61] "Pa. House of Representatives Can't Discriminate Against Non-Theists", press release, Americans United for Separation of Church and State, August 25, 2016, https://www.au.org/media/press-releases/pa-house-of-representatives-can-t-discriminate-against-non-theists-americans.

Commandments a religious display? "Of course", he said. But so what? "Simply having religious content or promoting a message consistent with a religious doctrine does not run afoul of the Establishment clause."[62]

Organized atheists constantly lean on the so-called establishment clause as justification for scrubbing society clean of every vestige of religious influence. The jurisprudence they rely on is deeply flawed, though that hasn't stopped many judges from making misguided decisions. "Congress shall pass no law respecting an establishment of religion nor prohibiting the free exercise thereof." That is the first part of the First Amendment. As judge John Noonan observed, there are no clauses there (calling them provisions is more accurate).[63] Michael Novak notes, "It is a mistake to make two clauses where the Constitution so clearly knits together one."[64]

Novak contends that the Framers "wished to protect the free exercise of religion in the states, *including* the establishment of religion in some states. To that purpose, they insisted that the *federal* government could neither establish one religion nor abolish the establishments existing in some states."[65]

Moreover, the author of the First Amendment, James Madison, made it clear that the "establishment clause" was meant to prohibit a national religion, such as existed in England, and government favoritism of one religion over another. It was not meant to stop George Washington, or any other president, from appointing a House chaplain.

[62] William Rehnquist, Van Orden v. Perry, 545 U.S. 677 (2005).

[63] John T. Noonan, "The End of Free Exercise?", *DePaul Law Review* 42, no. 2 (Winter 1992): 567, available at http://via.library.depaul.edu/law-review/vol42/iss2/2.

[64] Novak, *On Two Wings*, p. 114.

[65] Ibid., italics in the original.

Patrick Garry is a constitutional expert whose writings are a model of clarity and precision. He tears to shreds the argument favored by organized atheists and their intellectual mentors. They see the exercise and establishment clauses as being "at war with each other", interpreting them as if the former confers benefits on religion and the latter imposes burdens. Garry wryly notes that "it was as if the framers had intended the two clauses to cancel each other out, producing a kind of zero-sum result with regard to religion. This makes no sense whatsoever." He adds that "there is no constitutional basis for interpreting the establishment clause as contradictory to the exercise clause."[66]

Garry is correct, but the ACLU sees every religious expression not made inside a house of worship as a potential violation of the establishment clause. "The record will show a lot of foolish statements by somebody or other connected with the ACLU, like, for instance, taking 'In God We Trust' off of coins or postage or denying Congress its chaplains." The person who said that was not some civil-libertarian critic—it was the atheist founder of the ACLU, Roger Baldwin.[67]

The legal battles will continue, and although they are important, they may not be as important as the trashing of religion that takes place in the culture. From putting a crucifix in urine to smearing elephant dung on a picture of the Virgin Mary to plays that depict Christ having sex with the apostles, the artistic community has ravaged Christianity. And this is often supported with public funds: the Smithsonian hosted an exhibit that featured a video showing large ants eating away at Jesus on the Cross.

---

[66] Patrick M. Garry, *Wrestling with God: The Courts' Tortuous Treatment of Religion* (Washington, D.C.: Catholic University Press of America, 2006), p. 21.

[67] Peggy Lamson, *Roger Baldwin* (Boston: Houghton Mifflin, 1976), pp. 266–67.

TV shows based on sexual deviants who hate Catholicism are offered on prime time, but there is no show that puts Catholicism in a positive light. Movies are made that cast the Catholic Church as a corrupt institution. Students at every level are taught pernicious myths about the Catholic Church's role in the Inquisition and the Crusades, and they are indoctrinated with a secular orientation so as to make them question the Catholic Church's monumental achievements and contributions to Western civilization. Those who question these presentations are subject to ridicule, if not worse.

This is not an auspicious situation. Young people, led by those who consider themselves world-class intellectuals, are being presented with a vile and distorted picture of religion, especially Catholicism. The only saving grace is that most people have common sense and are therefore not likely to be seduced by ideology.

CONCLUSION

Donald E. Brown's list of human universals was never meant as a guidebook to good living, but we would be foolish to ignore what it portends: any society that does not address basic human wants and needs is bound to prove unsatisfactory. Matters only worsen when they are deliberately trampled upon by elites who think they know better. As Stella the nurse in Alfred Hitchcock's *Rear Window* says, "Nothing has caused the human race so much trouble as intelligence."

The social teachings of the Catholic Church are ordered toward the good of individuals and society. They work because they are in harmony with human nature, respecting the limitations of the human condition. To put it another way, there is a goodness of fit between Catholic social teachings and the wants and needs of men, women, and children, so much so that those teachings contain the best prospects of achieving the good society. If freedom, equality, and fraternity are to be realized, we can do no better than to heed what the Church instructs us to do.

For freedom to be enjoyed, we must adopt a realistic understanding of what it means. Our society sees freedom in terms of radical individualism, a condition in which all that matters is the rights of the individual. But this undermines the stability of the social order; individual responsibilities must be taken seriously. Catholicism is the antidote.

It teaches that freedom is the right to do what we ought to do, thereby putting responsibilities front and center. The Catholic conception of freedom is not focused on the individual—it is committed to the attainment of ordered liberty, a much more modest, yet realistic, interpretation.

Equality is another worthy goal, but it can also be misinterpreted. Instead of promoting a reasonable interpretation of equality, many in our society embrace a radical egalitarianism, a condition that totally ignores the ubiquity of hierarchy and the social needs that it meets. Equality before the law is a noble pursuit, as are attempts to ameliorate inequality based on unjust policies and laws, but, as with individual rights, when equality is pushed to extremes, it creates new problems. The Catholic understanding of equality rests on God's equal love for all people, regardless of personal or social circumstances. Moreover, the human dignity that inheres in all of us must always be respected.

Common sense tells us that there are fundamental differences between men and women, and fundamental differences based on individual abilities and ambitions, none of which can be denied. Recognizing these differences is not the problem; trying to deny them is.

Fraternity is a basic human need. Our desire for affection and recognition must be met, lest the individual succumb to pathologies that harm everyone. Unfortunately, the dominant culture has done a very poor job of providing for fraternity, so torn is it by the effects of radical individualism and radical egalitarianism.

The Catholic Church understands that a sense of community must begin with the family. If a child is not wanted in the home, then true fraternity can never be achieved. The Church also knows that if the individual is not taught to care for others, then the kinds of social bonds that make us whole will prove elusive.

The American people know we are in trouble. In 2017, Gallup released a survey that showed that only 1 percent of Americans think that our moral values are excellent; 81 percent rated them "only fair" or "poor". Is the state of our moral values improving or getting worse? According to 77 percent of the public, matters are getting worse. Just as disconcerting, the American people are badly conflicted on this subject. "Even liberals", Gallup says, "who seemingly should be pleased with the growing number of Americans who agree with their point of view on the morality of prominent social issues, are more likely to say things are getting worse than getting better."[1] The good news is that 55 percent of Americans say religion can answer most of our problems; the figure for those who attend church weekly is 85 percent.[2] Let's hope more Americans heed this message. In 2018, 49 percent rated our moral values as "poor"; this was the highest percentage ever recorded on this issue since Gallup first asked about it in 2002.[3]

There is a paradox here. We are loath to pass judgment on the personal choices of others—this is especially true of sexual matters—yet we are increasingly uneasy with the behavioral fallout that bad choices yield. It is one thing not to condemn the sinner and quite another to pretend that sinful acts do not exist. The negative consequences of an amoral conception of liberty are all around us, but

[1] Jim Norman, "Views of U.S. Moral Values Slip to Seven-Year Lows", Gallup, May 22, 2017, https://news.gallup.com/poll/210917/views-moral-values-slip-seven-year-lows.aspx.

[2] Art Swift, "Majority in U.S. Still Say Religion Can Answer Most Problems", Gallup, June 2, 2017, https://news.gallup.com/poll/211679/majority-say-religion-answer-problems.aspx.

[3] Justin McCarthy, "About Half of Americans Say U.S. Moral Values are 'Poor'", Gallup, June 1, 2018, https://news.gallup.com/poll/235211/half-americans-say-moral-values-poor.aspx.

the resolve to correct it is lacking. We reject the Catholic interpretation of liberty—freedom must be ordered toward the good of others—so we are left with the social debris occasioned by radical individualism.

It doesn't have to be this way: there is no iron law of culture that destines our future. But to reverse course takes courage. It also commands us to challenge theories and policies that defy common sense.

The Catholic corrective to this moral conundrum requires a renewed interest in grounding the law in the moral precepts of the Judeo-Christian ethos. To do this, we need to follow the advice of Philadelphia archbishop Charles Chaput: we need to get our own spiritual house in order first. "To recover the Church's identity", he contends, "we need to first recall our own." Then we can get on with the serious business of confronting our cultural crisis. There is much work to do. "The world hates the story Christians tell. It no longer believes in sin. It doesn't understand the forgiveness of sin."[4]

Changing the culture means a commitment to balancing the rights of the individual with the rights of others. This cannot be done without a pledge to begin all discussions about freedom with an emphasis on the relationship between rights and responsibilities. To continue down the road we have been going—separating the law from the moral foundations of our society—is to serve everyone poorly.

The public also needs to come to grips with the loss of common sense that marks contemporary discussions of sex differences. Sex is rooted in nature, not in society. As Donald E. Brown has shown, gender roles are universally acknowledged. Even when we allow for cultural and

---

[4] Charles J. Chaput, *Strangers in a Strange Land: Living the Catholic Faith in a Post-Christian World* (New York: Henry Holt, 2017), p. 218.

historical differences, the similarities in gender roles is evidence that they are largely a function of nature, not nurture.

The fact that some men and women are profoundly unhappy with their sex is regrettable, but it is not the sign of a mature society to pretend that their condition is normal. It is not normal for a transgender girl to be so repulsed by her genitalia that she wills herself not to go to the bathroom, suffering intestinal damage that requires surgery.[5] These young people need our help, not more policies, more laws, and a new industry to enable their pathology.

Dennis Prager sees this phenomenon in cultural terms. "The biblical view is that man and woman are entirely distinct beings, and human order in large part rests on preserving that distinctiveness. The Left is working to abolish this distinction. That is what its battle for the 'transgendered' is about."[6] And we know who is leading the fight to abolish sex differences.

"It is the intellectuals who are at war against the common man and the normal way of life. They defy common sense."[7] That is the way Chesterton scholar Dale Ahlquist interpreted what his subject said about the learned ones. One can only imagine what Chesterton might have said about intellectuals who think it is normal for men and women to be in constant rebellion against their nature.

Economic equality is another goal that will always elude us. Some are born into families of affluence, and others are not, and there is nothing that any policy can do to change

[5] Jack Turban, "How Doctors Help Transgender Kids Thrive", *New York Times*, April 9, 2017, section SR, p. 10.

[6] Dennis Prager, "The Left's Battle to Restore Chaos: Judeo-Christian Values: Part X", *The Dennis Prager Show*, April 5, 2005, http://www.dennisprager.com/the-lefts-battle-to-restore-chaos-judeo-christian-values-part-x/.

[7] Dale Ahlquist, *Common Sense 101: Lessons from G. K. Chesterton* (San Francisco: Ignatius Press, 2006), p. 276.

this reality substantially. Moreover, not all manifestations of inequality are inequitable. We are called to root out group inequalities born of unjust laws, but it is not a service to those at the bottom if we improve material conditions while fostering dependency on the government.

The adage about teaching the poor how to fish instead of giving them fish is as true today as it ever was. When Rudy Giuliani was elected mayor of New York City, one in seven New Yorkers was on welfare. Two decades after he instituted workfare—insisting that the able-bodied poor accept work—only one New Yorker in twenty-eight was on the dole.[8] Is this not preferable to giving the poor a government check, or underwriting their livelihood? What Giuliani did was very much in the Catholic tradition, which understands that work is necessary for human dignity.

To address the problems of unemployment and poverty, Catholic philosopher Jacques Maritain called for work programs that would be started and funded by the government but would be managed by private enterprises coordinated with one another and by the various communities of the people concerned, under the leadership of independent responsible appointees.[9] Underlying his idea is the Catholic principle of subsidiarity, which is based on the understanding that great harm is done to individuals and the communities of which they are a part when larger bodies (read "governments") take over their responsibilities. Such governmental overreach creates a permanently dependent underclass, with all the

---

[8] Myron Magnet, "What Ever Happened to the Civil Rights Movement?", *City Journal*, Spring 2017, https://www.city-journal.org/html/what-ever-happened-civil-rights-movement-15126.html.

[9] James P. Kelly, *Christianity, Democracy, and the American Ideal* (Manchester, N.H.: Sophia Institute Press, 2004), pp. 52–53.

social ills associated with it: crime, substance abuse, and illegitimacy.

A blend of public financing and private administration that would encourage individuals and families to take responsibility for themselves ought to win the hearts of everyone; but to radical egalitarians, it is unsatisfactory. They want more: they prefer redistributive policies on a grand scale, ones that take from the affluent and destroy all distinctions between rich and poor.

This explains why such an agenda was never part of Mother Teresa's outreach efforts—she focused exclusively, and from a state of poverty, on helping the sick, the infirm, and the dispossessed. She was not out to settle scores. She did not share the egalitarian goal of having the government act as the custodian of the poor, for if that were to happen, the poor would have no self-respect, and there would no place for people to share voluntarily and compassionately with one another.

Aside from the love that only parents can give their children, the human need for fraternity—at the level beyond the family—is best fulfilled by respecting the customs and the traditions that inhere in society. To be certain, there may be instances in which such practices do not accord with objective criteria of justice or the adopted goals of freedom and equality; tough choices not to honor them may be prudent. But overall, any democratic society that does not celebrate its heritage is headed in the wrong direction. What we are doing is worse.

In 2017, the student senate at the University of California–Davis decided to jettison the rule that the American flag be displayed at every meeting; displaying it was declared optional. The author of the bill, who had recently become a naturalized citizen, said, "The concept of the United States of America and patriotism is different for every individual."[10] This kind of subjectivism is very much in vogue on campuses across the nation. The United States is no longer a nation that men and women died for so that we could be free—it is a "concept" with no objective meaning.

It is not normal to sabotage one's own heritage, and this is especially true of free and prosperous nations, but that is what we have been doing, all in the name of multiculturalism. Just how far we are prepared to go in trashing our customs and traditions is uncertain. Statues and pictures of famous Americans are being torn down in communities across the country, simply because what they stood for is seen as objectionable by today's standards. Does denying our past really help us to overcome its most unsavory elements?

The Catholic Church, owing to its rich traditions, is well poised to lead on this issue. Pope Francis and his two predecessors have been quite frank in their denunciations of a deracinated West. By turning our back on Christianity, and all the good that it has bequeathed to the world, we are committing suicide. What exactly should take its place? Nazism and communism have been tried, and today we have sharia law in many parts of the world. Militant secularism, aided and abetted by multiculturalism, is in high gear in many other nations. Even its proponents are hard-pressed to name their achievements.

"Italy and Europe live in a pagan and atheist way", said Monsignor Carlo Liberati, the archbishop emeritus of Pompeii, and "they make laws that go against God and follow practices that are proper to paganism." He made those comments in 2017, and he was not optimistic about the future. "All of this moral and religious decadence favors

---

[10] Todd Starnes, "University Students Vote to Make American Flag Optional", *Fox News*, April 15, 2017, http://www.foxnews.com/opinion/2017/04/15/university-students-vote-to-make-american-flag-optional.html.

Islam", he observed. "In 10 years we will all be Muslims because of this stupidity."[11]

Despite current conditions, there is evidence that the Church's leadership is paying dividends. Gone are the days when Prime Minister Tony Blair heralded the importation of immigrants from the Middle East into Britain.[12] Now the leaders of England, France, and Germany have spoken out against multiculturalism. No one has been more forceful than Angela Merkel, chancellor of Germany. Multiculturalism, she said, "has failed, utterly failed". More important, she recognizes the cultural damage done when the West turns it back on Christianity. "We feel tied to Christian values. Those who don't accept them don't have a place here."[13]

We need to do a better job in America. When Christian students are punished by school officials for questioning a Muslim professor's distortion of history, we need to push back.[14] When students are denied the right to celebrate Christmas on campus because non-Christians might be offended, it is similarly indefensible.[15] Moreover, if

---

[11] Michael W. Chapman, "Catholic Archbishop: Europe Will Be Muslim in 10 Years 'Because of Our Stupidity'", CNSNews.com, January 19, 2017, https://www.cnsnews.com/blog/michael-w-chapman/catholic-archbishop -europe-will-be-muslim-10-years-because-our-stupidity.

[12] "Nigel Farage Blames Westminster Attack on Support for Multiculturalism", BreakingNews.ie, March 23, 2017, https://www.breakingnews .ie/world/nigel-farage-blames-westminster-attack-on-support-for-multi culturalism-782803.html.

[13] "Merkel Says German Multicultural Society Has Failed", BBC, October 17, 2010, https://www.bbc.com/news/world-europe-11559451.

[14] Bill Donohue, "Rollins College Drama Continues", Catholic League, March 29, 2017, https://www.catholicleague.org/rollins-college-drama -continues/.

[15] Bill Donohue, "Univ. of Tennessee Abridges Christian Rights", Catholic League, January 26, 2016, https://www.catholicleague.org/univ-of-tennessee -abridges-christian-rights-2/. I wrote a letter to the members of the Tennessee legislature on December 4, 2015. It was favorably resolved. See "Tennessee Triumph", Catholic League, July 5, 2016, https://www.catholicleague.org /tennessee-triumph/.

Christian values are not to be touted, should we accept as natural all cultural practices, such as the Islamic practice of female cutting? What about wife beating? "Men have approved wife beating in virtually every folk society", writes anthropologist Robert B. Edgerton.[16] Should we allow it here? Without guiding principles, such as the Catholic Church's embrace of natural law, we are left to whim and chance.

We need to make up our minds. Do we want to recapture our Christian past, breathing new life into its rich traditions, or do we want to succumb to the emptiness that secularism affords? If our cultural crisis is to be rectified, we will have to stop treating the public expression of religion as if it were a problem. We need to get over our public phobia of religion. We'll know when progress is being made when we stop sending grief counselors and consoling dogs to allay the fears of students following a school tragedy, and instead revert to summoning the clergy.

The diversity and inclusion game must end. When Christian clubs on campus are told they cannot exclude non-Christians from leadership positions—in the name of multiculturalism—we've been played. Inclusion means one size fits all; diversity means the opposite. The two are inherently contradictory principles, yet we ignore this obvious disharmony by mouthing "inclusion and diversity" as a mantra every time we seek to deny Christian beliefs and practices.

Are gay clubs told they must open their leadership positions to those who tout "Straight is great"? Why not? In 2017, a "Harvard University Black Commencement" was held on campus for the university's graduate schools, including the law, business, government, and medical

---

[16] Robert B. Edgerton, *Sick Societies* (New York: Free Press, 1992), p. 81.

schools. Following many other colleges, the University of Delaware flexed its diversity muscles by holding a "Lavender" graduation for LGBT students.[17] Does anyone ever ask these people how they can celebrate inclusion by excluding everyone who is not like them? Didn't white racists do this to blacks not too long ago? Why is segregation now chic on campus? Naturally, the professoriate is leading the cause.

Just as mad is the ongoing attempt on the part of activists and judges to remove religion from culture. It can't be done. Religion is not the only part of culture, but in every society it is its most defining element. When church and state overlap—as they often do—would we not be better off taking de minimis violations less seriously?

When parochial students who receive remedial education from public-school teachers during school hours are ordered to attend classes in a van parked across the street from the Catholic school—so that the teacher does not have to set foot on its premises—common sense has been abandoned. When I taught in a Catholic school in Spanish Harlem, before this 1985 Supreme Court 5–4 decision was rendered, public-school teachers were invited to take down a crucifix if it made them feel more at home. None did. This was a solution in search of a problem.

If we are to repair the damage done to our culture, we will have to end the practice of denying religious exemptions to laws that infringe on the autonomy of religious institutions. This is a fairly recent problem. For good reasons, some religious exemptions have been denied in the past (a child who needs medicinal help should not be overruled by his parents, no matter what their religious

---

[17] Anemona Hartocollis, "Celebrations of Diversity in Distinct Ceremonies", *New York Times*, June 3, 2017, p. A11.

beliefs are), but the pace at which such exemptions are being rejected has quickened. Worse, the reasons offered are increasingly suspect, if not unjust. This is due largely to instances in which the behavioral status of homosexuals comes into conflict with the religious convictions of those opposed to homosexuality.

The Catholic Church teaches that unjust discrimination cannot be tolerated, allowing, therefore, for cases in which it is just. Of course, this calls for prudence in decision-making, but not to differentiate between just and unjust discrimination is to work against the autonomy of religious institutions.

The Catholic Church holds the right prescription for American renewal. It should be given every constitutional right to exercise its prerogatives, though this cannot happen unless we realize that the First Amendment was written to *favor* religion over secularism. It is not an issue to say that the Founders never wanted a national church—they did not—or that they never wanted the government to favor one religion over another. No one seriously argues to the contrary. This account, however, is incomplete.

As law professor Patrick Garry observes, it was also never the intent of the Founders to "place religion and nonreligion on the same level". "Textually", he says, "the Constitution provides greater protection for religious practices than for any secular-belief-related activities."[18] Similarly, about a month before he died, Supreme Court justice Antonin Scalia gave an address in which he noted that the Constitution was never meant to be neutral about

[18] Patrick M. Garry, *Wrestling with God: The Courts' Tortuous Treatment of Religion* (Washington, D.C.: Catholic University Press of America, 2006), pp. 22–23, 100.

religion. In fact, he said, "there is no place for that in our constitutional tradition."[19]

We would do well to ponder the words of U.S. Supreme Court justice Joseph Story. This Harvard professor gave us his *Commentaries on the Constitution* in 1833, offering insight into the meaning of the First Amendment.

> Probably at the time of the adoption of the Constitution and of the First Amendment ... the general if not the universal sentiment in America was that Christianity ought to receive encouragement from the state so far as was not incompatible with the private rights of conscience and the freedom of religious worship. An attempt to level all religions, and to make it a matter of state policy to hold all in utter indifference, would have created universal disapprobation, if not universal indignation.[20]

Our cultural crisis is deeper than a flawed jurisprudence. "We have grown in numbers, wealth, and power, as no other nation has ever grown. But we have forgotten about God.... Intoxicated with unbroken success, we have become too self-sufficient to feel the necessity of redeeming and preserving grace, too proud to pray to the God who made us."[21] Lincoln uttered those words in his presidential proclamation appointing a national day of prayer and fasting in 1863. He sought to remind us of

[19] Bill Donohue, "Scalia—Religious Neutrality is Bunk", Catholic League, January 4, 2016, https://www.catholicleague.org/scalia-religious-neutrality-is-bunk/.

[20] Russell Kirk, "The First Clause of the First Amendment: Politics and Religion", Heritage Lectures, no. 146, Heritage Foundation, 1988, http://research.policyarchive.org/13422.pdf.

[21] Abraham Lincoln, Proclamation Appointing a National Fast Day, Washington, D.C., March 30, 1863, Abraham Lincoln Online, http://www.abrahamlincolnonline.org/lincoln/speeches/fast.htm.

the principles of the Declaration and our need never to forget them.

We can do no better than to honor Lincoln's plea. But to do that, we must confront those who are "too proud to pray to the God who made us".[22] They, of course, are the geniuses who look down their noses at the common man. They are leading the crusade against our Judeo-Christian tradition and are hell-bent on inspiring policies and laws that dismiss what nature and nature's God have ordained.

The good news is that the lack of common sense exhibited by blue-sky intellectuals need not be determinative. Cultures have a way of rejuvenating themselves—there is nothing inevitable about the vector of change. It is up to us to challenge the big thinkers and uphold common sense.

In an ideal world, these wizards would be quarantined, to keep them from contaminating the rest of us with their stupid ideas. There is an answer to what ails us, and it is found in the wisdom that inheres in the teachings of the Catholic Church. Miracles do happen—common sense Catholicism holds great promise.

---

[22] Larry P. Arnn and Douglas A. Jeffrey, *"We Pledge Allegiance": American Christians and Patriotic Citizenship* (Claremont, Calif.: Claremont Institute, 1998), p. 12.

ACKNOWLEDGMENTS

This book challenges many dearly held beliefs, among them being that human nature is a fiction. It is not. The real fiction is believing that life is nothing more than a social construction. More important, laws and policies that assume there is no such thing as human nature, or do not adequately pay homage to it, are not only bound to fail; they are likely to wreak havoc with the social order.

The seminal volume by anthropologist Donald E. Brown, *Human Universals*, plays a central role in my analysis. Brown courageously and perceptively noted the timeless human characteristics found in every society. My undertaking is to show how those attributes are in harmony with the teachings of the Catholic Church, while those of the dominant society are not.

Father Joseph Fessio and Mark Brumley of Ignatius Press read the manuscript and offered cogent advice. Vivian Dudro, my editor, was equally helpful. These are three serious Catholics, all with a keen eye for accuracy.

I also want to thank Bernadette Brady-Egan, Rick Hinshaw, and Don Lauer for sharing their insights with me on many of the issues addressed in this book. They are integral to the success of the Catholic League. Walter Knysz, the chairman of the board, is a strong supporter of our work and encouraged me to pursue this book.

My family, Valerie, Caryn, Paul, Caitlin, and Jay—and now Grant William—are always in my corner, pushing me to succeed. I would also like to thank Maggie and Mike Mansfield, Linda and Tom Boyle, the McGetricks, and the guys and gals at Doc's for their goodwill.

INDEX

abortion: and Obama's health-care mandate, 235; and rights, 31, 33, 80; and the sexual revolution, 77, 80

Adams, John, 51, 247

affirmative action programs, 161–63

Affirmatively Furthering Fair Housing database, 162

African Americans: affirmative action programs, 161–63; families, 150–52; students and school achievement, 163–64, 172–73

Afrocentrism, 207–9

Ahlquist, Dale, 265

AIDS epidemic, 72, 88–91

Aid to Families with Dependent Children, 158

Akerlof, George, 94

altruism, 244–45

American Association of Women Professors, 132

American Civil Liberties Union (ACLU), 35–40; Committee on Women's Rights, 133; and the establishment clause, 258; on freedom of speech, 37–40, 41, 42; New York, 36, 133; on obscenity laws, 54–55; policy on AIDS transmission, 88; position on

the ERA, 133; on refusals to say the Pledge, 196; and the Scout Oath, 197–98; Southern Regional Office, 50

American Enterprise Institute, 243

American Grace: How Religion Divides and Unites Us (Putnam and Campbell), 239

American Red Cross of Southern California, 195

The American Sex Revolution (Sorokin), 67

Anderson, Ryan T., 111–12, 116

anti-Catholicism: atheist intellectuals and, 205–6, 253–55; and attacks on Western civilization, 202, 205–6; blame for male dominance and sex inequality, 129–31; on college campuses, 73; cultural challenges to Catholic social ethics, 73–82; in television and movies, 259

Anti-Defamation League, 242

Aquinas, Thomas, 37

Aristotle, 47, 57–58, 142, 188–89, 208, 220

Arkes, Hadley, 32–33

Arnn, Larry P., 230

Asian American students, 171, 172–73